Language Assemblages

What are languages? An assemblage approach to language gives us ways of thinking about language as dynamic, constructed, open-ended, and in and of the world. This book unsettles regular accounts of knowledge about language in several ways, presenting an innovative and provocative framework for a new understanding of language from within applied linguistics. The idea of assemblages allows for a flexibility about what languages are, not just in terms of having fuzzy linguistic boundaries but in terms of what constitutes language more generally. Languages are assembled from different elements, both linguistic elements as traditionally understood, as well as items less commonly included. Language from this point of view is embedded in diverse social and physical environments, distributed across the material world and part of our embodied existence. This book looks at what language is and what languages are with a view to understanding applied linguistics itself as a practical assemblage.

ALASTAIR PENNYCOOK is Professor Emeritus at the University of Technology Sydney. His notable publications include *The Cultural Politics of English as an International Language* (1994) (now a Routledge Linguistics Classic), *Global Englishes and Transcultural Flows* (2007), *Language and Mobility* (2012) and *Posthumanist Applied Linguistics* (2018) (all winners of the BAAL Book Prize).

KEY TOPICS IN APPLIED LINGUISTICS

Series Editors

Claire Kramsch (University of California, Berkeley)
and Zhu Hua (UCL Institute of Education, London)

Books in this series provide critical accounts of the most important topics in applied linguistics, conceptualized as an interdisciplinary field of research and practice dealing with practical problems of language and communication. Some topics have been the subject of applied linguistics for many years and will be re-examined in the light of new developments in the field; others are issues of growing importance that have not so far been given a sustained treatment. The topics of the series are nuanced and specialized, providing an opportunity for further reading around a particular concept. The concept examined may be theoretical or practice oriented. Written by leading experts, the books in the series can be used on courses and in seminars, or as succinct guides to a particular topic for individual students and researchers.

Language Assemblages

ALASTAIR PENNYCOOK
University of Technology Sydney

Shaftesbury Road, Cambridge CB2 8EA, United Kingdom

One Liberty Plaza, 20th Floor, New York, NY 10006, USA

477 Williamstown Road, Port Melbourne, VIC 3207, Australia

314–321, 3rd Floor, Plot 3, Splendor Forum, Jasola District Centre, New Delhi – 110025, India

103 Penang Road, #05–06/07, Visioncrest Commercial, Singapore 238467

Cambridge University Press is part of Cambridge University Press & Assessment, a department of the University of Cambridge.

We share the University's mission to contribute to society through the pursuit of education, learning and research at the highest international levels of excellence.

www.cambridge.org
Information on this title: www.cambridge.org/9781009348652

DOI: 10.1017/9781009348638

© Alastair Pennycook 2024

This publication is in copyright. Subject to statutory exception and to the provisions of relevant collective licensing agreements, no reproduction of any part may take place without the written permission of Cambridge University Press & Assessment.

When citing this work, please include a reference to the DOI 10.1017/9781009348638

First published 2024

A catalogue record for this publication is available from the British Library.

A Cataloging-in-Publication data record for this book is available from the Library of Congress

ISBN 978-1-009-34865-2 Hardback
ISBN 978-1-009-34862-1 Paperback

Cambridge University Press & Assessment has no responsibility for the persistence or accuracy of URLs for external or third-party internet websites referred to in this publication and does not guarantee that any content on such websites is, or will remain, accurate or appropriate.

Contents

Acknowledgements   page vi

1 Why Language Assemblages?   1
2 Language, Knowledge, Myths and Being   20
3 Structures and Practices   50
4 Linguistic, Semiotic and Sociomaterial Assemblages   81
5 Other Language Ontologies   109
6 Applied Linguistics as Practical Assemblage   136

Suggested readings   154
Glossary   156
References   163
Index   192

Acknowledgements

Bujari gamarruwa Diyn Babana Gamarada Gadigal Ngura. I would like to acknowledge the Gadigal of the Eora Nation – Saltwater People – the traditional custodians of the country (land and water) around Warrane (Sydney Cove), where much of this book was written. I pay my respects to the Elders past, present and emerging, and recognize the importance for all of us of the knowledge they hold, and the significance of listening to what they have to say about language and other matters of concern.

'*Jede wissenshaftliche Arbeit, jede Entwicklung, jede Erfindung, ist die Frucht allgemeiner gemeinsamer Arbeit. Diese ist zum Teil eine Zusammenarbeit von Zeitgenossen, zum Teil eine Verwertung der Arbeiten früherer Geschlechter*' (Karl Marx, cited in Ahner, 1963).[1]

Books always emerge from multiple collaborations, *die Frucht allgemeiner gemeinsamer Arbeit*, the fruit of general collective labour, sometimes, as Marx suggests, with *Zeitgenossen*, contemporaries, sometimes with the work of previous generations (*früherer Geschlechter*). Several major thinkers with whom I had long and lasting friendships and critical discussions have alas recently moved to become members of those previous generations no longer with us. As I write, we are mourning the death of Tim McNamara, a great intellectual who was always ready to engage in long and thoughtful discussions about language, poetry, art, deconstruction, life. We recently saw the departure of Tove Skutnabb-Kangas, such a fierce advocate for language rights. Bernard Spolsky, who did so much for language policy, will be sorely missed. And it is still hard to accept that as we constantly refer to Jan Blommaert's remarkable body of work, he is sadly no longer with us.

---

[1] 'Every scientific work, every development, every invention is the fruit of general common work. This is partly a collaboration of contemporaries, partly an exploitation of the labours of previous generations.'

Acknowledgements

Among the many contemporary thinkers, thanks first to Claire Kramsch, a long-term interlocutor on questions of language and (symbolic) power, who first invited me to contribute to this series. And to her co-editor, Zhu Hua, who has also been a collaborator with whom many of the ideas developed here first started to emerge (Zhu Hua et al., 2017). They have given me space to explore my ideas and have provided very helpful feedback on the first draft of this book. Anonymous reviewers also provided extensive and valuable commentary on the initial proposal. The team at Cambridge University Press – Becky Taylor and Izzie Collins – have been very supportive and made the publishing process smooth.

Books such as this – as Marx suggests – are the fruit of many labours and collaborative work, with colleagues both past and present. I am grateful to the members of MultiLing in Oslo (under directors Liz Lanza and Unn Røyneland) who have made many stimulating discussions possible through invitations, seminars and informal discussions. A summer school run by Gavin Lamb provided the chance to engage further with questions of posthumanism; Haley de Korne and Pia Lane have been insightful in discussions of Indigenous language reclamation, truth and reconciliation; Rafael Lomeu Gomes has been an important interlocutor on language and the Global South; Bente Svendsen has been very helpful in talking through the implications of citizen sociolinguistics; and Bjørn Torgrim Ramberg has been most generous in taking time to discuss at length, and for taking seriously, my questions about language, ontology and realism.

I'm also very thankful to all those who've been pushing forward thinking on assemblages, posthumanism, new materialism and related questions through seminars, papers, journal special issues, and so on, especially Britta Schneider and Theresa Heyd (the Unthinking Language project), and the various contributors and long-term collaborators on these ventures, such as Leonie Cornips, Ana Deumert, Kellie Gonçalves, Adam Jaworski, Catherine Kell, Annelies Kusters, Crispin Thurlow and Kelleen Toohey. I have also been fortunate to be part of an extended engagement on questions of ontology, and I thank Chris Hall and Rachel Wicaksono for that opportunity.

My two longtime collaborators and co-authors, Emi Otsuji and Sinfree Makoni, still inspire me with their constant ideas, suggestions and ongoing projects. The co-editors of our book series, Critical Language and Literacy Studies, Ryuko Kubota and Brian Morgan, have also provided a vibrant model of intellectual collaboration over many years. Critical colleagues with whom I have long been in dialogue are part of the background to this book: Samy Alim, Ros Appleby, Adrian Blackledge, David Block, Brigitta Busch, Suresh Canagarajah, Angela Creese, Sender Dovchin, Ofelia García, John Joseph, Li Wei, Beatriz Lorente, Stephen May, Lynn Mario Menezes de Souza, Tommaso Milani, Ricardo Otheguy, Sari Pietikäinen, Elana Shohamy, Kleber Aparecido da Silva, Shaila Sultana, Ruanni Tupas, Theo van Leeuwen and many others. And thanks as always to Dominique Estival, who asks many searching questions about what I write while also supporting my endeavours in multiple ways.

1 Why Language Assemblages?

Thinking of language as an assemblage, according to Wee (2021), has a number of advantages over other views of language, particularly those that suggest that language is a system with defined boundaries. Thinking in terms of assemblages can help us understand how languages are constantly under construction, how they are put together through social processes and why it is better to start with an understanding of social action than an assumption about pregiven languages. The idea of assemblages also allows for a flexibility about what languages are, not just in terms of having fuzzy linguistic boundaries (languages blend together) but in terms of what constitutes language more generally. Languages are assembled from different elements, both linguistic elements as traditionally understood (words and grammar, for example) as well as items less commonly included (bodies and things). An assemblage approach to language thus raises questions about what constitutes the linguistic as well as giving us ways of thinking about language as dynamic, constructed, open-ended and in and of the world. This is to approach language not as a pre-existing or circumscribed entity but rather as something created, produced in social action. Language from this point of view is embedded in, indeed part of, diverse social and physical environments, distributed across the material world and part of our embodied existence.

In this book I want to unsettle regular accounts of knowledge about language in several ways and for several reasons. Something of an *ontological panic* seems to have gripped some areas of linguistics recently. There is nothing new in questions about the ontological status of language and languages. In one of the earliest introductions to applied linguistics, when the field was still heavily reliant on formal linguistic accounts for an understanding of language, Corder (1973, p.27, emphasis added) warned of the dangers of following a 'linguistic approach to language' since it is the 'most objectivizing. But *language is not, after all, a thing with real existence.*' This caution was already pointing to the problem that approaches to language developed within the field of linguistics tended towards the reification of its object. The ontological status of language and languages, and thus the subject matter of linguistics, has always been a topic in need of serious discussion (Santana, 2016), though for obvious reasons linguists have tended to tiptoe around this problem (the discipline defines itself in no small measure around the idea of separate and comparable languages).

Questions about what language is, or what languages are, or how the two are related, are a necessary part of any *ontologically curious* position (Wee, 2021). Yet such curiosity has been met recently with a rather panicked response, a concern that if the status of languages is questioned, so too are the possibilities of language policy, language maintenance, bilingualism, second language acquisition and much more (MacSwan, 2020, 2022a). All this seems rather alarmist, as well as mistaken: the obvious problems with the status of 'languages' as commonly conceived doesn't mean that language learning practices and policies will somehow cease to occur; it simply challenges the terms with which these are described. Integrational linguists have long raised questions about the status of languages in the field: 'linguistics does not need to postulate the existence of languages as part of its theoretical apparatus' (Harris, 1990a, p.45). Questions that have pushed this concern further, however, asking where the boundaries around language should be drawn – whether we can study animal communication with sociolinguistic tools (Cornips, 2022, in press) or what roles artefacts may play in social relations (Kell and Budach, 2024) – have brought warnings of a 'neo-pagan apocalyptic linguistics' (Pablé, 2022, p.6).

As Sinfree Makoni and I (Makoni and Pennycook, 2007, p.2) pointed out some years ago, languages do not exist as pre-formed entities in the world; they are, by contrast, 'the inventions of social, cultural and political movements'. This is to acknowledge that languages are social creations, and to warn against the reification of languages that comes from treating them as bounded systems. Like others who have pointed to the obvious problems with the ontological status of languages within linguistics (Otheguy et al., 2018), we also emphasized that languages nonetheless exist as social entities with very real effects, and that once we have raised questions about the status of languages, we need to develop alternative ways of thinking about this focus of our work. We talked about this in terms of 'a project not only of critique but one of reconstruction' (Makoni and Pennycook, 2007, p.3), while García and her colleagues have taken this up, arguably

Why Language Assemblages?

more productively, in terms of *translanguaging*. As we shall see in the discussion in Chapter 3, translanguaging itself is also a term that needs to be handled with a degree of caution, but these projects are by no means an abandonment of language, language education or language planning. They do not, as some suggest, undermine minoritized speakers' possibilities for social justice (Tannenbaum and Shohamy, 2023) so much as shift the grounds on which such campaigns are fought.

The question of whether and how languages exist is an ontological one. The ontological panic that follows ideas such as disinvention, integration or translanguaging is also about whose knowledge counts. As Jakobs and Hüning (2022, p.46) warn, a rejection of the concept of (different) languages is not necessarily a very useful direction for linguistics because it goes against both the disciplinary investment in different languages and everyday concepts of language. This should not mean, however, that it is not worth trying to find better ways of grasping linguistic realities than are currently presented in both domains, or of trying to understand how common concepts of language and linguistic understandings of language are related. There is a tension in linguistic approaches to this question: on the one hand a not unreasonable position that, as academic linguists, we know best; on the other, an egalitarian acknowledgement that other people's views matter. As discussed in this and the next chapter, how everyday knowledge about language is understood without falling into the descriptive-prescriptive dichotomy or labelling popular views as myths or errors in need of correction is another theme of importance here.

Corder's (1973) observation about the existence of language was also an *applied linguistic* concern.[1] It has been common in applied linguistics to see our work as applying existing linguistic knowledge to real-world contexts. This might seem fairly obviously to be what we do – inherent perhaps in the disciplinary terminology we inherited – and this has traditionally been the way that linguistics and applied linguistics have operated, with the one providing theories of language and the other putting them into practice, or at least mediating between the two. Alongside the hierarchical understanding of

---

[1] In places where there are important differences in purpose, I draw distinctions between linguistic and applied linguistic work. In other contexts I treat both as forms of linguistics since they share common foundations. Emphasizing the difference is not always helpful and if we all see ourselves as linguists, we potentially set a better agenda for change than if we insist on deep disciplinary schisms.

knowledge distribution that this view espouses, it also raises the question of what it means to 'use linguistics' for applied purposes. For Kramsch (2015, p.455), applied linguistics is not so much 'the application of linguistic theory or any other theory to the real-life problem of language learning and teaching' as 'the practice of language study itself, and the theory that could be drawn from that practice'. That is to say, the work we do in applied linguistics – translation, language in the workplace, language education, language policy and so forth – is itself the study of language, not the application of someone else's version of language.

Like Kramsch's (2015) call for a theory of language practice and Li Wei's (2018) call for a practical theory of language, this book makes central an applied linguistic view of language based in practice. Both views are part of a broader critical orientation that argues that practice and theory should not be separated and certainly not placed in a hierarchical relationship. Also known as *praxis*, this view suggests that theory derives from practice and that theory therefore needs to be practical: 'The process of theorization, or knowledge construction, involves a perpetual cycle of practice-theory-practice' (Li Wei, 2018, p.11). There are a number of reasons why it is important to develop practical theories of language: the knowledge about language drawn from linguistics may not be fit for purpose; if we are trying to deal with real-world contexts, it doesn't really make sense to draw on theories of language that haven't emerged from such contexts.

This book therefore sets out to look at what language is and what languages are (noting these may be quite different questions) with a view to arriving not at *one* practical theory of language, but rather at ways of assembling practical ways of thinking about language or, as I discuss in Chapter 6, understanding applied linguistics as a practical assemblage (Pennycook, 2018c). Rather than thinking about applied linguistics in disciplinary or interdisciplinary terms (approaches that keep structures of knowledge in place), this view suggests the coming together of language-oriented projects (social or educational endeavours that involve language), practical theories of language (different ways of approaching linguistic questions) and critical appraisals (ethical, material and political concerns). As applied linguists, we may not be interested so much in developing theories about language as in doing stuff with language: language policies, translations, language education, language in aviation and so on. To do so, however, we have to start to take responsibility for the ways we think about language. Approaches to language that derive from attempts to describe language structures or to account for language use in structural terms may be counterproductive. The terrain has changed from when applied linguistics was first seen as the application of linguistic knowledge to real-world contexts. We can now start to think seriously about practical theories of language or ways of thinking about language that derive from contexts of practice.

1.1 RELATIONAL ONTOLOGIES, SOCIAL EPISTEMOLOGIES AND CRITICAL APPRAISALS

Following Latour's (2004) warning that critical work has focused for too long on the *construction* of reality (regimes of truth, orders of discourse, discursive production) rather than also making its own claims to reality, I extend the critical realist position developed by Block (2022), though with a number of twists. Drawing on Bhaskar's (1989) work, Block (2022) makes a case for a form of critical realism based on an argument for an external reality (there is an external, real world), a relativist position on epistemologies (there are different ways of getting at this reality) and a rationalist mode of judgement (we need to be able to decide between these competing takes on the world). Drawing on Haslanger's (2012) *critical social realism*, the implications of the *ontological turn* in the social sciences (see later in this chapter and Chapter 2) and a concern about how to ground any critical project in the field (Pennycook, 2021a), I take a slightly different view. I argue for a form of *relational ontology* (Barad, 2007; Escobar, 2016, 2018) that emphasizes both the multiple and the relational qualities of existence. A key argument throughout this book will be that there is not just one ontology: the world is plural. This ontological stance has implications for the discussions of languages in other chapters, not as different understandings of the same thing but as different things. This focus derives from various quarters: the ontological turn in the social sciences (and particularly anthropology), a response to the recent ontological panic about what it means to question the existence of languages and an increased interest across the field in raising ontological questions (Demuro and Gurney, 2021; Hall and Wicaksono, 2020; Kell and Budach, 2024).

This perspective cuts across the book but is discussed in greater detail in the next chapter, where I outline what it means to look at questions of being from a pluralist (relational) stance and questions of knowing from a social stance. In line with Haslanger's (2012) *critical social realism*, and her scepticism about the usefulness of positing some kind of independent reality (neither a dependent nor an independent reality is very plausible), I am interested in the implications of social construction, or rather the importance of understanding different kinds of social construction, the ways things may be socially distinguished, constituted or caused (Haslanger, 1995; Sveinsdóttir, 2015). Epistemologies are obviously plural – we have many different ways of thinking about the world – but rather than Block's epistemological relativism, following Haslanger (2012),[2] I insist on social epistemologies, entailing a focus less on the relativism of epistemologies than on their social nature.[3] This view of epistemology aims to understand the social, cultural and political interests of different epistemological positions, how social epistemologies work, how forms of knowledge derive from social orders. It also, as will be argued later, by no means suggests that things that are social constructs are not real.

Critical social realism needs ways of deciding between alternatives. From Block's (2022) point of view, a form of *rational judgmentalism* enables the critical realist to link a critical project to an ontological realism by looking analytically at the different epistemologies. I take a slightly different approach in this book: while we should be cautious not to throw rationalism out just because of its ties to particular modes of so-called Enlightenment thought (rationalism can be salvaged from this history), we need a clearer set of ethical and ideological principles on which to evaluate ways of thinking. Once epistemologies are viewed in social rather than relativist terms, the seeds of critical evaluation have already been sown: we can look at different understandings of the world in terms of the interests they serve. By assuming relational ontologies, the goal is no longer to use this judgemental position to decide on which epistemologies best account for a given reality, but to explore how ontologies, epistemologies and ideologies are intertwined (or assembled).

A key framework for this book, therefore, is a form of critical social realism that allows for more than one reality, grounds epistemologies in social relations and takes a critical-ethical position on choosing between different versions of the world. The next chapter lays out these basic concerns, explains why they matter and discusses questions of ontology – what language is – and the ontological turn in the social sciences. In Chapters 3 and 4, in line with the thinking of

---

[2] Neither Haslanger's metaphysical realism nor Bhaskar's transcendental realism, however, accords with the relational ontological position I am trying to establish here.

[3] Although Block names his epistemological stance as relativist, emphasizing the array of ways of getting at reality, he also, as I understand his position, emphasizes the importance of the social bases of knowledge.

Why Language Assemblages? 7

Demuro and Gurney (2021), I focus on language as structure, language as practice and language as assemblage. These by no mean exhaust possible language ontologies, as will be discussed in Chapter 5. If we ask what ontological position has been taken on language by mainstream linguistics over the last century or so, the answer is, fairly uncontroversially, language as structure (or object or system). For much of its modern history, linguistics has taken an ontological stance on language as a structural entity, with a wide set of implications for how languages are understood as bounded entities. Linguists might immediately object to this, suggesting that structuralism was a passing phase of linguistics, and that things have moved on since then, but this is to confuse ontological and epistemological stances. Structuralism was a particular epistemological position, related of course to the ontological position on language as a structure, but the ontology of language as a structure has outlasted structuralist epistemologies.

This is not about the different epistemological approaches to a structural version of language – various schools of linguistics, or whether structuralist linguistics was superseded by generativist or even functional schools of linguistics – but about the basic ontological assumptions about what language is. A structural ontology made it possible to treat language as an object amenable to scientific study, enabling descriptions of languages around the world and facilitating many advances in our understandings of languages as structural entities. Yet this very tendency towards seeing languages as autonomous systems has enabled those forms of thinking that emphasize boundedness. A significant argument in this book is that this ontology – language as structure – has remained a cornerstone of linguistic analysis and may only be helpful in limited sociolinguistic and applied linguistic cases. It is this ontology – with its underlying assumptions about bounded systems – that often leads to confusion when linguists are criticized for assuming languages to be discrete, countable entities, a position they may also disavow.

This discussion will be of particular importance in Chapter 3, where I try to disentangle some of the translanguaging debates: simply put, the two sides of the discussion are often talking about different things, language as structure and language as practice (though without always being clear about their own ontological assumptions). Because structural and social (practice) language ontologies are so different, the debates about translanguaging have become mired in misunderstandings. The idea of 'a language', Blackledge and Creese (2014, p.1) suggest, 'may be important as a social construct, but it is not suited as an analytical lens through which to view language practices'. The discussions around codeswitching versus translanguaging often hinge on this problem: people are talking about different things, some focusing on language as structure (How do we account for one language or another being used in a particular context?), others on language practices (What are people doing with different linguistic elements?). Language as a social practice (not to be confused with sociolinguistics) puts the emphasis on language as something we do.

The idea of language as something we do is not always easily expressed in English, hence either the addition of the term 'practices' to language, literacy and so on, or the creating of variants of 'languaging', a term with a longer history than we might expect (Cowley, 2019). Proponents of *polylanguaging* (Jørgenson, 2008) and *translanguaging* (García and Li Wei, 2014) have insisted not only on the *poly* or *trans* aspects of this terminology but also on the *languaging*, while others have opted for *translingual* or *translinguistic practices* (Canagarajah, 2013; Lee and Dovchin, 2020). This focus on practices has a long history in sociology and anthropology, and it is revealing to reflect that the common linguistic assumption that systems or structures produce processes or practices, rather than the other way around (systems are the products of rather than the precursor to what we do), renders linguistics something of an outlier in the social sciences on this score (Ahearn, 2001; Van Leeuwen, 2008). From a standard (socio)linguistic point of view, languages as entities pre-exist their instantiation, so it is possible to think in terms of 'language use' or 'language in context' or 'codeswitching' where the language systems come before the social activity. From an integrational linguistic point of view, by contrast, 'first-order' activity is seen as communicative practice, while languages as structures are only 'second-order' concepts (Thibault, 2011). As discussed in Chapter 3, a practice ontology turns the tables on the language-as-structure perspective and makes languaging or social practices primary.

Taking different views of language seriously may mean entertaining the possibility that languages are different things to different people. What a linguist means by language may not be at all what a nonlinguist means by language. This is a question of ontology rather than epistemology. The shift from questions of knowledge to questions of being urges us to consider not so much that there is one reality that we cut up differently from different perspectives (knowledge, culture, worldview, ideology) but rather that we are dealing with different realities. For Van Dooren (2019, p.8), it is important to escape the dominant Western belief in a single reality over which are layered various perspectives and cultures that provide different takes on this otherwise consistent world. 'Our worlds', he suggests, 'are not preexisting, static entities'. We live in a world of many worlds, or a *pluriverse* (Escobar, 2020), a means for thinking about 'ecologies of practices across heterogeneous(ly) entangled worlds' (de la Cadena and Blaser, 2018, p.4). Such a view rejects the assumption that there is a given, independent world cut up by different worldviews, moving instead towards an understanding of entangled relationships, or assemblages.

Ontological questions cut across the book but are discussed in greater detail in the next chapter. As will be discussed in the following two chapters, the recent, rather panicked reactions to discussions about whether or how languages exist need to be seen within a much longer history of sceptical appraisal, and the concern, particularly from an applied linguistic point of view, that linguistics has tended to reify its objects of inquiry, to lose the connections between language, people and the world (Corder, 1973), and to fall into the trap of the *methodological nationalism* with which languages are associated (Schneider, 2018). If we acknowledge that languages are 'social constructions, artifacts analogous to other constructions such as time' (Makoni and Pennycook, 2007, p.1), this does not mean the end of all language learning, activism or politics, but rather a need to think through the implications of the 'social' and the 'construction' more carefully.

What flows from the observation that languages are social constructs? If, as Cummins (2021) suggests, in the context of arguments about translanguaging (see Chapter 3), there is no dispute about the fact that languages are socially constructed, the question is what is actually therefore under dispute? If it is no longer controversial to see monolingualism and multilingualism as *inventions* (Gramling, 2016, 2021), then what is at stake here? The problem in part is that social construction can be understood in multiple ways and is often seen as implying that something constructed is not real. Hence MacSwan (2022a) assumes that a *critical constructivist* position on language (what he calls *deconstructivism*) implies that languages are fictions, while Cummins (2021) understands this in terms of languages being social artefacts with unclear edges that can nevertheless also be described in terms of their *linguistic reality* (we will return to this). Yet if we consider Haslanger's (2012) point that gender and race are both social constructs and real, and if we draw an analogy with language, there is clearly more at stake here.

If 'we decide that languages exist', argues Hutton (2002, p.121), we would likewise have to concede that 'races exist'. This point is not necessarily under dispute if we understand that to concede the existence of language or race is to concede that they are social constructs: they do not exist as anything other than socially created entities that pull together certain features – words, morphemes, hair colour, facial features – into a supposed unifying construct. As Haslanger (2012) makes clear, if we want to resist reality (oppose racism or sexism), we first have to acknowledge that race and gender are socially constructed realities. If 'any attempt to classify and characterize different races is unscientific', Hutton (2002, p.121) continues, 'then any attempt to classify and characterize different languages must similarly be pseudo-science'. That is to say, it is one thing to accept that language, gender and race are real as socially produced constructs, but it is quite another to turn a scientific gaze onto each as objects of study beyond the social.

As recent *raciolinguistic* work has made clear, language and race are deeply entangled in many contexts (Alim, 2016; Rosa and Flores, 2017). Linguistics is 'both the parent and the child of race theory'; the parent in the sense that linguistic categories were crucial in the development of physical anthropology in the nineteenth century, the child 'in the sense that linguistics has reclaimed its role as the premier science in the classification of human diversity, elaborating a "characterology" or "typology" of the world's languages, and therefore of the world's ethnic groups' (Hutton, 1999, p.3). On this score, we have to appreciate the 'contribution of linguistic theory and linguists to the murder and mayhem of twentieth century ethnic politics' (Hutton, 2002, p.137). For these and other reasons it is incumbent on linguists of whatever sort to consider carefully what kind of realism we want to pursue: a realism that insists that languages are scientifically analysable entities or a critical social realism that insists on relational ontologies, social epistemologies and critical appraisals.

1.2 WHOSE VERSION OF LANGUAGE COUNTS?

Alongside ontological questions about what language is and what languages are, a related concern is whose version of language counts. A practical theory of language surely needs a strong relationship to how language users think about language. For Bauer and Trudgill (1998b), like Pinker (1994), the important linguistic distinction between descriptive (linguistic) and prescriptive (lay or pedagogical) approaches to language enables a focus on *language myths*, or popular but erroneous views on language that need to be rectified. There are, to be sure, many mistaken views about language across different social worlds, some that evidently matter – that women speak too much, or that some languages are primitive, for example – and others that may appear less consequential but may still have serious implications – that 'Eskimos' have a hundred words for snow, for example, or that there are 7,117 languages in the world. The descriptive/prescriptive distinction itself, however, is something of a myth. It assumes that scientific descriptions of language are somehow above and distinct from social norms; it overlooks the ways that attitudes towards language, or language ideologies, are part of the social world of language and cannot therefore be dismissed as outside the linguistic purview. Above all, however, it conceals the point that linguists' attitudes to language are similarly value-laden, and their pronouncements about what is and is not possible in language can be equally normative (Cameron, 1995). As will be discussed further in Chapter 3, once decisions have been made about how a language system works, or how two such systems can work together, linguists are as capable of prescriptive pronouncements as those they denounce.

It is certainly true that people are interested in language: like the weather or families, it is something many people like to comment and have views on. Whether this fits a descriptive/prescriptive dichotomy, however, is another matter. Take this recent comment by a young woman to her friends on a tram in Melbourne: 'Isn't it weird the way English doesn't have a word for, like, the day before yesterday but has some, like, really complicated word for throwing someone out a window.'[4] Such everyday commentary on language is far more descriptive than it is prescriptive, and suggests both a general interest in how language works, as well as intimated comparisons of languages that can express the day before yesterday more easily – *avant-hier* in French, 一昨日(*ototoi*) in Japanese, 前天(*qiántiān*) in Chinese, *vorgestern* in German and so on – and languages such as English that struggle to do so. Common utterances about language along the lines of 'words cannot express how I feel' likewise have little to do with prescription and more to do with a perceived gap between emotional states and our capacity to express them: 'Words are not enough, mate'; 'There are no words to explain what we've been through'; 'Words can't describe what they're going through'; 'Words cannot express how much she

---

[4] Defenestrate, presumably. APLA (Alastair Pennycook Language Archives) language notes, Melbourne, 4 August 2023.

will be missed'; 'Words cannot express how devastated we have been by this'; 'Words cannot express the depth of our sorrow.'[5] The idea that words can't do some of this emotional work for us seems commonplace and arguably reveals a popular attitude towards language and its limits (though I have not yet pursued this interest across other languages). It has become interestingly formulaic (words cannot express), suggesting a popular discourse that expressing grief, anguish, distress, amazement or shock cannot be done well with language (defined in terms of words). Maybe language can do more than people think, but I certainly have more respect for this view than to try to question it, and it is more useful in any case to understand this in pragmatic rather than propositional terms. It might therefore have the potential to be seen as a language myth, though not in terms of being untrue so much as a common way of thinking about language.

If we look at newspaper or other media, where people write in to comment on language matters, it is true that a more normative attitude is common, though as discussed in Chapter 3 such normativity may be equally shared by linguists. In letters to the *Sydney Morning Herald* on the last day of 2022, people wrote to suggest that the term 'hero' was being overused, that a medical receptionist's use of 'gorgeous' to confirm an appointment was a bit over the top, or to inquire when 'snuck' (rather than 'sneaked') became the past of sneak, and so on.[6] As (applied) linguists, we like to step back and look at such views as examples of everyday language ideologies, though as daily language users we may also agree with the comment about heroes (how did health workers, firefighters, teachers and many others all become heroes by doing their commendable jobs?), feel some sympathy with the reaction to 'gorgeous' (how have common terms of verification now become 'fantastic', 'gorgeous', 'terrific' and so on?) and feel we may need – a little hypocritically – to look up 'sneak' (I thought the past tense *was* 'snuck'). Such letters, of course, don't necessarily give us insight into popular views on language, since this is a self-selecting group who choose to write to a particular newspaper about language. They perhaps have prescriptive overtones in their comments on change but they are also descriptive in their observations about contemporary language use, and as both linguists and language users we often have rather mixed reactions to such commentary.

The *language myths* position (common views about language are mistaken) can be seen as a form of the 'error correction' approach

[5] APLA language notes, various sources, 2016–23.
[6] APLA language notes, 31 December 2022.

that, it has been suggested, fails to engage with the reasons and interests in particular views on language (Lewis, 2018). If we simply try to disprove arguments, we overlook the investments people have in their views about language, the wider political and ideological contexts from which such ideas emerge, and the material conditions they support. Arguments aimed to counter raciolinguistic or homophobic ideologies that attempt to put people right about language fail to address the material, institutional and historical aspects of racism and homophobia from which such views emerge. This is also a question of what we mean by 'myths'. If we assume myths are simply falsehoods, we fail to understand their power as 'communally shared narratives told in the construction of an ideological set of beliefs' about structures and functions of language (Watts, 2011, p.10). Since these myths are the shared properties of groups – stories about language that are one of the ways people make sense of the world – 'deconstructing language myths is unlikely to have much effect on how people, on an everyday basis, view language' (Watts, 2011, p.17).

Drawing a distinction between popular and scientific views of language – where the former are seen as myths and the latter as truths – fails to acknowledge both the social nature of academic work (particularly when something like language is at stake) and the social embeddedness of beliefs about language. It suggests that one set of beliefs are social, cultural, political or ideological while denying such elements in linguistic knowledge. As discussed in Chapter 3, the liberal egalitarian beliefs common in linguistics – that all languages are equally complex, for example – may be estimable but they also need to be seen as ideological positions. Various alternative positions on everyday views on language have suggested that rather than dismissing popular views about language, they should be the starting point for any useful linguistics. Integrational linguistics, for example, claims a lay-oriented position, arguing that any study of language needs to take into account common views about communication (Pablé, 2019b). Indeed integrational linguistics turns the tables on the science versus myth position, suggesting that everyday views on language should be our starting point and that the real *language myth* is the one upheld by mainstream linguistics (Harris, 1981).

Folk and citizen linguistic projects, by contrast, may be less critical of orthodox linguistic principles but insist nonetheless on the importance of everyday views of language and even on putting scientific analysis in the hands of the participants (Rymes, 2020; Svendsen, 2018). A linguistic anthropological approach, meanwhile, takes language ideologies seriously as local ways of understanding language. As

Blommaert (2013) makes clear, we can no longer assume static languages in a landscape that can be interpreted by linguists. We need instead an appreciation of mobility, complexity and unpredictability, and we will only be able to approach an understanding of language by 'close ethnographic inspection of the minutiae of what happens in communication' and by 'keeping in mind the intrinsic limitations of our current methodological and theoretical vocabulary' (2013, p.8). The idea of *language ideological assemblages* (Kroskrity, 2021) urges consideration of the entanglements of people, ideology, place and material arrangements in any consideration of what languages are. How these different approaches may contribute towards a practical theory of language is discussed in much greater depth in Chapter 2.

The question as to whose version of language counts takes on a much sharper political focus when placed in the context of global knowledge production and distribution. In light of the decolonial demand to question Western or Northern ways of thinking about language and to take seriously not just different contexts around the world but different ways of thinking about languages, and indeed different language ontologies, the focus is on all that has been dismissed and denied in contemporary linguistic approaches. Language activist-scholars have asserted their own community ways of thinking about language, questioning the power linguists hold to define and describe Indigenous languages, and calling instead for the need to decolonize standard ways of considering what language is (Leonard, 2021). This links to a similar call to decolonize orthodox views of multilingualism in the Global South, challenging mainstream understandings of multilingual education, mother tongue education, language policies and so on (Ndhlovu and Makalela, 2021). For MacSwan (2022a, p.1), this kind of questioning 'implies that multilingualism and a vast array of related topics on linguistic diversity are fictions'. This is not what is being argued, however. Rather, the point is to try to understand how multilingualism is not the same thing in different contexts. Such moves, discussed further in Chapter 5, not only raise questions about whose version of language counts but pose major challenges for how the field thinks about language.

1.3 LANGUAGE AS ASSEMBLAGE

A central interest of this book (given the title) is the notion of language assemblages. On one level, the entire book is about language assemblages: languages are not pregiven entities but rather are assembled, gathered from a range of different elements and experiences, the products of social and ideological processes. Languages are made by both linguists and non-linguists, and the question about whose version of language counts asks whose language assemblage prevails in which contexts. On another level, however, there are more specific ways of thinking about language as an assemblage, discussed in depth in Chapter 4. This perspective eschews assumptions about languages as structural entities, focusing instead on the spatial gathering of linguistic and other material elements. A focus on languages as assemblages reconfigures what counts as language and how social, spatial and material worlds interact.

This understanding of assemblages as entangled groupings of different elements allows for an appreciation of the ways in which different trajectories of people, semiotic possibilities and objects meet at particular moments and places. This emphasis draws on the wider interest in assemblages and entanglements in the social sciences to understand how different kinds of things – bodies, words, artefacts, space, emotions, policies and so on – come together at particular moments and in particular configurations, creating a dynamic arrangement that is greater than the sum of its parts. Thinking in terms of assemblages points to ways that social life happens as an unfolding set of uneven practices. It insists that we explore social life not through broad abstractions about language, society or culture but in terms of local combinations of things that become happenings. This does not mean turning our back on the possibility of thinking about political economy or structural racism, for example, or indeed language in some of its more traditional senses, but insists instead that these only make sense when looked at in their local entanglements.

There are three slightly different ways that language and languages can be considered in relation to the idea of assemblage: assemblages as combinations of linguistic items (language assemblages), assemblages as semiotic gatherings (semiotic assemblages) and assemblages as material arrangements that involve language (sociomaterial assemblages). While these three different approaches often overlap, the different implications of each are discussed further in Chapter 4. Thinking about language as an assemblage, Wee (2021) suggests, can account for how languages are assembled through varied experiences with language in the world. Looking at language in terms of assemblages emphasizes the processes of communication as people draw on their prior linguistic encounters to create meaning. The notion of semiotic assemblages opens up ways of thinking that focus not so much on language use in particular contexts – as if languages pre-exist their instantiation in particular places – but rather on the ways in which particular assemblages of objects, linguistic materials and places come together. This is to approach language not as a pregiven or circumscribed entity but rather as something that is constantly being compiled from a range of semiotic possibilities. Sociomaterial assemblages similarly focus on the gatherings of things, places and linguistic elements, and consider language to be embodied, embedded and distributed, where language is not so much an abstract system of signs as changing sets of material relations.

The idea of language as assemblage therefore suggests an ontological commitment that differs in a number of ways from structural or practice-oriented ways of thinking. In structural ontologies, language is rarely seen in material terms, any relation to the material world being largely symbolic or representational. This interest in materiality does not propose that matter is all there is, as if language, thought, consciousness and so on can be reduced to material explanations, nor that material relations in terms of political economy or worldly circumstances define all other concerns. The point is to take matter seriously and to find ways of understanding language and its connections in material terms. This is of particular concern for a practical theory of language, for while practice cannot be reduced to material processes, it makes little sense to extract practice from its material surrounds. Whether language is understood as an assemblage of linguistic items, semiotic gatherings or sociomaterial arrangements, an assemblage ontology is a move away from autonomy and towards complexity.

Language cannot be separated from human or other life but provides potential meanings that participate in social and material events. An assemblage focus emphasizes the dynamic relations among people, things, places and artefacts, enabling a view that languages may be socially, materially and politically reassembled. While emphasizing human action in the assembling of languages, it also downplays the centrality of the individual actor, drawing attention to the ways human, non-human, technological and material actants combine. An assemblage ontology is a much better candidate for a practical theory of language than a structural ontology, since it urges us to understand how language operates in the world. It can give us a better handle on language learning, social interaction, semiotic landscapes and much more by opening up ways to see how language is not so much an abstract entity confined to our minds that escapes now and then when we talk and write, but rather is part of the symbolic and material world we inhabit.

1.4 OTHER LANGUAGE ONTOLOGIES

If a focus on language assemblages is central to this book, an approach based on relational ontologies also emphasizes the importance of considering how different language ontologies are related. This is not just the liberal egalitarian focus of folk or citizen linguistics that asks how people ordinarily think about language, but rather of taking alternative views of language much more seriously. As argued in the discussions of whose version of language counts, this is a political question, a concern about how some versions of language have been discounted, disparaged and dismissed at the expense of others. Of particular importance here are Indigenous and minoritized languages. Taking seriously other ways that languages can be understood is of significance for both practical and political reasons. If language revival or other applied projects need practical theories of language, they have to be drawn from concerned communities rather than imported from elsewhere. A difficulty with such work is that community activists and language experts are not always trying to reclaim the same thing.

The 'very idea of "language"', as identified and delimited in Western ideological frameworks, corresponds, as Dias (2019, p.90) reminds us, 'to an invention arising from seventeenth- and eighteenth-century coloniality and nationalism' and an 'assumption that such a notion, as a preconceived, independent object, is readily transposable to all locations and populations'. If this is particularly true of the notion of language as object or structure, it is also important to ask what structure, practice and assemblage as ontologies may exclude. An argument can be made that in their emphasis on social and material or human and non-human relations, practice and assemblage ontologies are closer to Indigenous and other Southern ways of thinking. The focus on land, Country and a more-than-human world that runs through many accounts of what language is from different Indigenous perspectives echoes a number of the themes discussed in relation to assemblages. Yet such relations need to be drawn with great caution lest we reduce Indigenous cosmologies to Western ontologies or assimilate a diverse range of ways of thinking about language into Northern ways of thinking. The focus on ontologies that runs throughout the book derives in part from attempts to grasp these different worlds.

The material focus developed in the discussion of assemblages can shed light on connections to land, water and surrounds, yet it runs the danger of overlooking what are often deeply spiritual relations.

Assemblage-oriented thinking may point to more grounded views of language, but the material can also be connected to the spiritual. At the same time, to focus on Indigenous ways of knowing is not to cast such knowledge in terms of spiritual at the expense of rational, or local at the expense of extendable, or other such troublesome binary thinking. Approaches to *radical Indigenism* (Garroutte, 2003) or *Indigenous standpoints* (Nakata, 2007) emphasize the importance of understanding Indigenous philosophies of knowledge as coherent logics for understanding the world and to appreciate that these have also developed in relation to colonial forms of knowledge that surround them. The issue is far more than one of exclusion or distortion – Indigenous languages have been overlooked or misunderstood – but of taking marginalized knowledge seriously for what it can bring to contemporary thinking and applied projects.

For many Indigenous people, language is deeply connected to land, or what is commonly known as *Country* in Australia. Country encompasses far more than earth, dwellings and place. It can include not only rocks, trees and many physical features (and the particular significance they may have) but also water – sea, rivers, water holes – as well as animals – linked to people and their stories – and many other things such as wind and other beings (including humans) (Bawaka Country et al., 2022). Language within these ways of thinking is not connected primarily to people but to land or Country. It is because these ways of thinking about language are so different from a consideration of language as structure, as object, as separate from people and the world that many language revival projects have foundered. As long as Indigenous languages are thought of in terms of non-Indigenous ontologies, there will always be at best misunderstanding, if not appropriation and extractivism. On these grounds, Indigenous language activists have called for local control of language reclamation projects and the need to *decolonize* what is meant by language (Leonard, 2017).

1.5 CONCLUSION

Taking up ontological questions has implications for both what we think the world is and for what we think language is. As Grace (1987, p.9) pointed out long ago, an orthodox linguistic standpoint is 'implicitly committed to the strong ontological assumption that there is an objectively given world common to all people which defines for all time what can be talked about'. It is on these grounds that it is commonly assumed that despite various differences, the same thing can be said in different languages: there is, after all, one world to be spoken about and all languages are ultimately cut from the same linguistic cloth. Part of that one world is a general property called language, which can then be subdivided into different but equal entities called languages. Apart from lacking philosophical and anthropological curiosity, such a view does not account either for the possibility that the world may be more ontologically diverse than this, or that the languages that are the focus of linguistic inquiry are as much objects of our own making as they are entities waiting to be described (Jakobs and Hüning, 2022). Above all, such a view does not do enough to question the interests – national, ethnic, political and economic – behind these linguistic divisions.

What if we listen to other worlds and start to consider both that the world may be plural and that languages may not necessarily be comparable things? Once we ask whose version of language counts, taking into account people's investment with language as well as the demand to decolonize language, once we engage with local language accounts, we have to base any practical theory of language on what language is within a local ontology. This necessitates an engagement with language ideological assemblages and an understanding that languages are inevitably locally made assemblages (linguistic, semiotic and material), and that applied linguistics as an epistemic assemblage is one way we can start to address the needs for a practical theory of language that can remain both plural and political (Pennycook, 2021c). This will be developed further in Chapter 6. In the next chapter, I will discuss questions of whose version of language matters and what it means to talk in terms of language ontologies.

2 Language, Knowledge, Myths and Being

The historical relationship between linguistics and applied linguistics, whereby the one produces knowledge about language and the other applies it to real-world contexts, creates a hierarchy of knowledge, with linguistic knowledge at the top, everyday popular views on language at the bottom and applied linguistics somewhere in the middle, mediating between the two. This relationship has started to shift, however, as applied linguists have sought to develop their own views of language based on their engagements with language users and contexts. As will be argued in Chapter 3, this is arguably the case for an idea such as *translanguaging*, which emerged from, and is generally applied to, contexts of language in education. For Li Wei (2018) it is the practical nature of translanguaging theory that commends it. Approaches to everyday views on language have also unsettled this relationship, insisting that ordinary people's knowledge about language needs to be part of how we understand it: linguistics should be lay oriented (Harris, 1998b), and we need to take more seriously *folk linguistics* (Albury, 2017) or *citizen sociolinguistics* (Rymes, 2020). This will be of significance in this book, particularly when considered within a broader politics of knowledge.

2.1 EVERYDAY KNOWLEDGE ABOUT LANGUAGE

Much is made among integrational linguists of Roy Harris' (1990b) dialectology epiphany when he asked whether the patois of one peasant's Alpine village was the same as that of another. The response he received turned the question back on Harris, pointing out that while other villages used different words, they all seemed to understand each other anyway, but that in any case young people spoke differently. The response undermined the question and its assumptions about dialectal variation and mutual understanding. It was not just the response of a dialect informant (this is how we say this and they say that) but an informed metalinguistic comment. To his credit, Harris apparently took these comments seriously (they might have been dismissed) and started as a result to question many of the foundations of linguistic thought (the *dialect myth* to start with). To researchers with a more ethnographic background – such as linguistic anthropologists – to make a great deal out of a researcher taking the worldview of an informant seriously is a rather remarkable indictment of a research tradition that has typically not done so. As we know, however, from critical accounts of language research, particularly in Indigenous contexts, linguists all too often find the languages they are looking for (Stebbins, 2014); that is to say, the linguistic ideologies that linguists bring to their contexts of study have profound implications for subsequent analyses.

Aside from various armchair linguistic approaches (such as so-called native speaker intuition), getting people to supply linguistic information has always been essential to linguistic endeavours. The great *Oxford English Dictionary* (OED) project, for example, sought to derive the meaning of words by citing their earliest known use and asked for help from the public at large (as well as members of the Philological Society of London). One of the most regular contributors was William Minor from his prison cell in the Broadmoor Criminal Lunatic Asylum (Winchester, 1998). Over five million citation slips were received, though the project was always biased towards particular sources from literature, reference works and journalism (Willinsky, 1994). As Harris (1988, p.1) has noted, the OED, by drawing on such sources to describe the 'myth of standard English' was a 'remarkable example of self-fulfilling prophecy', a 'myth which had been invented to serve the purposes of a typically Victorian brand of national idealism' (1988, p.26). Asking linguistic informants, therefore, particularly in the form of providing examples to substantiate a claim, may only serve to bolster preconceived ideas about languages. There is nothing methodologically that opens the investigation to alternative views about what matters.

In recent times, and with the ease of online platforms, it is still common for linguists to ask the general public what terms they use to refer to common items, such as swimwear (a more important issue in Australia than in some other countries): bathers, swimmers, togs, cossie, swimsuit, boardies or budgie smugglers? (The Linguistics Roadshow, 2023). This is largely in the tradition of dialectology – asking what words people use – rather than the stronger orientation in folk or citizen linguistics to discover what people think about language, or even getting them to set and ask the questions. Harris' reported regard for the views of the Alpine peasant 'later became one of the pillars of Harris's perspective on language: the primacy of the lay perspective' (Bade, 2021, p.22). Harris takes a strong view on lay-oriented language viewpoints, arguing that the ordinary language user 'has the only concept of a language worth having and everyone is a linguist' (Harris, 1998b, p.20). For Harris, a 'linguistic theorist speaks with no greater authority and insight about language than a baker or a bus-conductor' (1997, p.237). The grounds for this strong and, it would seem at times contradictory, if not self-defeating, position on language (Roy Harris was, after all, professor of linguistics at Oxford University) are on the one hand a profound dissatisfaction with orthodox linguistics: thus it is really the orthodox linguist who has nothing to say here rather than the integrational linguist. On the other hand, Harris' position derives from his commitment to a vision of the experience of communication that unfolds moment by moment: hence an interest in everyday experiences of communication rather than authoritative accounts of language. As Pablé (2019a, p.2) explains Harris' integrational perspective, 'there are no linguistic experts because there are no scientifically describable objects called "languages".

From the integrational perspective, therefore, since there is no good reason for linguistics to posit the existence of separable languages (Harris, 1990a), there is no good reason to claim some form of linguistic expertise. While these arguments seem commendably opposed to the overbearing authority of the linguist, there are also grounds for some circumspection. Linguistic expertise need not depend on the separability and description of languages, as many a generative linguist might also suggest: Chomsky's importance has been described as demonstrating that 'there really is only one human language' and the apparent variations across languages are really only 'variations on a single theme' (Smith, 1999, p.1). Linguistic expertise, from this point of view, has to do with the scientific study of more general notions of language, and it seems implausible to suggest that a lack of interest in separate languages has led to a lack of claims to expertise among transformational grammarians. For integrationists to focus instead 'on the notion of "activity" as a fundamental lay concept when it comes to understanding human communication' (Pablé, 2019a, p.2), furthermore, raises at least two questions. Firstly, while the notion of 'activity' does point in the direction of an understanding of language as social action and reaction (Enfield and Sidnell, 2017) or of language as a social practice (Pennycook, 2010) – what people *do* with language (discussed further in Chapter 3) – and thus potentially

Language, Knowledge, Myths and Being

gives us categories of social language use (chatting, greeting, texting, mansplaining), without closer ethnographic study of such social activities (a perspective often lacking in integrational work), it is less clear how we can determine the salience of such categories.

Secondly, is it not also very common for people to talk in terms of languages? If we're looking for a good example of a 'lay' category of language, speaking different languages ('Do you speak Thai?' 'How many languages can you speak?' 'English is not my native language' and so on) would seem a common starting point. This takes us to a broader concern that has been raised in relation to recent work that questions the usefulness of positing different languages, particularly under the umbrella of translingual practices. Jaspers and Madsen (2019) point to the problem that for all the emphasis on fluidity of language use and the questioning of named languages, we live nonetheless in what they call a *languagised* world, a world in which people talk about languages in terms of these named entities. As Joseph (2006, p.27; emphasis in original) notes, 'so long as people *believe* that their way of speaking constitutes a language in its own right, there is a real sense in which it *is* a distinct language'. Even if we grant that what people may mean by talking of French, Navajo or Turkish may not at all accord with what linguists and sociolinguists take these things to be, and even if we suggest that what people are describing with these linguistic labels might actually be translingual practices (though never named as such; Pennycook and Otsuji, 2016), language labels are nonetheless the common terms by which languages are often spoken about, and are arguably a good category for a 'lay' language category.

More careful engagement with ordinary views on language can be found in *citizen* and *folk (socio)linguistics*, though neither term is used very consistently. Folk linguistics sometimes describes popular language ideologies, in the same way that *language myths* discussed in Chapter 1 and in Section 2.2 refer to popular misconceptions about language. The folk linguistic fear that texting among young people may undermine their ability to write more extended prose, for example, can be disproved by research on their actual writing practices (Finkelstein and Netz, 2023). Thurlow (2014, p.483) similarly contrasts 'folk-linguistic beliefs about young people's digital discourse' with the findings of studies of 'their actual text messaging practices', conceding nevertheless that it is not necessarily useful to substitute 'one set of metalinguistic judgments for another' (2014, p.494). Echoing concerns about 'error correction' discussed in Section 2.3, this suggests that while it is important to critique folk linguistic misconceptions – such normalization of forms of prejudice are a 'means of rehearsing or reproducing the social order' (2014, p.495) – simply replacing such beliefs with better information may not bring about change. Other approaches to folk linguistics seek to understand everyday views of language not as misconceptions but as views about language that are important for a more general understanding of language use. Folk linguistics (or folk dialectology), as initiated by Preston (1993, 1996), argues the need to incorporate everyday understandings of language into the analysis (how people evaluate dialect variation, for example). Although this approach to ordinary views on language takes them more seriously, it has been critiqued for still leaving the analysis and data-gathering in the hands of the researchers, keeping the position of the professional sociolinguistic analyst in place, and thus not letting everyday views unsettle linguistics more broadly (Rymes, 2020).

Citizen sociolinguistics draws on *citizen science*, which aims to involve more people in science, and thus both to demystify scientific processes and to broaden the base of research. By asking people to report on bird or animal sightings, for example, or the best growing conditions for conservation of the recently discovered (1994) and critically endangered Wollemi pine (*Wollemia nobilis*; made available as a garden plant around the world in 2005) (Home Gardeners, 2023), citizen science engages ordinary people in wider scientific enterprises. Citizen sociolinguistics focuses on 'the study of the world of language and communication by the people who use it' (Rymes, 2020, p.5). Rather than 'looking to experts in the field of Linguistics for definitive diagnoses of language issues', Rymes (2020, p.2) suggests that 'these institutionally centered voices are just one of many different interesting and personally invested views on language'. In an era when people's observations on each other's language use are now readily available in online forums, much of this work draws on metalinguistic commentary on social media to shed light on common language values and ideologies. Rymes focuses particularly on aspects of English use in Philadelphia – the pronunciation of certain streets (Passyunk Avenue, for example), the use of terms such as 'hoagies' to refer to a long sandwich (a 'hero' in New York) – and the ways people talk about these (debates over how 'croissant' should be pronounced: kwuh-SAHN, kruh SANT, Kwar-SOR, CREscent and so forth).

Rymes distinguishes her work from other related approaches, particularly folk linguistics, on the grounds that citizen sociolinguists do not assume a capacity to analyse the language ideologies of others but rather take a more linguistic democratic approach to knowledge,

Language, Knowledge, Myths and Being

sharing viewpoints and valuing different views on language. Citizen sociolinguistics 'offers a means to explore alternative sociolinguistic knowledge: everyday opinion about language, how it functions in context, and how it is created and disseminated' (Rymes, 2020, p.27). Citizen sociolinguistics is therefore concerned with understanding how ordinary people understand language. Citizen sociolinguistics 'entails a redistribution of expertise' and an aspiration towards a greater democratization of a 'culture of knowledge exchange' (Lee, 2022, p.174). Gamification as a tool of citizen science can provide access to larger and more natural forms of data than other research approaches, Kim and colleagues (2023) claim. While folk linguistics might be understood as a sociolinguistic interest in everyday attitudes towards language, citizen linguistics draws more on linguistic anthropological interests in language ideologies. This more inclusive orientation draws us closer to what Silverstein (1985) called the *total linguistic fact* and Blommaert (2017) the *total semiotic fact* (discussed further in Chapter 4). As suggested in Chapter 1, linguistic anthropology, and particularly an understanding of language ideological assemblages (Kroskrity, 2021), has generally assumed that everyday views about language must, at the very least, be part of the picture.

As Svendsen (2018) notes, however, this approach to citizen sociolinguistics may be little different from a folk linguistic perspective since it studies what people think about language rather than involving those people directly in language analysis. It is common, as noted in Chapter 1, for people to comment on language: I recently noted cricket commentators (cricket is a slow game so there's plenty of time to talk about other things) discussing how to pronounce 'debutant' (one had pronounced the word deBUTent, while another suggested it should be DEbutahn – compare with Rymes' croissant discussion earlier in this section). The conversation then moved on to a more regional and class-based discussion (cricket really is a slow game) as to whether one was a Queensland way of speaking as opposed to 'that's how we say it in the working suburbs of Perth [Western Australia]'. For Svendsen (2018, p.155), observing such language debates is much more in the line of folk linguistics than *citizen sociolinguistics*, which implies the 'engagement of citizens in *doing* sociolinguistic research'. There are a number of questions, therefore, as to who directs the research, whether people are informants, participants or analysts, and who the research is for: is it of interest for sociolinguists to see how others think about language or is it for the participants to gain deeper knowledge about language? Citizen sociolinguistics, from Svendsen's perspective, has to involve ordinary citizens in sociolinguistic research, from designing the research project and forming questions to collecting and analysing data. While Rymes (2020, p.27) claims to offer a way to explore 'alternative sociolinguistic knowledge', Svendsen (2018, p.140) pursues the question of citizen science further and asks questions about 'who can claim to possess (sociolinguistic) knowledge, who is qualified to collect it and which data are "legitimate" (Svendsen, 2018, p.140).

Of importance in these various discussions is the significance given to everyday understandings of language. As Rymes (2020) concedes, while her emphasis on citizen linguistics is very different from linguistic claims to scientific knowledge (discussed in Section 2.3), it shares much with the linguistic ethnographic interest in language ideologies and everyday language use. It is arguably from this direction that the focus on *translingual practices* (under various names; Pennycook, 2016) has emerged, drawing on the ways ordinary language users think about language rather than imposing a framework from outside. It is this emphasis on working *with* people rather than writing *about* them, on seeking local rather than outside knowledge, that can potentially tie such approaches to decolonial perspectives (Svendsen and Goodchild, 2023). 'What if the participants do not orient to the juxtaposition of languages in terms of switching?' asks Møller (2008, p.218) in his study of three young Turkish-Danish men talking over dinner. It is not satisfactory to categorize a conversation as 'bilingual or multilingual, or even as language mixing', he suggests, if the participants instead see themselves as using 'all available linguistic resources' to achieve their linguistic goals. While there are also good reasons as linguists not to reject all our accumulated knowledge about language, there are also many grounds on which we need to question what we think we know, particularly in light of the insistence on rethinking linguistic knowledge from a Southern perspective (Deumert et al., 2020; Pennycook and Makoni, 2020).

2.2 MYTHS AND NORMATIVITY

For Pinker (1994, p.371), by contrast, the important distinction to be made is between 'a scientist and a layperson', with language knowledge resting with the former rather than the latter (contrary, for example, to Harris' lay-oriented linguistics). For Pinker and likeminded linguists, the most significant distinction to be made is between descriptive and prescriptive approaches: the language rules one learns at school are '*prescriptive* rules, prescribing how one "ought"

Language, Knowledge, Myths and Being

to talk. Scientists studying language propose *descriptive* rules, describing how people *do* talk' (Pinker, 1994, p.371; emphasis in original). Pinker is interested in debunking so-called *prescriptive* language norms (views on split infinitives, ending a sentence with a preposition and so on) by presenting *descriptive* scientific correctives. Authors in Bauer and Trudgill's (1998a) edited book address various *language myths*, such as erroneous views on language change: that languages shouldn't change, that languages are being ruined by poor use or the media, or that children can't speak or write properly any more, a perspective still alive and well, as shown in Finkelstein and Netz's (2023) discussion of folk linguistic views about texting. Also taken to task are views that some languages are better than others: that French is more logical or beautiful than other languages, that some languages lack grammar, that certain languages are not up to the task of educational or scientific work. They also critique discriminatory views about particular speakers: that women talk too much, that Black children are verbally deprived, and so on.

Unlike the language myths discussed in the next chapter – where disgruntled linguists turn the tables on the field and suggest it is linguistics itself that is the purveyor of myths – this version of language myths takes aim at everyday misconceptions about language. The goal of the authors is to show why popular beliefs about language may be mistaken from a linguistic point of view, and why such myths persist: 'linguists have not been good about informing the general public about language' (Bauer and Trudgill, 1998b, p.xv). One problem, as they rightly explain, is that linguistics has become a highly technical discipline, and most of what is written in linguistics is linguists talking to each other. Leaving aside questions of who holds the views they critique and how widespread they are (their book is not so much an exercise in folk linguistics as in correctional linguistics), the chapters usefully set the record straight: women still struggle to gain the floor in a male-dominated world; 'gossip' is a term steeped in historical bias, and 'not speaking up' can be better understood in terms of silencing (Holmes, 1998). If someone asks whether Indigenous Australian languages (or even worse, the 'Aboriginal language') are as complex as English, linguists are quick to point out the opposite: the complexity and diversity of First Nation languages (Evans, 1998).

At the same time as it criticizes these language myths, however, Bauer and Trudgill's book also reveals some of the underlying ideological positions of linguistics that are less evident, particularly the normative values embedded in its descriptive assumptions and 'error correction' as a methodology. Let us take the case of linguistic normativity first. The descriptive/prescriptive divide is fundamental to linguistics as commonly taught (Lyons, 1981), and is one of the first lessons that any linguist learns. A distinction is made between the scientific and objective study of language, on the one hand, and the social dictates of those in authority on the other hand: 'Linguistics is a **descriptive** field, meaning the aim is to describe language and all its wonderful, varied features. Linguistics is NOT **prescriptive**, meaning it does not endorse a "proper" way to speak a language. Linguists believe that all languages, dialects and forms of human communication are equal' (The Linguistics Roadshow, 2023, np; emphasis in original).[1] Linguistics is 'presented as a liberation struggle from the tyranny of traditional grammar' (Hutton, 1999, p.1). From this point of view, languages as systems work to their own internal logic – 'self-regulating systems' that operate independently (Trudgill, 1998, p.8) – while changes brought about by human activity are somehow less real (Milroy and Milroy, 1991). Appealing though such a distinction is, it assumes that language is a system that undergoes natural processes of change (changes within the system) while the social activities of humans that affect language are not part of this picture (Cameron, 1995). As Straaijer (2016, p.235) explains, 'linguists should realise that despite their descriptive aims, there is hardly any descriptive practice that comes without some form of norm setting, if not actual prescriptivism'. For Cameron (1995, p.8), 'the overt anti-prescriptive stance of linguists is in some respects not unlike the prescriptivism they criticize' in that they 'invoke certain norms' about language. Description and prescription are 'aspects of a single (and normative) activity'.

A good case can be made that notions such as grammaticality are not so much descriptions of a system as projections of standardization, that 'many of the grammaticality judgments on which linguistic theorizing relies do little more than recapitulate the normative dynamic of the standardization process' (Armstrong and MacKenzie, 2013, p.3). At the very least, discussions of grammatical norms and well-formed utterances can be seen for the normative statements they are, while assumptions about standard, prestige or 'inner circle' norms – where a particular version of the standard language remains the benchmark, the core from which other varieties diverge – distort the understanding of language variability (Milroy, 2001). This covert

---

[1] To be clear, I am interested here in the reiteration of forms of linguistic dogma rather than critiquing projects such as this that seek to bring education about language to a wider audience.

adherence to standard norms and the strong position against prescriptivism that posits languages as natural objects and social interventions as somehow unnatural are clearly ideological stances based on various undisclosed norms. Linguists have often placed themselves beyond public debates on language – one obvious reason for the limited take-up of their advice (Bauer and Trudgill, 1998b) – and 'often actively place themselves in polar opposition to prescriptivists and the general public' (Straaijer, 2016, p.235). This refusal to account for processes of standardization ignores social practices and takes up a strong ideological commitment against standardization (seen as a form of control opposed to creativity, diversity, authenticity and linguistic democracy) (Hutton, 2022). The descriptive–prescriptive distinction therefore is a means to distance linguistics from everyday views on language, to insist on precisely the opposite to a form of lay linguistics (even though many lay linguistic views may not in any case be as prescriptive or normative as those of linguists).

While linguists tend to emphasize their descriptive over their prescriptive agenda, 'criticising the prescriptivism of laypeople while indulging in it themselves' (Bird, 2020, p.3508), they nonetheless adopt normative versions of language, many of which derive from the structural ontology of linguistic orthodoxy. A key linguistic tenet is that 'normative ideology about language structure is anathema to linguists' (MacSwan, 2020, p.327). This is the descriptive versus prescriptive position restated: by claiming not to follow normative principles, linguists insist that they only describe what is, rather than suggest what should be. There are two main historical reasons for this claim: the first is to distinguish themselves from those who stand in judgement on others' language, the arbiters of good and bad language. The second is to establish themselves as scientists: linguistic judgements are not based on moral or aesthetic views of what is good or bad, but rather on scientific descriptions of use. This remains an important ideological but contradictory standpoint. The linguistic tradition going back to Saussure, by dint of its methodological nationalism (Schneider, 2018) and belief in stable language structures, 'placed theoretical constraints upon the freedom of the individual speaker no less rigid than the authoritarian recommendations of the old-fashioned grammarian-pedagogue' (Harris, 1981, p.46). Rather than being prescriptive rules imposed by educational systems, these, by contrast, were 'imposed from within the language itself' (p.46).

Here, then, is the first broad set of problems faced by a linguistics that tries to maintain a descriptive stance while doing so from a framework that claims linguistic neutrality in relation to its linguistic rules. If we look, for example, at recent debates about bilingualism and translanguaging (to which we shall return in Chapter 3), various tensions become apparent. In trying to show that some elements of bilingual competence must be separate (there are different systems for different languages), MacSwan (2017) points to various impossible structures when one is mixing Spanish and English. Drawing on data on Spanish–English bilinguals in the USA, as well as knowledge about the two languages involved, MacSwan insists that while it is possible to use a Spanish determiner (equivalent to English 'the') with an English noun, as in phrases such as 'los teachers', to do this the other way round, to put 'an English determiner before a Spanish noun is *ill formed*' so that examples such as 'the casa' are not possible (2017, p.181; emphasis added). Not so, reply Otheguy and colleagues (2018): not only is 'the casa' possible and used but so are many similar phrases from 'the escritorio' (the desk) to 'the caja de los juguetes' (the toy box).

Without going into the arguments on each side – structural and supposedly descriptive arguments on the one hand, and language user arguments on the other (Otheguy et al., 2018, are using their insider lay-linguist insights here as much as their disciplinary knowledge) – it is clear that while normative statements are supposedly anathema to linguists, this is exactly what these arguments about what is possible and not possible are. Looking at adjectives and nouns (in English, adjectives generally come before the noun – 'the tall building' – in Spanish generally after the noun – 'el edificio alto'), MacSwan (2017, p.181) asserts that 'the underlying linguistic system of a Spanish-English bilingual' can generate 'the white house', 'la casa blanca' and 'the white casa' (English adjective before Spanish noun) but never 'la blanca casa' or 'the casa white' (where the adjective is in the 'wrong' position for the assumed language). Not so, point out Otheguy and colleagues (2018, p.18), since this is based on 'the false claim' that a supposed Spanish rule 'forbids preposed adjectives', contradicting the evidence of many common phrases such as 'la blanca nieve' (the white snow) or 'el buen amigo' (the good friend).

It is not useful here to get bogged down in this kind of argument. The point is that linguistics may be as normative (and as misguided about its normative assumptions) as the prescriptive foe it denigrates. As Armstrong and MacKenzie (2013, p.106) explain, 'the grammar constructed by a professional linguist is simply an alternative codification to that provided by a normative grammarian'. On the one hand, as I will argue in the next chapter, arguments about bilingualism and translanguaging are often dealing with different language ontologies, one structural and the other practice oriented. On the other hand, when we see them arguing on the same ground – the claimed structural limitations of languages – we can see that the traditional linguist may take a far more prescriptive stance (under the guise of 'structural constraints', 'underlying linguistic systems' or constructions being 'ill formed') than they like to admit. The 'distinction between grammatical and ungrammatical word-sequences' Sampson (2017, p.39) explains, is 'a dogmatic article of faith' rather than any empirically verifiable idea. Although it is clear that judgements about grammaticality depend on 'a collective body of received beliefs', linguists treat grammaticality as 'an empirical primitive, assuming uncritically that the question whether a given linguistic datum is grammatical or not has essentially the same scientific status as a measurement in physics' (Armstrong and MacKenzie, 2013, p.54).

2.3 *ERROR CORRECTION AND KNOWLEDGE DEMOCRACY*

All of this presents various difficulties if we are to move towards a practical theory of language in applied linguistics. The descriptive/prescriptive distinction is unconvincing, relying on the one hand on fragile claims to a scientific knowledge of language and on the other casting everyday views of language as normative while overlooking the normative position from which this is articulated. As applied linguists we need to engage with everyday views on language as part of our work. Folk, citizen and lay linguistic approaches argue for the need to take ordinary people's views on language seriously, integrationists proposing that only the lay users' perspective on communication is useful. While Harris' position on a lay-oriented linguistics usefully questions 'the legitimacy of orthodox linguistics' (Pablé, 2019b, p.151), it is less common from this perspective to actually investigate how people think about language.[2] A folk linguistic viewpoint, by contrast, investigates people's beliefs but often does so from a fairly orthodox standpoint, mapping what people think against what we actually know to be the case. The citizen sociolinguist, meanwhile, aims to put scientific analysis in the hands of the participants (though the two approaches are sometimes conflated). A linguistic

---

[2] Integrational linguists, one might suggest, take something of an armchair view of lay linguistics, assuming they know what people think about language without really investigating the question in any depth.

anthropological approach to language ideologies aims to understand and take seriously the ways languages are understood locally.

Yet an applied linguistic agenda may also involve the promotion of some version of language over others, whether as a multilingual language policy or a language curriculum. There are a number of reasons to be sceptical about too great a democratization of knowledge about language. While there are good reasons to question the liberal egalitarian spirit of linguistics (the idea that all languages are equal is a nice idea but is also fairly meaningless; see Chapter 3), so too should we be sceptical about a notion that all language ideologies or metalinguistic commentaries are equal. There are reasonable grounds to see ourselves as better informed about questions of language than many other people:[3] informing parents and teachers that bilingualism may be beneficial rather than harmful (even if done from a somewhat constricted vision of what bilingualism can mean), advising governments on the benefits of mother tongue education (even if the discussion often lacks insights into more complex language ecologies), and explaining that language is always undergoing change and that alarms about deterioration are mistaken (even if such positions often fail to grasp the broader politics of the arguments) are positions we may need to take if only to oppose much more detrimental options. We should also be cautious about too great a faith in knowledge equality. One lesson we have learned from recent concerns over the 'media bubbles' created by social media, or just by reading comments posted on popular platforms, is that it can be a grave mistake to assume all knowledge is equal or that scepticism about scientific knowledge is necessarily progressive. The rise of the Internet, social media such as Twitter (now X) and platforms such as Wikipedia promised and partly delivered the democratization of knowledge – knowledge would have many sources and would be less bound by narrow academic concerns or the influence of major media outlets – but this has also brought about mistrust of science, unreliable information, alternative truths, conspiracy theories and ugly commentary.

At the same time, as critiques of 'error-correction' approaches to knowledge have made clear, it may be equally ineffective to insist on better knowledge without engaging with wider political and affective

---

[3] A well-educated friend asked me recently, for example, whether Norwegians have their own language. Well, of course, it depends what you mean by language ... Norwegian and Danish ... mutual comprehensibility ... historical background ... the Scandinavian continuum ... Nynorsk and Bokmål ... etc., etc. Much more information than he needed, but as linguists we know a lot about language(s) and it would be foolish to disavow this knowledge.

investments (Cutler, in press). An error-correction position tends to overlook the interests behind views about language. It aims to disprove arguments rather than seeking to understand the wider political and ideological contexts from which such ideas emerge and the material conditions they support. Arguments to counter raciolinguistic ideologies aim to overcome inaccurate understandings of language by providing better information, but fail to connect them 'to the material and historical aspects of racism' (Lewis, 2018, p.335), or to ask 'HOW language is represented, WHAT material circumstances these representations support, and WHICH social positions are occupied by actors representing language in these ways' (2018, p.329). This can also be seen in terms of the *locus of enunciation* from which views are expressed: observations on language are articulated by historical bodies within particular configurations of material, racial, gendered and class positions (Figueiredo and Martinez, 2019).

The continuation, and even resurgence, of 'language gap' ideologies that assume that children from working-class, migrant and Black families suffer from a linguistic deficit by dint of their background (Cushing and Snell, 2023; Johnson and Johnson, 2022), cannot be corrected simply by better information. There is always more at stake in terms of interests, ideologies, positionalities and materialities that need to be engaged with (Cushing, 2022a, b). A raciolinguistic rather than an error-correction perspective seeks a more radical transformation of institutions, addressing more directly ideologies that 'maintain the power of the white listening subject and the onus it places on minoritised speakers to modify the way they talk' (Cushing, 2022b, p.21). Error correction can also miss its target by assuming that the language it is trying to put straight is the same language that is being wrongly described by its antagonists. A linguist's language may be very different from a lay person's language, and rather than assuming either that lay views or linguistic views should be our preferred starting point, it may be more productive to try to understand how and why each is being articulated in particular ways and with particular interests.

There are therefore important reasons to question our linguistic orthodoxies and the position from which these are presented. Leonard (2021, p.223) gives an account of linguists suggesting that his attempts at reclaiming his language, myaamia, would fail. They 'were trying to uphold their academic territory – manifested here as the power to define, describe, and control the fate of Indigenous languages'. Along with 'a racialized assumption of inferiority' and 'a more general logic of failure that gets applied to Native Americans engaged in language work' (Leonard, 2021, p.223), this is about assumptions of expertise, of superior knowledge about language. Investigating te reo Māori in Aotearoa (New Zealand), Albury's (2016, p.291) version of folk linguistics has a strong impetus to 'decentralise knowledge authority, question universal truths, and seek out alternate epistemological biases that exist within language communities themselves'. His concern is that current theories 'continue to define language vitality in western ontological terms' and are thus less applicable for revitalization projects (Albury, 2016, p.306). From this point of view, 'folk linguistic research methods can contribute to the decolonisation of sociolinguistic theory and method by understanding, voicing, legitimising, and indeed ultimately applying more ontologies and epistemologies of language than those that generally premise current scholarship' (Albury, 2017, p.37).

This emphasis on different, relational ontologies, will be explored in greater depth with respect to First Nation languages in Chapter 5. More generally here it points to the importance of thinking about language rather than just languages in plural terms. It is in such propositions that we can finally see how a greater emphasis on local understandings of language can be important. This is about opening up our understanding as linguists that there are multiple language ontologies. For some linguists, linguistic ethnographic perspectives that seek not only to locate language use in carefully described contexts but also to incorporate language user perspectives may add very little if anything to the knowledge of language based around descriptive techniques. Such disciplinary arrogance, such 'lazy thinking' (*razão indolente*) (de Souza, 2017; Santos, 2002, 2004), avoids 'representing the public interest in the realm of thinking' (Dasgupta, 1997, p.24). We need instead to engage with how language is understood locally in order to unsettle our assumed knowledge about language without at the same time undermining our capacity to say something useful about, or at least to listen carefully to, others' views about language. This, as will be argued at greater length in Chapter 6, is about developing applied linguistics as an *epistemic assemblage*, about bringing together language matters of concern, practical theories of language and critical appraisals of what is at stake (Pennycook, 2018c).

2.4 THE ONTOLOGICAL TURN

As discussed in Chapter 1, one of the ways we can approach these difficulties is by taking ontological questions seriously, a major theme

Language, Knowledge, Myths and Being

of this book. Ontology is the study of being (what things are) rather than epistemology (what we know).[4] It also becomes, as a result, a study of classifications of being: what kinds of being are there? There are several reasons for taking up ontological questions here, most obviously because I want to ask what language and languages are, or how they come to be, how they are assembled. This is partly in response to a lot of recent discussion about what it means to take an ontologically curious or sceptical stance about languages (Wee, 2021). It is also in response to what has been called an 'ontological turn' in the social sciences and particularly anthropology. In a general sense this refers to a renewed interest in questions of what things are. Povinelli (2016) suggests that this turn towards ontological questions is a result of the threat to human ways of life as a result of climate change and other ecological threats. It raises questions about the ways humans have elevated life forms (and particularly human life forms) over other entities. Posthumanist and new forms of materialism have started to ask searching questions about the ontological distinctions we make between humans, other life forms, the world around us and objects (Pennycook, 2018a). This line of thinking takes us in the direction of assemblages (a major theme of the book and of Chapter 4) and of other ways of conceiving of the world (explored further in Chapter 5).

In more specific terms, and particularly in relation to anthropology, the ontological turn refers to a move away from cultural difference – assuming the same reality viewed from different perspectives – towards ontological difference – suggesting that we are actually dealing with different things (Holbraad and Pedersen, 2017). This ontological turn is generally seen as originating in the work of Viveiros de Castro (2014), who argues that for all its focus on cultural difference, anthropology remains stuck in a divide that renders nature universal, solid and unchanging (there is one reality) and culture as the vastly different ways in which the world is represented. We need to move, he argues, from this multicultural framework (same reality, different ways of looking at it) to a *multinaturalist* view (different realities): 'in a multinatural metaphysics, there is no stable ontological ground'

---

[4] There are many different versions of what ontology means. In semantic modelling within computer science, for example, ontologies are systems of knowledge conceptualizations based on simplified categorizations of a field. There are also questions, discussed further in Chapter 6, as to whether the ontology–epistemology distinction (the separation of being and knowing) is sustainable. Much of the discussion around the ontological turn also potentially confuses ontological and epistemological categories (Graeber, 2015).

(Kohn, 2015, p.319). The challenge that emerges from this way of thinking is that if we take difference seriously, and we do our ethnography carefully, we need to start to question more profoundly the categories through which we understand difference. We can, following Holbraad and colleagues (2014), distinguish between a traditional philosophical concept of ontology that seeks a single truth about *how things are*; a sociological critique of such a position (as essentialist) that nonetheless ends up affirming through its ideology critique a vision of *how things should be*; and an anthropological approach to ontology as a multiplicity of forms of existence enacted in concrete practices or *how things could be* (Escobar, 2020).

The standard framework for thinking about difference – in anthropology and elsewhere – is that there is one world, one physical environment, but different ways of getting at it. These are cultural differences, that is to say different human ways of framing the world. The notion that humans inhabit different worlds was, as Pickering (2017, p.135) puts it, 'defanged academically by adopting a social constructivist or relativist perspective'. People might talk and act as if their worlds were different, but this was just talk, just human ways of constructing difference. This consensus has started to fail, however, as human hubris has come in for more critical scrutiny. What if we go beyond the liberal democratic 'respect for difference' – the idea that we cut the world up differently and each way of doing this should be respected – and instead ask whether the worlds we inhabit actually are different?. The problems of Western anthropology were not so much epistemological questions about the knowability of Indigenous practices, but ontological questions to do with underlying assumptions of Western researchers about objective and universal nature and subjective and plural cultures. Much of this work has emerged from anthropologists' engagement with Indigenous worldviews, going beyond an interest in how people shape the world differently and asking whether these worlds may in reality be different. The notion of the *pluriverse* – a way of looking at reality as a plurality of entangled but distinct worlds in contrast to assumptions that there is only one world – derives, according to Escobar (2016, p.22), from the ontological turn on the one hand and the engagement, on the other, with non-dualist relational understandings of life from outside Western modes of thought. We can also see an engagement with a pluriverse as a multiple-level disengagement from universality. Ontologically it rejects the insistence on one world; on an epistemological plain it discards claims about the knowability of this world from one perspective; and from an ideological position it refuses Northern assumptions to be the knowers.

This view has, not surprisingly, encountered considerable opposition and critique, some seeing it as a kind of 'linguistic relativity' in overdrive: not only do different languages affect the way we think, but they actually create new worlds. The ontological turn is not, however, a matter either of the linguistic construction of reality or of the linguistic representation of reality (different worlds are reflected in different languages and cultures). It is rather a non-representational view in which the practices, performances, doings and sayings of humans and other animals are part of a pluriversal world. Other critiques restate the need for a realist ontology and theoretical relativism (following the critical realism of Bhaskar, 1989; and see Block, 2022) rather than the ontological anarchy and epistemological limits of the ontological turn (Graeber, 2015). Of particular concern is the critique that a focus on a radical ontological alterity obscures common struggles faced by many Indigenous and minority people, such as climate change, incarceration, loss of land and habitat, and neoliberal economic policies (Bessire and Bond, 2014). Perspectivism, as this view is also known, has been described as 'indifferent to the historical and political predicament of indigenous life in the modern world' (Ramos, 2012, p.489), while the claims of researchers to give voice to the world 'can easily sound like the height of white or colonial hubris' (Chandler and Reid, 2020, p.495).

The ontology–epistemology distinction, furthermore, is one with deep roots in Western ways of thinking, and there are clear problems in using an ontological turn to better understand Indigenous ways of thinking when that very framework derives from a way of thinking that has done violence to those communities. The ontology–epistemology distinction is one we would do well to get beyond (Barad, 2007; Savransky, 2017), an issue discussed further in Chapter 6. For Todd (2016) the problem is that while ontological and posthumanist turns draw on, and at least sometimes recognize their debt to, Indigenous understandings of the world, the tendency is either to ignore these connections – to draw on both old and contemporary understandings of humans and the natural world without adequate attribution – or to appropriate and deracinate these ideas from their close affiliations with languages, communities and land (or water). This presents a serious challenge: you are damned if you take up forms of posthumanist thinking without connecting adequately to Indigenous cosmovisions, but equally damned if you make the connection but extract them from their contexts.

Constructing an ontological turn supposedly through the worldviews of Indigenous people runs the danger of 'projecting our theoretical ambitions on indigenous peoples' (Ramos, 2012, p.489), while the tendency to confuse white, Western Eurocentric concerns about a crisis in modernist thinking with Indigenous communities' real political and life struggles for security and freedom from colonialism has been described as both dishonest and parasitical (Chandler and Reid, 2020, p.499) There are therefore real reasons for circumspection when taking up any strong version of the ontological turn. While it may focus on material difference rather than cultural difference, it can still overlook material disparity; it potentially appropriates the very frameworks it claims to engage with; and it can map Northern epistemological crises onto Indigenous communities. It can nevertheless present some very real possibilities for alternative politics: it takes difference seriously rather than relativizing in terms of human construction; it suggests alternative ways of thinking about materiality; and it insists that researchers need to work much more carefully with the communities with which they are engaged. It is not that posthumanist or ontological-turn thinking cannot serve useful purposes in rethinking language and knowledge but rather that the tendencies to absorb Indigenous knowledge without accounting for location (Sundberg, 2014) or Indigenous Place-Thought (Watts, 2013; and see Chapter 5 for further discussion) need to be strongly resisted.

It can also be understood in terms of a form of recursivity (it has also been termed a *recursive turn*) that demands that the terms by which we try to frame cultural difference need themselves to be subject to greater openness to the terms by which others frame their world. This is a radical challenge to the ways we think about difference, a challenge not just to understand different classificatory systems but to grasp in relational terms the implications of these different ways of dividing up the world. It involves asking whether we need to also consider different kinds of difference, not just cultural difference but material and corporeal difference (Heywood, 2017). The ontological turn can be understood in terms of an open-ended critical project in which the critical academic-activist is not so much imposing ideas upon the world as enabling the world to speak back to power (Holbraad and Pedersen, 2017). As Kusters and colleagues (2017b) remind us, thinking in terms of ontologies – in their case deaf ontologies – enables a focus on the lived realities and embodied experiences of deafness that top-down concepts such as 'Deaf culture' or 'Deaf community' can end up obscuring. Similarly, thinking in terms of language ontologies can make possible an emphasis on what language is in the everyday lives of people, rather

Language, Knowledge, Myths and Being

than making assumptions from above about what languages are and how people think about them. Linguists, from this point of view, need not only to be *activist* in their orientation towards working with (rather than for) communities, but also to move beyond their *extractivist* approach to knowledge (Pennycook, in press).

2.5 LANGUAGE ONTOLOGIES

From a linguistic point of view, we might be content to let the anthropologists struggle over these questions without letting them disturb our thinking too much. There are nonetheless several reasons why we need to take this seriously. Linguistics, and particularly the more open fields of socio- and applied linguistics, cannot be immune from such concerns. Anthropology, and particularly linguistic anthropology, furthermore, has become increasingly influential in areas such as sociolinguistics. The split between sociolinguistics and linguistic anthropology into different social and cultural domains has been partly reconciled; Bucholtz and Hall (2008) suggest that it is perhaps time to recognize this reunion by talking of *sociocultural linguistics*. Indeed, a more constructive way forward in the anxieties about language ontologies would be to engage with the influence of linguistic anthropological interests in *language practices* (see Chapter 3) and the *decolonial imperative* to delink from colonial ways of thinking (Chapter 5) so that we can better focus on the ways languages are constantly under assemblage.

It was the work of Jan Blommaert (2010) and others with a background in linguistic anthropology, as well as the rapid growth of interest in linguistic ethnography, that unsettled the normative vision of languages that had established itself comfortably within sociolinguistics (languages were givens, the task being to look at their variability). This argument will be developed in much greater length in Chapter 3. From the point of view of linguistic anthropology, this has meant that when people talk about their languages in different terms, we are at least open to the idea that these languages may be different things rather than different representations of the same thing. An ontological focus on language, as Demuro and Gurney (2021) explain, moves away from a focus on language ideologies, which, like cultural analysis, is more concerned with how humans view the same world differently. The notion of language ideologies potentially leaves intact the object of inquiry: these are beliefs about things (languages) whose ontological status we have already established (Hauck and Heurich, 2018). A deeper inquiry into the nature of language requires us to ask ontological questions about what language and languages are.

The answer to the question 'What is language?' must, according to Hauck and Heurich (2018, p.5), 'remain plural' just as the answer to the question 'Where is language?' (Finnegan, 2015) needs to remain open. Based on studies of Amerindian language they argue that language remains 'an equivocal term, that is sometimes virtual and sometimes actual, sometimes part of pan-spiritual communication and sometimes confined to intra-kin-conversation' (Hauch and Heurich, 2018, p.5). Looked at from an ethnographic point of view, the Americas are not only a region of great linguistic diversity in terms of what are usually known as 'languages' but also in terms of different genres, styles, chants, songs, dreams, wailing, and narrative conventions within and across communities. 'These diverse phenomena', Hauch and Heurich argue, 'should not be understood as easily commensurable instances of a general phenomenon "language"' since they 'all may have different linguistic natures' (2018, p.5). As Course (2018, p.5) suggests, the idea of 'language' possibly 'obscures a fundamental diversity of ultimately irreconcilable practices, that Mapudungun and Spanish are understood to be fundamentally different kinds of things'. From this point view, the question is not only whether Mapudungun and Spanish (two languages spoken in Chile) 'are two different kinds of the same thing' but also whether 'they are two different things' (2018, p.5).

Some of these themes will be explored in greater depth in Chapter 5, where questions of Indigenous linguistic worldviews are discussed. This is not by any means, however, only a question of Indigenous languages but also of language more broadly. A central ontological focus in linguistics has been on the classification of human language as an entity distinct from all others. Language is what distinguishes humans from other animals. This gives an ontological status to the human capacity of language that is different from all other forms of communication (Finnegan, 2015). This cornerstone of linguistic thought is unsettled by challenges to the status of humans and their unique linguistic capabilities (Cornips, 2022). Once an ontological challenge is made to the status of language as an underlying monolithic category, or the idea that all languages are cut from the same cloth, the field is opened up to some very different explorations. In a similar vein to the arguments in this book, Demuro and Gurney (2021) suggest that we can look at language in at least three different ways, each suggesting not just a different take on the same thing, but a different thing: language as object, language as practice and language as assemblage. The first we can see as the fairly traditional linguistic approach to language as an identifiable system that exists independently of human action. The second focuses on language as part of broader social practices. The third looks at how linguistic resources come together in momentary assemblages of people, places and artefacts.

2.6 LANGUAGES AND REALITY

Ontological questions can also be understood as questions of reality (Kohn, 2015), which takes us back to concerns about what it means to say languages are real. This has been a particular topic of discussion in the wake of the claim that languages are 'inventions' (Makoni and Pennycook, 2007). To suggest that languages are inventions was clearly to suggest a greater social role in their creation than many were comfortable to admit. The argument was not that languages do not exist (this was perhaps not always clearly articulated, but inventions do, after all, produce something), but that they are social constructs. That languages are social constructs should be uncontroversial: 'There is no dispute about the fact that languages are socially constructed with porous boundaries, but languages are also experientially and socially *real* for students, teachers, policymakers, curriculum designers, politicians and most researchers' (Cummins, 2021, p.17). Like race or gender, language is not so much a biological entity as a human artefact (Haslanger, 1995, 2012). To say languages exist, like saying race or gender exist, is to acknowledge that social facts are real: 'socially constructed facts cannot be real or unreal; they are real because they are social facts' (Auer, 2022, p.137).

The key question is what flows from this observation about what languages are. For Rambukwella (2019, p.128), 'to argue that languages are not ontological realities is one thing but that has little or no impact on how language continues to be reproduced institutionally and societally as a site of inclusion and exclusion'. This is exactly the point, however: languages are social artefacts that are institutionally embedded and continue to be used to reproduce social inequalities; they are *socially real* for many people. We need to recognize this social reality – languages are a major site of exclusion and discrimination – without then falling into the trap of attributing to them some kind of reality beyond these social relations. Cummins (2021, p.17), for example, acknowledges the social construction of languages but also 'challenges the convention of using the term *named languages* to signify that socially constructed languages do not have linguistic reality'. Such *linguistic reality*, however, independent of social reality, needs more substantiation than such affirmations. The term *named languages* (e.g. Li Wei, 2018; Otheguy et al., 2018) is used to highlight the social and political status of what we call languages; if we also assume a *linguistic reality* beyond such naming, we are dealing with two different ontologies. Similarly for MacSwan (2020) the ontological question concerns the real existence of languages, a claim that needs to be upheld because of the ways languages are embedded in social institutions. The critical constructivist (deconstructivist in his terminology) position supposedly suggests languages, language communities or bilingualism are 'merely socially reified fictions' (MacSwan, 2022a, p.19). Yet this is to misunderstand the point that languages are not fictions but facts, social facts with social and political implications.

This takes us further into discussions of what it means to talk of reality. To get a better handle on this, it may be useful to consider further the notion of an artefact. When we consider the existence, the being, the reality of things, it is fairly easy to deal with objects such as rocks, rivers, seaweed or trees that evidently exist largely irrespective of human interference: they have to some extent an independent existence. It becomes more complex when we deal with artefacts (made objects) such as tables, sushi, fishing rods or ships, since these evidently share properties of being with other objects but have only been brought into being by human intervention. A table is no more or less real than a tree but it is less independently real. It is not always clear where something like a wood or a forest sits in this way of thinking, since humans have often had a hand in their making, and they play a not insignificant role in both human livelihoods and storytelling. This is in part the difficult territory of the natural and the cultural. We might observe that in the divide between 'natural' and 'cultural' sites in the UNESCO World Heritage categorizations of the world – the Great Barrier Reef (natural) and the Sydney Opera House (cultural), or Ethiopia's Simien National Park (natural) and the rock-hewn churches of Lalibela (cultural) – there are also sites such as the Val d'Orcia near Sienna in Italy which is a cultural rather than a natural landscape (an example of Renaissance agricultural landscapes), while the Uluṟu-Kata Tjuṯa National Park (formerly known as Ayers Rock and Mount Olga) in central Australia is a mixed natural and cultural site (both spectacular geological formations and part of the traditional belief systems of the Anangu).

This raises various considerations. The very existence of UNESCO World Heritage sites, whether buildings or landscapes, suggests an entangled relationship between the world and humans. We might also question the distinction between cultural and natural entities (Barad, 2007; Descola, 2013), or between the human and the natural, a separation that, as Latour (2015, p.146) has observed, 'has paralysed science and politics since the dawn of modernism'. There is an anthropocentrism at the heart of distinctions between culture and nature or the human and the natural that can be usefully overcome if we ask different questions about why we have for so long considered things in terms of mere objects, or why we have assumed that discourse matters while matter doesn't, or if we ask what nature looks like to other beings within it (What is a mountain, a minaret or molehill to other creatures?). We shall return to some of this discussion in later chapters. For now it is worth considering again what status we want to give to a world 'out there' independent of humans. This question by no means leads towards a kind of metaphysical idealism by which the world is only understood in terms of human perception; rather, it is an argument in favour of a more entangled, relational understanding of how humans, other animals, physical objects, artefacts, landscapes and so on are bound up with each other.

The question is what role humans should be seen as having in relation to what might otherwise be seen as an independent reality. The two extreme cases posit either a strong realist position (transcenendental realism in Bhaskar's terms) or a strong cognitivist position (transcendental idealism in Kantian terms) that continues in arguments about discursive production (Teubert, 2013), of reality being wholly dependent on the human mind. Neither position – a wholly independent or a wholly dependent reality – is very convincing. When we consider both the entangled relations of humans and the world as well as the world as lived by other animals such as dogs, cuttlefish or cows, and possibly plants such as trees, it is clear we need to move away from anthropocentric assumptions about a human-dependent world but also away from a natural world independent of other relations. Pushing further, we might also wish to consider how objects exist for each other (Bogost, 2012). When we consider more complex things such as gender, race or language, however, it would seem impossible to consider these outside human life. They are real too, but they are also very much human creations.

Social constructions can be understood as artefacts (Haslanger, 1995). Human intention or design are not always necessary in the process of construction, so although 'natural languages and cities are certainly artifacts' (1995, p.97), they are not necessarily the work of an intentional agent or artisan: languages may be assembled (Wee, 2021) but not intentionally. Languages are social constructs. To avoid the slippage into an anti-realist stance – or that everything is socially constructed so no differences apply – we need to distinguish between different types of social construction (Sveinsdóttir, 2015). In thinking about social construction – of gender, for example – we can distinguish between causal and constitutive construction. The first refers to social factors bringing about the existence of something; the second to social factors crucial in defining something. Genders are not less real for this but they are also differently real. They are also much more clearly tied to cultural, ideological and epistemological relations, and arguably plural: neither race, nor gender, nor language is one thing. This is not the same as talking about races or languages in the plural, which is to assume an underlying concept of language or race and then to accept its subdivisions along various lines. Rather, the argument here is that the reality itself is plural. Rather than being one thing, language may be plural not along the lines of methodological nationalism that has divided language into different entities but in ontological terms.

We shall return to some of these debates in Chapter 3, where the argument will be developed that in the discussions about social construction and translanguaging, we are dealing with different ontologies rather than epistemologies. That is to say, part of the difficulties in sorting out these arguments about the reality of languages rests on the fact that proponents of different sides of the argument are talking about different things, different ontologies. The general idea of an 'independent reality' – a reality independent of its relations to human sociality – is suspect, particularly when applied to concepts such as languages, but so too is a world only constructed by humans. We need to understand the relational aspects of being, and that humans do not have a relation to the world so much as they are part of it. To posit either a wholly independent world or a wholly constructed world is to concede too much to two particular worldviews. Instead, like Haslanger (1995, p.119) it is useful to think in terms of 'alternative, modestly realist, ontologies that enable us to come to more adequate and just visions of what is, what might be, and what should be'.

As explained in Chapter 1, in order to come to grips with what is, might be and should be, I have been working with a form of critical social realism.[5] *Critical realism* (Bhaskar, 1989; Fairclough, 2003) can be

---

[5] This is in part a move to resist arguments that critical constructivist approaches are somehow anti-realist or idealist. As suggested earlier, it is also in response to Latour's injunction for critical work to reclaim the real. We might nevertheless remind ourselves of the potential dangers and particularities of all claims to reality.

an appealing way to avoid what are seen as the pitfalls of either strong versions of realism and positivism (an emphasis on external and independent reality) or of relativism and constructionism (an emphasis on the world as only knowable from divergent human dispositions). A reworking of Block's (2022, p.41) take-up of *critical realism* presents a more dynamic understanding by introducing *relational ontologies* (Escobar, 2016) rather than *ontological realism*: different realities are entangled with human relations rather than constituting an independent reality beyond human experience. This does not mean that all reality is dependent on humans: that would be to accord too much to human hubris and to overlook, for example, reality as experienced by other animals. It is also not to dismiss the possibility of thinking in terms of a 'ready-made world' into which humans emerged – for some First Nations people this may include language that predates the arrival of humans (Chapter 5) – since it is to work from an ontologically plural position. Many realities – social realities – are nonetheless inseparable from human social life. This includes categories such as class, race, gender and language. They are social constructs, which means they are dependent on human sociality, they are real, but they are also open to challenge and resistance.

Rather than epistemological relativism, therefore, I focus on *social epistemologies* (Haslanger, 2012), so that the emphasis is necessarily on the social relations that produce forms of knowledge. As Haslanger (2012, p.197) suggests, there are reasons to take a *critical social realist* stance that aims to reveal 'differences that are socially constituted but not recognised, or fully recognised, to be so'. From this point of view, the focus is not so much on global claims to social construction but rather on 'particular social structures, and their impact in spite of their invisibility' (2012, p.197). Finally, such thinking needs a concept of *critical ethicalities* rather than *judgemental rationalism* (we need ways of deciding between alternatives that are based in political, ethical and affective modes rather than supposed forms of rationality). This means that neither language nor languages should be considered in terms of an independent reality beyond human experience but as social constructions that derive from social structures, relations and practices. This does not mean that languages do not exist but rather that they exist in so far as they are social facts. This position avoids normative assumptions in ontological terms (an assumed objective world), epistemological matters (an assumed way of getting at the world) or ethical concerns (a fixed position on the politics of language).

2.7 EXAMINING ONTOLOGICAL PREMISES

While one implication of the ontological turn is the argument that there are ontologically different worlds, another, more mundane consequence is that there is a lot of discussion of language in terms of ontologies. Ontological questions are not new to language studies: the 'ontological question', as Sampson (1980, p.36) asked a long time ago, is 'what kind of things Saussure thought languages are'. For Seargeant (2010), the ways that 'language is conceptualised as a feature of the human experience, and what existential form it is understood to take within the world' is an ontological question of 'fundamental importance in that it sets the parameters for any subsequent discussion of language' and linguistic research (2010, p.3). Seargeant is pointing to the problem that research generally proceeds based on a range of largely unexamined suppositions about the ontological status of what is being examined. Assumptions about language as a set of sentences, as a structured system of internally distinguishable features or as a way of representing the world are largely unquestioned research premises: 'Within contemporary linguistics, the ontological status of language and languages tends to be taken for granted' (Hall and Wicaksono, 2020, p.5). Researchers in the second language acquisition (SLA) tradition, Ortega (2018, p.65) similarly observes, leave their 'ontologies of language unquestioned, adhering without much public discussion to received ontologies from Saussurean structuralism or Chomskyan generativism'.

While a great deal of research leaves language ontologies untouched, work that has sought to examine the ontological status of language and languages presents a range of different possibilities. For Santana (2016, p.502), there are three classes of ontologies – psychological, social and abstract – while for Hall (2020) language ontologies can be understood in terms of I-language as the internal and individual capacity in a language (Santana's psychological) and E-language as the external expression of the language (Santana's social) (this I-language/E-language distinction more or less follows a Chomskyan categorization of internal and external language). To this Hall (2020) adds N-language as the national construction of a language and P-language as a Platonic abstraction of language

Language, Knowledge, Myths and Being

(Santana's abstract). Although Ramberg and Røyneland (in press) question whether linguists ever adhere to such Platonic ideals of language – where languages are held to be natural kinds beyond the realm of human activity – for Hall (2020) and Santana (2016) they clearly are part of the ontological map of linguistics. Pablé (2021) makes a case for three different approaches to language ontology: Southern theory (based on Indigenous ontologies and epistemologies, which I explore in Chapter 5), ontogenesis (based on the prelinguistic dispositions of the neonate) and integrational (based around the radical indeterminacy of the sign and the primacy of individual communication over concepts such as language).

Ortega (2018) stresses the importance of examining the language ontologies we work with: what is language, what is its nature? This will enable us not only to understand better what assumptions we are making about what language and languages are but also to appreciate alternative ontologies, such as those developed in the sociolinguistics of globalization (Blommaert, 2010) or educational linguistics (García and Li Wei, 2014). For Ortega, there is a basic choice to be made between 'essentialist and non-essentialist ontologies of language' (2018, p.69) as epitomized by SLA on the one hand and world Englishes on the other. This contrast between essentialist, idealized, monolithic or standardized versions of language versus more fluid, plurilithic accounts of real language use and diversity runs through a number of accounts of language ontologies (particularly with respect to English). Schaller-Schwaner and Kirkpatrick (2020, p.235), for example, drawing on Ortega's distinction, compare 'traditional ontologies of language' that tend to be 'essentialist' and to 'treat language as a thing' with more fluid and contextual accounts of language 'as a form of social practice'. The English as a lingua franca (ELF) framework, they suggest, provides a more flexible ontology of language use than do other frameworks.

The distinction many of these authors draw between essentialist and reified version of language on the one hand and more flexible practice-based versions of language use on the other hand mirrors in some ways the structural and practice ontologies discussed in more detail in Chapter 3. Whether ELF and World Englishes approaches really escape structural ontologies, however, is less clear. O'Regan (2016) critiques proponents of ELF for assuming its a priori existence. While they promote a flexible and non-normative vision of English as it is used by speakers of other languages, they nonetheless assume the prior existence of something called English that is being used, a view that 'proceeds from the reduction of ontology (reality) to epistemology (what can be observed) so that what is presumed to be real is interpreted and understood – or misrecognized – primarily in terms of what is observed' (O'Regan, 2016, p.207). [6] The world Englishes paradigm may suggest a more diverse way of framing language than does work in SLA, as Ortega (2018) argues, but it is still hampered by a tendency towards reification.

Like ELF, World Englishes has been important in challenging the primacy of native speakers (of English) and monolingual norms, but in many cases it does not move beyond the traditional sociolinguistics from which it emerged, describing in structural and methodologically nationalist terms (Schneider, 2018) the different kinds of English to be found in different parts of the world. World Englishes diversifies language by focusing on many (national) varieties (Indian, Malaysian, Nigerian etc. English) – and to this extent moves beyond essentialist beliefs about English being only one kind of inner circle English – but at the same time it reproduces a structural ontology of languages as systems located in different countries. As Hall and Wicaksono (2020) remind us, *ontologies of English* refer to what we think English is, an exploration of considerable importance for applied linguistics in language education: 'applied linguistics must be more explicit about the ways in which English is conceptualised in and for the domains of language learning, teaching and assessment' (Wicaksono and Hall, 2020, p.368). While heeding this call to understand English ontologically, we also need to consider that English itself is rather a special case, implying that the ontologies of English may be quite different from ontologies of other languages. Ontologies of English, world Englishes, ELF and so forth may tell us little about other language ontologies since different languages are assembled in very different ways, and the global status of English(es) makes it hard to compare with other languages.

In asking 'What is language?' and 'What are languages?' this book does not seek to answer from some overarching metaphysical standpoint but rather to follow the line of thinking initiated by Foucault (1984) in terms of historical ontology, asking how we came to arrive at the present (Seargeant, 2010). By what processes and practices have languages been assembled? As Hacking (2002) explains, this approach is not one of grand abstractions but rather rests in specific local

---

[6] By talking of 'what is observed' as epistemology, O'Regan is presumably not talking only in terms of empirical observations, but rather of the ideological frameworks that inform such observations. Like Seargeant (2010) he is pointing to the unexamined ontological assumptions that drive such work.

formations. While on the one hand, I want to make a case for an assemblage-oriented ontology, I am also interested, like Santana (2016), in making a case for pluralism. The ontological turn points towards accepting multiple ontologies (Pickering, 2017) rather than opting for one. In a similar vein to Demuro and Gurney (2021), therefore, I want to map out different ontologies of language rather than provide either an overarching narrative to choose between them or a set of subcategories to describe them. If we take ontological questions seriously in our thinking about languages, we can start to see 'Language not in the singular – or in the case of multilingualism, as the multiplication of the singular – but as an umbrella term under which a range of entirely different phenomena have been organised' (Demuro and Gurney, 2021, p.2). This ontologically pluralist approach questions the status of some abstract unity of language outside human interaction. To posit some kind of linguistic constant, whereby all language(s) share a commonality is to 'presume that there is a metaphysically invariant and ontologically real phenomenon called "language" apart from its materiality' (Wee, 2021, p.26). Such a proposition – language as an invariant metaphysical entity beyond its worldly engagements – is both an unlikely and impractical concept. Ontological questions are therefore central to this book.

3 Structures and Practices

I made a case in the first two chapters of this book for the need for applied linguistics to work with a practical theory of language, an understanding of language based in everyday contexts of language use, in the ordinary ways language is part of people's lives. In order to get there, two considerations are important starting points: whose version of language counts and what do different people think language is? To explore these two questions I looked at various ways of taking more account of how people think about language themselves – lay-oriented or folk or citizen linguistics – and suggested that while these open up significant avenues for a more inclusive linguistics, we should also be cautious not to let an egalitarian ideology take us too far towards giving up all claims to knowledge about language. More important were wider considerations of global knowledge politics and the question of whose knowledge counts in the context of North–South relations. Also important was an understanding that what we call languages are assemblages that bring a range of elements together, including language ideologies, knowledge about language, and other local factors to do with people, place and varied semiotic possibilities. As a result, these assembled languages are not just different languages but different things.

I made a case therefore for thinking in terms of language ontologies, and to do so in relational terms. It is to two different language ontologies that I turn in this chapter, structural and practice ontologies. The first is the most common understanding of language in orthodox linguistics and is often attended by epistemologies based in scientific description and a politics focused on liberal egalitarian ideals. While these political stances are not often made explicit, this chapter shows the importance of these ideological underpinnings through a discussion of the idea of the equality of languages. This will be followed by a brief discussion of the recent translanguaging debates, since these disagreements can be partly explained through different language ontologies, language as structure or language as practice.

I try to show here why we need to pay much more attention not only to different ideological stances but also to different language ontologies. The last part of the chapter considers more broadly the notion of language as a social practice – making it clear that this cannot be reduced to 'sociolinguistics', which can be either structural or practice oriented.

3.1 A PRISONER OF ITS OWN INVENTION: LANGUAGE AS STRUCTURE

The most common way to view language from an orthodox linguistic perspective is in structural terms. This not only entails being interested in linguistic structures – often, though not limited to, syntactic structures – but also seeing the whole of a language as a structure itself. A structuralist ontology suggests 'not only that a language-system has a structure, but that it is a structure' (Lyons, 1981, p.60). The answer to Sampson's (1980, p.36) 'ontological question' (see Chapter 2) as to what kind of things Saussure (widely accepted as the originator of modern linguistic thought) considered languages to be is a *structure*. Linguistics is the study of language structures (Grace, 1987). For Saussure, as Crowley (1996, pp.17–18) explains, 'language is a systematic structure of sound-patterns and concepts, and rather than being the means by which we name the world, it is in fact a system of representation which does not necessarily, if at all, involve the world'. From this point of view, language structure is regular and rule governed, and 'at the heart of language lies a structured relationship of elements characterizable as an autonomous system' (Newmeyer, 1988, p.20). This was Saussure's move to focus on *langue* (language as a synchronic system) as opposed to *parole* (language as used in everyday life). It is the system of signs (*langue*) that the Saussurean structuralist takes as their object of study, not the speech events involving particular people in place. 'A dominant and rather naturalised way of ontologising Language in many contexts is as autonomous object: that is, language-as-object. Here, language is approached as an abstract system which can also be conceptualised in the plural, through languages' (Demuro and Gurney, 2021, p.6).

While some will argue that linguistics has moved on from its structuralist phase – structuralism was a mid-twentieth-century focus that has been superseded – this is to confuse epistemological (structuralism) and ontological (language-as-structure) concerns. Structuralist linguistics – or descriptive linguistics as it was also called – put a particular emphasis on describing 'different structures for different languages' so that these 'structural descriptions' can be used in 'the cataloguing of language structures, and in the comparing of structural types' (Zellig Harris, 1951, p.3). The key emphasis on languages as self-standing structures, or language as a mental capacity, was little changed by generativist or other challenges to the structuralist emphasis itself. While Chomsky repudiated aspects of structuralist linguistics (and the framework of his teacher, Zellig Harris), making it possible to do linguistics without necessarily worrying about the troublesome nature of different languages, the linguistics he developed 'still espouses a reified and systemic view of language' (Zhou, 2020, p.35). Although a particular form of structuralism was indeed challenged by transformational generative and other linguistic paradigms, the language-as-structure ontology has remained central to much of the discipline of linguistics.

When linguistics came into being, Calvet (2006, p.21; emphasis added) explains, 'it needed to define its field of study in order to guarantee its scientific status. This definition transformed and even hardened practices into an object, but while structuralist linguistics needed to invent language, it does not realise that it is now *a prisoner of that invention*.' Languages, according to many linguists, 'are to be envisaged as systems of abstract entities' (Love, 1998, p.148). From this point of view, to describe a language is not just the imposition after the fact of a structural analysis on utterances, but to claim underlying structures that are constitutive of utterances. That is to say 'communication itself is often *defined* as a matter of making use of an abstract system of the kind envisaged by descriptive linguists' (1998, p.149; emphasis in original). Language, from this point of view, is taken as 'something waiting to be scientifically described', after which the described language is 'projected back onto the community as a system shared among individual speakers' (Zhou, 2020, p.29). Languages, from this perspective, 'exist ontologically as self-contained, systematic and countable entities which enable speakers to match a certain form with a certain meaning' (ibid.).

Such a vision of language assumes not only that it is possible from a formal perspective to describe a language structurally, but that *this is in fact what languages are*. To use a language is therefore to draw on an underlying set of structures and to put them into play in the social realm of socio- or applied linguistics. 'Language, the scientific concept', as Santana (2016, p.501) explains, is 'descriptively whatever it is that linguists take as their primary object of study'. The power of scientific description and analysis rendered languages as structures of comparable complexity. From a structuralist position (both ontological and epistemological), 'each human language is a self-organizing system in which both the syntactic and semantic properties of a word are established purely in relation to other words' (Ellis, 2011, p.654). Of particular significance in this way of thinking is the insistence on systems that are (self-)organized in terms of their internal relations, entailing not only syntactic structures but also semantic relations, so that users of a particular language are assumed to share a set of meanings: 'speakers of a language all share a well-defined set of "normal" senses for words' (Sampson, 2017, p.103).

It is the emphasis on structure as the internal combinatorial and contrastive relations within a language system (and separation of that system from the world around it) that defines language as structure, a broad category of many contemporary forms of linguistics, from generativist to functionalist approaches. To talk of structure is not to limit the discussion to a particular structuralist school, but rather to understand that approaches such as systemic functional linguistics may be equally focused on language as structure despite their functional claims (Watkins, 1999). In arguing that language was not a means to describe the world, but a system in and on itself, Saussure was able to make a claim that the world and language 'belong to the same ontological order' (Crowley, 1996, p.18), that is to say that language was understood 'as a thing to be found in the world of other things' (p.18). This was not a materialist move to focus on language in its material being (a different way of thinking discussed in Chapter 4) but rather to consider language as a thing in and of itself. 'Once liberated from its status as but a pale shadow of the world of things into its proper place standing alongside those things, then language could join those other items of reality in the privileged status of scientific object' (Crowley, 1996, p.18). Language as structure was therefore an ontological claim, an assertion about both the nature of language and its status among other identifiable objects.

There are a number of implications of thinking structurally, including the centrality of the idea of 'the sign' with its separation of form and meaning, the independence of this self-contained structural system both from the social and material world around it and from the effects of use, and the emphasis on languages as finite and identifiable systems (Roy Harris, 1980, p.154). This approach to language, treating languages ontologically as structures, was 'built on hard-won theses about the inherent systematicity and coherence of individual languages' (Gramling, 2021, p.111). It is common among linguists to acknowledge that languages have fuzzy boundaries and that language change is constant and inevitable, and thus to reject claims that they deal with ontologically fixed and stable systems. The fact that the boundaries of languages are unclear and that languages change, however, reinforces the central uniformity and stability of the thing itself. According to Wee (2021, p.42), 'dominant modern ideologies of language lead us to conceive of language as an entity with clear boundaries, typically correlated with geographical or social boundaries and with an autonomous structure, uniquely definable through a fixed set of formal features'. 'Linguistics', as Blommaert (2006, p.512) observes, 'has contributed in no small degree to the cultural construction of language in general as a stable, contextless individual mental object' (p.512). 'Traditional ontologies of language', Ortega (2018, p.69) explains, 'conceive of language as a thing, a bounded object'.

In these 'essentialist ontologies' (Ortega, 2018, p.69) structure becomes the object so that language change can, as far as possible, be accounted for by *internal* factors, the 'continual readjustments that are made by a language-system as it moves from one state of equilibrium (or near-equilibrium) to another' (Lyons, 1981, p.209). The structuralist legacy in linguistics leads to an emphasis on systems that leaves little space for people and their views: 'Languages are self-regulating systems which can be left to take care of themselves' (Trudgill, 1998, p.8). Once structure becomes a self-organizing system, with individuals, agency (or people more generally) relegated to a secondary role in relation to language as structure, there is little place for any outside influences, whether social, political, cultural, economic or material. From this point of view, it is possible to overcome the thorny language versus dialect problem, for example – the difficulty that these are evidently social and political rather than linguistic distinctions – by structural criteria alone: 'Once political considerations are firmly discarded, it is generally not a difficult matter to decide whether one is dealing with one language or with more than one in a given situation' (Dixon, 1997, p.7).

Languages as structures are therefore explained in terms of internal coherence or in relation to other structures when they rub against each other. As a result, it has been common when two such language systems come into contact to talk in terms of 'mixing' or 'borrowing' since different elements are deemed to belong to different systems. The ontology of language as structure (or system, or object) has a number of ramifications. It has enabled a remarkable amount of linguistic description of languages around the world: by creating its objects of study, it has made it possible to describe and compare linguistic structures that have brought a range of insights into how language works at one level. Structuralism as an ideological and epistemological position has been highly influential across many areas of the social sciences (many developments in sociology and anthropology can be traced back to the structural turn in linguistics). Structuralism in linguistics developed an egalitarian ethos – all these languages are structurally equal – with positive effects for minority languages and bilingual education (Newmeyer, 1986). At the same time, it turned languages into objects and removed them from their social environment. In this pursuit of autonomy, linguistics 'has insisted upon the independence of language from everything else' (Grace, 1987, p.8). This makes it possible to 'analyze the synchronic structure of a language without considering anything extra-linguistic – without considering anything beyond the kinds of features which figure in linguistic descriptions' (Grace, 1987, p.8).

As Harland explains, once this structuralist tenet took hold and linguists 'started explaining language hermetically', there was no obvious reason to stop, so a 'methodological decision to exclude the outside world' became a 'general philosophical principle of unlimited scope' (1987, p.91). A structuralist epistemology became an ontological assumption. It is as if to understand a bridge one decided to look only at the ways the bridge operates structurally, the girders and rivets, forces and tensions. For an engineer, this might be fine – the commission is to build a bridge of a certain size and capacity that is safe and durable – but for others, building bridges (not coincidentally a common metaphor) is more than this. 'Many linguists', Joseph (2018, p.8) explains, 'go about their work of analysing language as if in engineering mode, dealing with something self-standing, autonomous, part of the brain though disconnected from other parts'. Beyond the structural properties of the bridge we might also want to consider its position, the river (or harbour, or land) it crosses, the people and vehicles that use it, the cost and struggles over its design and placement, its effect on communities either side of the water, its shape and aesthetic appeal, its part in the social and economic changes to the region.

Engineering plays a very important part in society, but when I look at Sydney Harbour Bridge (with the sun setting behind it from a boat on the water or a promontory nearby, as part of the cityscape as viewed from the window of a light plane, as a means to get to the North Shore, its giant girders surrounding me as I follow the cycle path or ride a train across its span), I see more than an isolated structure whose bits hold together well. This language ontology may work for some applied linguistic projects – it can provide usable grammars of languages (or at least pedagogical grammars that can be used for some curricular purposes) – but to the extent that language models are likely to be more practical if they derive from contexts of use, then a linguistic model aimed at structural description often falls short. The fixity of languages that a structural ontology inevitably implies (however much appeal is made to fuzzy boundaries and historical change) can easily hamper a project in need of a more dynamic language ontology. As far as Zhou (2020, p.66) is concerned, 'linguistics as a discipline needs to be more aware of the limitations of this system myth and explore new ways of thinking and imagining language beyond the notion of system'. The ontological assumption that languages are structures comes at a cost: linguistics has become a prisoner of its own invention.

3.2 LANGUAGE MYTHS

While it is commonly assumed that the adherence to a structural ontology at least allows for a separation of analysis from social and ideological concerns, this is not necessarily so. Along with the methodological nationalism (Harris, 1981; Schneider, 2018) that continues to reproduce languages along national lines, there are also a number of related ideological stances that are commonly taken within linguistics. We have already looked at normative accounts of language and the problematic description versus prescription position in the previous chapter. Here I want to address several further positions taken within linguistics which flow in various ways from a structural ontology: discussions of how language relates to thought, culture and reality, a commitment to universality, and the equality of languages. In Chapter 2, I discussed a book on language myths (Bauer and Trudgill, 1998b) that takes aim at everyday views about language, aiming to put people right about how language really works. Here I want to return to the question of language myths, but to a different kind of book that turns the tables on this position and, in a similar manner to Zhou's (2020) comment in Section 3.1 about the 'system myth', looks at language myths as purveyed by orthodox linguistics. There are quite a surprising number of such books.

While some, such as Roy Harris' (1981) classic *The language myth*, deal broadly with linguistics, others, as evident from their titles, focus on more specific concerns about linguistic ideologies: Evans' (2014) *The language myth: Why language is not an instinct* is concerned particularly with generativist claims about a supposed innate human capacity for language (the title is a reference to Pinker's (1994) popular book *The language instinct)*; Watts' (2011) *Language myths and the history of English* is concerned with myths such as the longevity of English and the development of standard English; McWhorter's (2014) *The language hoax: Why the world looks the same in any language* argues against the view that languages have a deep effect on how we think; and Sampson's (2017) *The linguistics delusion* takes as its principal focus the development of linguistics as an alleged science, with its problematic claims about universality, grammaticality and so on. While these books can usefully inform a discussion of the particular views about language maintained by linguistic orthodoxies – problems of normativity or of assuming that languages as systems can be mapped onto cultural systems – some are also attempts to establish one epistemology over another (cognitive over generative linguistics, for example), and thus do not challenge in more profound ways the ontologies that are of interest in this book.

While Harris (1981, 1998a) is similarly making a case for his own version of integrational linguistics, his argument is that a language myth – that languages are fixed codes into which we translate ideas to pass back and forth between each other (the fixed code and telementational fallacies) – 'pervades the whole of Western culture' (Harris, 2002, p.24). For Harris, not only are different schools of linguists going about things the wrong way (he has little good to say about the last hundred years of linguistic theory), but this is a deep-seated Western cultural tradition. Western linguistic traditions have mistakenly constructed a vision of languages as autonomous objects which can be studied without reference to their contexts or communicative functions. For an integrationist, by contrast, it is possible to study language without positing these discrete codes called languages, and there are certainly no grounds to treat them as self-contained systems. More broadly, integrational linguistics recognizes that 'human beings inhabit a communicational space which is not neatly compartmentalised into language and non-language' (Harris, 1981, p.165).

As Seargeant (2010, p.3) notes, this 'would appear to provide an alternative ontology for language which would involve the re-evaluation of much of the history of the language sciences'. Pablé (2021) makes an analogous case for integrational linguistics as an alternative ontology. Similar in some ways to Harris' language myth, Grace (1987, p.4) suggests that 'our society has a particular perspective on language, a particular way of looking at it and talking about it', a view shared by both linguists and the public at large. Grace does not clearly specify who 'our society' is but seems, like Harris, to be referring to a broad Western cultural orientation towards language shared by linguists and non-linguists alike and, at least in Grace's estimation, one that is at odds with reality: 'our culture in general and the science of language in particular ... have a false view of the nature of language' (1987, p.139). By talking of the 'nature of language' Grace is here making ontological claims, critiquing the autonomous view of language outlined in Section 3.1 not only as 'false', but also as 'a serious obstacle to progress in learning what language is really like and how it affects various aspects of our daily lives and of human existence' (1987, p.10). By viewing these as widely shared Western views, he is opening the discussion to the more recent critique (in which 'Northern' replaces Western; see Pennycook and Makoni, 2020) of global knowledge disparities, where one culturally derived view of language is mapped onto the world as a universal construct.

At the same time, however, as sympathetic but critical readings of Harris suggest, his claim that there is *one* myth about language is surely too grand a claim: 'Harris contributes to the process of linguistic myth-making which he claims to undo' (Joseph, 1997, p.39). This is a product of 'an archemyth of his own designing, namely the idea that one single language myth, with all its various components, has characterized the whole of Western linguistic thinking' (Joseph, 1997, p.39). By claiming that there is *one single language myth*, Harris creates his own myth that is as equally segregational as the segregational linguistics he decries. In Seargeant's (2010, p.4) terms, 'there is not simply one myth which constitutes the ontological foundations for Western linguistic science' so much as an array of ways of thinking about language that emerge from particular social, cultural and historical contexts. It is more useful to think in terms of language-ideological assemblages (Kroskrity, 2021), where a wider array of interests are considered than one cultural myth. Rather than an overly broad language myth, it may be more useful to think about specific myths such as the *linguistic worldview* or *all languages are equal* myths (see Sections 3.3 and 3.4) or the *bilingual advantage* or *creole exceptionalism* myths (see Chapter 6).

Unlike the use of the term 'myth' in Bauer and Trudgill (1998b), which largely focuses on the sense of a myth as untrue, or the even stronger claims to falsity that Grace (1987) makes, Harris is using the idea of 'myth' here in the broader sense of a cultural explanation of an aspect of the world. He over-reaches himself, however, by claiming its ubiquitous and unitary status. Watts (2011) is also careful to explain that his understanding of myths is based on different ways of understanding the world. For Watts, 'every discourse on language is ultimately based on myths representing beliefs about language' (2011, p.260). His focus is on the constellation of myths about homogeneity, standardization, superiority, and so forth that construct their central ontological entity, the English language. He nonetheless sees what he calls the 'linguistic homogeneity myth' as central to the ways people have come to 'accept the "truth" of the existence of languages' (2011, p.120). In other words, although his focus is centrally on the various myths around English, his more general points that a myth about linguistic homogeneity is central to language ontologies and that all discourses about language can be traced to various longstanding myths (unlike Harris' single Western language myth) is useful for an understanding of how languages are understood within different traditions.

3.3 LANGUAGE, THOUGHT AND WORLDVIEWS

Two sets of belief that flow from thinking in terms of language structures have to do with language and worldviews and language equality, both a result of the commitment to a structural ontology (as well as a descriptive epistemology and egalitarian politics). If we ask the general question as to whether language affects thought, the answer would seem fairly obvious: of course it does. Whether cultural, ideological or discursive, language plays a role in our thinking (without getting into discussions of whether we think in language). It is fairly obvious that listening to rap music, texting a friend, chatting to a colleague, bartering in a market, checking the news online, following a recipe, asking directions, reading a novel, writing a poem, singing with friends, and much more affect how we think. The question over which there has been continued debate, however, is whether separate languages affect our thought, either on the micro-level of structures within languages (grammatical gender, for example, or certain lexical items) or at a more general level of languages expressing a worldview: 'Each language encapsulates the world-view of its speakers – how they think, what they value, what they believe in, how they classify the world around them, how they order their lives. Once a language dies, a part of human culture is lost forever' (Dixon, 1997, p.144).

The problem here is that there is a very big jump from suggesting that language use, and possibly even some particular structures, may affect the way we think to claiming that languages as whole structures can be mapped against cultures as whole structures and thus encapsulate a particular way of thinking. Like variationist sociolinguistics that sought to map language entities against social systems, this view seeks to map structures of culture against structures of language (Eckert, 2018; Williams, 1992). Languages are seen as containing the worldview of the speakers who use that language, as storehouses of knowledge. If they are no longer used, forms of culture and knowledge disappear with them. The fact that different languages may influence their speakers' minds in varying ways because of various structures or lexical items – time, colour, gender and so on – which tend to point us in particular habitual directions (Deutscher, 2011) is well attested. The main issues in these debates are on the one hand how important this effect is: if it is only a slightly discernible effect, it may not be very interesting, and certainly doesn't constitute a worldview; and on the other hand, the direction of effect: to what extent does a language *cause* a mental orientation, and to what extent is it part of a wider set of relations among material conditions, cultural orientations and linguistic items?

For Pinker (2007) the proposition that 'Eskimos' pay more attention to types of snow because of the many words for it (rather than have many words because of their environment) is the wrong way round. It is not clear who adheres to the view critiqued by Pinker that language is causative in this sense, but it does point to the problem of trying to map language and culture in this way. The 'many words for snow' is, of course, in any case yet another of those myths that does not hold up to scrutiny (Martin, 1986; Pullum, 1989). McWhorter (2014) devotes his book *The language hoax* to this topic, addressing both linguistic and popular myths about the effects of language on thought. In a similar vein to Pinker, he looks at another of these commonly cited cases, the use of cardinal directions (north, south, east, west) rather than relational terms (in front, behind, right, left, and so on) among speakers of Guugu Yimithirr and other Indigenous languages of Australia (N. Evans, 2010; Levinson, 1996). These speakers do not refer to something being, say, in front of them but use instead directions akin to compass bearings, with obvious implications for knowledge of directionality beyond relative positions (east rather than in front of). They do not orient this way *because of* their language, McWhorter (2014) insists, but because of their environment (reflected in their language). McWhorter's central concern is to refute what he sees as inappropriate causal claims or overstated views about worldviews, insisting – quite reasonably – that '*language structure does not correlate meaningfully with culture*' (2014, p.150, emphasis in original).

The problem, however, both for some proponents of a language/culture correlation and for these antagonists, is that a starting point of languages as structural wholes that can be mapped against cultures is never going to shed much light on the complexity of linguistic meanings, cultural orientations, thought patterns and material conditions. The somewhat parodic refutations of linguistic determinism – that it is languages themselves that determine thought – and the counter-argument that languages are as they are because they reflect the environment – that languages are representational systems – by Pinker (1994, 2007) and McWhorter (2014) are themselves stuck in structural assumptions about languages. In another of the *language myth* books, Vyvyan Evans (2014, p.228) rejects Pinker's attempts to discredit ideas about language, culture and thought, and concludes that 'human languages and minds are inexorably interconnected'. Akin to the discussion in the previous chapter about the limitations of trying to decide whether human thought and reality are dependent or independent, Vyvyan Evans suggests that language and thought are intertwined. As most of those who have directly dealt with such cases (rather than their parodic versions), and who have sought to understand their complexity, the issue is inevitably more subtle than a causative relation between language and culture: language differences 'guide our attention to different facets of reality' and 'nudge our reasoning in different directions by suggesting different metaphors and analogies' (N. Evans, 2010, p.179).

A structural ontology, by presenting languages as unitary wholes, lends itself to a view that a language, by dint of its relation to a culture, presents a consistent worldview. Each language, from this point of view, contains and limits its speakers' view of the world (Dixon, 1997; Skutnabb-Kangas, 2000). According to Mufwene (2017, p.204), 'conceiving of languages as systems' suggests that 'every population has developed in their language their own ways of packaging information, which in some cases are not replicable in other languages'. This position has been particularly important in the field of language revival (discussed in greater depth in Chapter 5) since it provides an argument not only that a language might be lost but also a culture, a knowledge system, a worldview: when a language is no longer used, a particular take on the world goes with it. This container view of language – a language as an entity holds a view of the world in its lexical and grammatical structures – has been widely critiqued for exoticizing certain cultures, for overusing examples from various Indigenous contexts without adequate consideration of the interests of those communities, for placing the rights of languages to be spoken before the rights of speakers to adapt to changing socioeconomic conditions, and thus for placing linguistic interests over community concerns and language ideologies (Duchêne and Heller, 2007; Gal, 2018; Mufwene, 2008).

The container view of languages as structural entities that hold the worldviews of their speakers and the accompanying endeavours to save endangered languages arguably overlook the more radical implications of Whorf's (1956) work where he sought to challenge the assumptions of Western/Euro-American thought. Methodologically and empirically weak, and likewise focused on languages as structures, his ideas nevertheless conveyed the possibility that 'there may well exist a completely different but internally coherent model of the physical universe, right down to base ontologies of time and space' (N. Evans, 2010, p.163). This starts to sound like an ontological turn. These ontological questions then need to be pointed back at language, however, and to the possibility not only of completely different spatial and temporal ontologies but also of linguistic ontologies. Summarizing the arguments about language and thought, Nick Evans (2010, p.180) suggests that 'the process of learning a language goes hand in hand with constructing a particular thought-world, and the pervasive web of integrated cultural practices that go with it'.

Rather than mapping structures against each other, this approach considers learning processes and integrated practices, thus pointing in the direction of social practices (as discussed in Section 3.7) – what we do with our available bits of language – or language assemblages (discussed in the next chapter) – how linguistic elements, cultural practices and material conditions combine at different moments. If languages are assembled in the ongoing practices of daily life, rather than pregiven structures, then any effects of language use on thought are going to be far more variable and dynamic than structural, container-based worldviews suggest. As Kramsch (2009, p.188) explains, if we understand language in terms of symbolic power, then 'speaking or writing another language means using an alternative signifying practice, that orients the body-in-the-mind to alternative ways of perceiving, thinking, remembering the past, and imaging the future'. This is to work from a notion of language practices (drawing on Bourdieu) and to suggest not that a language itself structures thought but that doing language, with all that comes along with such social activity, can change how we orient to the world.

3.4 ALL LANGUAGES ARE EQUALLY COMPLEX

Another objection to the linguistic worldview arguments – that languages cut the world up differently – is an insistence on an ontological universality for both the world and language so that 'any content that can be expressed in one language can be expressed in any other language' (Grace, 1987, p.7). The subtitle of McWhorter (2014) *The language hoax* is *Why the world looks the same in any language*. This position is based on a transcendental view of reality and an assumption that all languages, despite their differences, can describe it. For Harris (1980) this is a European tradition whereby languages are considered to be 'superficially different but fundamentally equivalent systems of expression' (p.21). While the strongest version of universalism was evidently in Universal Grammar (irrespective of language differences, an underlying set of linguistic principles is shared across all humans), a more common linguistic goal was to establish not so much universal underlying principles as universally shared grammatical structures (Greenberg, 1963). For many linguists, Sampson (2017, p.35) argues, 'the alleged existence of language universals represents the chief claim linguistics has on the attention of the public at large' since it allows for inflated claims about human commonality and mental hard wiring. Despite convincing evidence that 'languages differ so fundamentally from one another at every level of description (sound, grammar, lexicon, meaning) that it is very hard to find any single structural property they share' (Evans and Levinson, 2009, p.429), and although it is clear that 'what are treated as universals in language ... prove on investigation actually to be *norms* – what most people tend to do' (Joseph, 2018, p.8), many linguists still cling to this universal dream.

This insistence on universality is both a claim to speak beyond the frame of methodological nationalism and also a commitment to questions of equality on the assumption that the two are deeply connected.[1] As Hutton (1999, p.1) explains, modern linguistics 'sees itself as a forward-looking discipline, and regards the activity of linguistic analysis as either ideologically neutral ("scientific") or ideologically positive, in that most linguists rhetorically claim the equality of all language systems'. A central ideological belief is therefore the all-languages-are-equal position taken by many linguists. A commitment

---

[1] While these relations between structuralism, universalism and liberal egalitarian politics were common in the twentieth century, they by no means necessarily go together. In other fields such as sociology, structuralism was much more commonly allied with Marxist analyses of the social world.

to a structural ontology and an ethics based in liberal egalitarianism suggest that any comparisons between languages will imply structurally comparable entities. Because of its ideological commitment to being a descriptive science, linguistics generally denies any such underlying ideological orientation, though a closer examination of the politics of linguistics shows that in its dominant Western form it has typically been against, for example, forms of standardization (as a form of control that denies freedom and authenticity) – hence some of the confusions over the description/prescription distinction – and in favour of forms of liberal equality (Hutton, 2022; Newmeyer, 1988).

The argument that all languages are equally complex emerged in the twentieth century to become a key axiom of much linguistic thought. It was centrally an argument against ethnocentric and racist descriptions of primitive languages and people, where it was assumed that people and their languages and cultures could be ranked on scales of civilization (from higher to lower). Arguments in favour of universality had similar origins in attempts to refute accounts of difference that also became accounts of deficit. There was some evidence to back up arguments in favour of complexity – work on the grammars of a range of languages (Indigenous Australian languages, for example) showed that they were complex in a range of ways that made European languages look uncomfortably simple – but to argue that all languages were equally complex was never supported by either a framework for deciding what this exactly meant or empirical evidence showing that this was so. Arguments about linguistic complexity nevertheless became ubiquitous across linguistic textbooks (Joseph and Newmeyer, 2012): 'No one can claim that of any of the five thousand or so human languages is more advanced or more developed or more complex than any other' (Bickerton, 1995, p.67); or 'Although there are innumerable languages in the world, it is striking that they are all equally complex (or simple) and that a child learns whatever language it is exposed to' (Smith, 1999, p.168); or 'It is a finding of modern linguistics that all languages are roughly equal in terms of overall complexity' (Dixon, 1997, p.118); or 'Linguists believe that all languages, dialects and forms of human communication are equal' (The Linguistics Roadshow, 2023, np).

Although Sampson (2017) complains that once challenged on this topic, linguists denied making this claim, it is still common enough to read both that languages are equally complex and that linguistics has shown this empirically: 'linguists have tirelessly engaged in clear empirical demonstrations that every human language is as rich and complex as the next' (MacSwan, 2020, p.327). This fitted well with the relativism of structuralist linguistics (languages are made up of internal structures that are different but all generally comparable) and the claims of the generativist branch, for whom language was one general human capacity that was realized in different ways in different languages (but all generally reflected the same underlying linguistic capacity). It was useful to show how things that were done one way in one language (say grammatically framed politeness) might be realized differently in other languages (the same things might be done through lexical choice or even through non-verbal means). It was, in short, an ideologically driven argument – an argument on estimable grounds supporting equality – but one that did not really have evidence to back it up, nor a consensus with more popular views on language. This view, without any real evidence, was constantly restated as 'an uncontroversial axiom' (Sampson, 2017, p.8) and eventually as a 'self-fulfilling prophecy' (2017, p.162).

The doctrine of equal complexity, as Joseph and Newmeyer (2012) explain, was a well-intentioned ideological stance against racist views about language, evolution and development. It was a very important view to hold in the twentieth century, though once the tables were turned on racist evaluations of language, once it was ascertained that many Indigenous languages were highly complex, the preferred option was to argue for the equality of all languages rather than pursue this point to its logical conclusion. The problem was, however, that it didn't really seem to hold up to critical scrutiny. It also undermined linguists' strong claim to political neutrality and, as Joseph and Newmeyer (2012) explain, it also in the end perpetuated exactly the view it sought to overcome: why should we insist dogmatically that all languages are equal as if to concede that the opposite implies something unacceptable about different groups of speakers? It was eventually challenged, not (apart from a few exceptions) from a position that aimed to reassert racial distinctions, but one that pointed out that there were absolutely no grounds to equate linguistic complexity with any sort of superiority or inferiority. As Dixon (2016) notes, having spent about a hundred years aiming to redress racist evaluations of languages with the 'all languages are equal' trope, it is now possible to start to look more carefully at how different languages do things differently and to reopen the question of whether some languages might be better at doing some things than others (a question for language users rather than linguists). It is a myth that has done its work but can now be dropped. The problem, now more broadly acknowledged, is that on the one hand, it could never really be empirically demonstrated and, on the other, though well-intentioned, it is largely an irrelevant claim. It hinges on old and discredited ideas about language, thought and mind that should have been discarded long ago, a prisoner of its own invention.

We may still want to maintain part of the egalitarian sentiment of the all-languages-are-equal argument, but with a sharper, critical understanding of what is at stake. As applied linguists, it is important that we can appreciate such ideas for what they are: an ideological commitment to equality (based on the idea of similarity) coupled with an ontological commitment to structure. There is nothing wrong with ideological positions – it depends on the ideology rather than a distinction between science and ideology – but it is important to understand the politics behind them. A commitment to equality may be estimable, but when it is based on a politics of similarity we need to ask what it does and does not do. The discussion in the first two chapters concerning ontologies, epistemologies and ideologies suggests that linguistics generally has a commitment to a structural ontology accompanied by epistemologies that insist on scientific description and an ideological stance committed to liberal egalitarianism or, as Williams (1992, p.226) once described sociolinguistics, 'an overriding desire to support the underdog, accompanied by a sociological perspective which reflects the power of the dominant'. This framework differs from my own linguistic orientations: rather than one language ontology, I am interested in relational ontologies; rather than an epistemological orientation towards description, I am interested in understanding how knowledge is constructed socially; and rather than an often-unacknowledged commitment to liberal egalitarian ideals, I am concerned with a more overt engagement with ethical and political concerns.

3.5 TRANSLANGUAGING AS A PRACTICAL THEORY

In the first two chapters, I referred to an ontological panic in areas of sociolinguistics: what is our work about if we question the reality of languages? As also became clear, these arguments are often confused when it comes to separating ontological, epistemological and ideological matters, and in terms of understanding what critical-constructivist claims to reality imply. This concern over the status of languages has emerged particularly in debates about the notion of *translanguaging*. While there has been disquiet over the remarkable popularity of this term, whether it is consistently used and whether some of the claims to effect social change are realistic (Jaspers, 2018;

Pennycook, 2016), of interest to the discussion here is the fact that the idea of *translanguaging* has emerged from contexts of practice – in Li Wei's (2018) terms it is a *practical theory of language* – and derives from an ontology of language centred around the notion of practice. These two understandings of practice need not be aligned – a theory derived from practical concerns to do with education, families and communities and an ontology of language practices are not the same thing – but it is also not surprising that they are combined in many discussions of translanguaging, with their focus on 'both the complex language practices of plurilingual individuals and communities, as well as the pedagogical approaches that use those complex practices' (García and Li Wei, 2014, p.19).

The idea of translanguaging is usually traced to Cen Williams' (1996) use of the term (a translation of the Welsh *trawsieithu*) in an educational context. This linear historical tracing perhaps overlooks the wider influence of a 'trans turn' across the field (an interest in transnationalism, transculturalism, translation and so on) or what Joseph (2022) calls a 4T approach involving translingual, transmodal, transindividual and transspecies themes. The revelation that translanguaging is a common practice also overlooks common knowledge in the Global South and 'astonished southern scholars immersed in complex multilingual societies where horizontal modes of multilingual crossing and fluidity were documented decades earlier' (Windle et al., 2023, p. 281). It is important to appreciate the educational impetus that has been central to the development of translanguaging. Two large and influential studies of bilingual and complementary schools in the USA (García, 2011) and UK (Blackledge and Creese, 2010) played an important role. For Blackledge and Creese (2010), it became clear that the ways of framing languages in structural terms could not account for how languages were being used in schools and families. After many years advocating for bilingual schools, García came to realize that the separation of languages into distinct entities (taught or used separately at different times) was very different from the ways language operated in her own bilingual home. It is not of course the case that schools should necessarily reflect what goes on in homes, streets or other places of informal interaction, but when the differences run so deep, and appear to do so in unproductive ways, there are good reasons to question the ways languages are separated in particular ways. Why do we treat languages in this way in schools, she and her colleagues asked, when we don't in daily life? Bilinguals, Otheguy and colleagues argue, 'have at their disposal a large, full, unitary linguistic system that is not partitioned into the linguistic compartments that schools create' (2018, p.25).

Languages may be distinguished for certain social, cultural and political purposes and along various lines, but that does not mean that this is how languages are used, work inside the brain or should be taught. Translanguaging can be understood in a number of ways, As Canagarajah (2013) points out, a translingual perspective suggests not only a questioning of the ways in which named languages are seen as separate, but also a questioning of the boundaries around language in general. This suggests the importance both of translingual practices (using elements from what are categorized socially as different languages) and of translingual semiotics (material, spatial and semiotic options). It is a language-ideological stance that takes multilingualism as the norm and questions the ways languages are assumed to operate in separate domains. In this respect, it also operates as a theoretical stance on bilingualism, suggesting a unitary view of multilingualism whereby the importance of languages as sociocultural concepts is acknowledged but a corresponding belief in multiple linguistic systems in the brain is refuted (Otheguy et al., 2018). This in turn leads to a research interest in translingual practices, into the ways in which people draw on multiple semiotic possibilities in their daily interactions. Translanguaging is 'an approach to bilingualism that is centered, not on languages as has often been the case, but on *the practices of bilinguals*' (García, 2009, p.140; emphasis added).

A focus on translinguistic practices, therefore, suggests that linguistic boundaries are 'the result of ideological invention and sedimentation' that 'do not guide communication in everyday contexts' and that such communication is 'not limited to "language" insofar as interlocutors draw on a range of semiotic and spatial repertoires' (Lee and Dovchin, 2020, p.1). Translanguaging is a 'Practical Theory of Language, therefore an applied linguistics theory, that comes out of practical concerns of understanding the creative and dynamic practices human beings engage in with multiple named languages and multiple semiotic and cognitive resources' (Li Wei, 2018, p.27). The fact that translanguaging derives not from an attempt to describe languages as pregiven entities but rather from an interest in language as it used in schools, conversations, family settings and so on gives an indication of why it has been so avidly taken up in such contexts. Translingual projects have focused on 'the rights of racialized *people* to be educated on their own terms and on the basis of their own language practices' (García et al., 2021, p.206; emphasis in original). This should tell us something about its usefulness for looking at common language use. Those who decry its popularity and trendiness also need to account for why it has appealed so widely to so many, especially in education.

This is not to suggest, by any means, that the widespread adoption of the notion of translanguaging should be uncritically celebrated. Its extensive espousal in educational contexts – often to mean little more than the use of the first language in second-language education classes – may provide a useful opposition to the dominance of, for example, English-only ideologies in English language teaching (ELT). In such contexts it can expose the complicity of an ELT industry bent on the promotion of English-only textbooks and English monolingual teachers, and release teachers from the dogmatic proscription of first-language use and the accompanying denial of multilingual identities and practices. Yet an overly zealous insistence on first-language use in minority-language classrooms (particularly when this may mean in a dominant language such as English) may be a regressive step. If a translanguaging focus undermines, say, a Māori-only policy in Māori-language classrooms in Aotearoa, it may weaken such language revival projects. Opposing over-enthusiastic engagement with translanguaging may be the 'best means of retaining (some) linguistic *autonomy* for Indigenous languages in the classroom (for if not there, where?)' (May, 2022, p.337; emphasis in original). While linguistic autonomy may be a concept itself to be questioned, at the same time a practical theory of language is only a good theory if carefully used.

Of central importance to the discussion here is this idea of a practical theory of language, that is to say an understanding and an ontology of language that derives from practice and aims to describe practice: what are people doing with the linguistic elements available to them? It is such an approach to language that was important in our attempts to understand what we came to call a *translingual family repertoire* (Hiratsuka and Pennycook, 2020) in our studies of a multilingual family. The question of interest concerned the role of a set of shared multilingual practices within the family in creating and maintaining family life. When the father, for example, warns his elder daughter that her sister has a stomach ache by saying '*No, Morci is itaiitai panzita, amor*' (English 'no'; 'Morci' Colombian Spanish abbreviation of 'morcillita', a type of sausage, the younger child's nickname; English 'is'; Japanese diminutive/doubled form of 'itai' – to be in pain; Spanish 'panzita', diminutive term of 'panza' – belly; and 'amor' – love, a term of endearment to the daughter), our question concerns the ways that these different linguistic elements are combined within the family repertoire. It is this idea of a translingual repertoire shared among the family and not dependent on individual competence – with, for example, three different words for egg ('eggy', 'huevos' and 'tamago') all available – that seemed the most helpful in understanding how this family engaged in daily language practices. The focus is not on language structures (which underlying grammatical system(s) could account for the string '*is itaiitai panzita*'?) or why certain supposed switches are made, or what kind of underlying competence would one need to posit to explain this multilingual use, but rather on the translingual practices that are part of a repertoire spread across the family: how do they 'do family' linguistically?

3.6 THE TRANSLANGUAGING BATTLES

One of the questions of importance for this book, however, concerns the meeting of different language ontologies – structural and practical – and the confusions around different claims to the ontological status of languages. Translanguaging, Otheguy and colleagues (2018, p.627, emphasis added) argue, offers a '*different ontology* for the languages of the bilingual'. They are not questioning the reality of languages as sociopolitical constructs but rather what that reality is: the 'dual ontology of the two separable named languages is anchored in sociocultural beliefs, not in psycholinguistic properties of the underlying system' (2018, p.628). This is what Bell (2014, p.9) calls a 'critical-constructivist' stance (as opposed to a more traditional orientation) that focuses on language 'as a social practice, with speakers drawing on all kinds of linguistic resources for their own purposes'. For MacSwan (2022a, p.19), by contrast, this critical-constructivist stance is what he calls a *deconstructivist* position, [2] which claims that 'discrete language communities do not exist, and that community- and individual level conceptions of bilingualism are merely socially reified fictions'. On the one hand, then, is a position that sees languages as sociocultural constructs: we engage in various language practices but these are only constructed as languages by certain language ideologies. On the other hand, there is a position that starts with 'discrete language communities' which are not so much constructed as they are pre-existing communities with a given language.

---

[2] It is not very clear why MacSwan uses this term from an architectural movement in the 1980s that sought to break down the sense of a building having a unitary form, such as Frank Gehry's Guggenheim Museum in Bilbao. None of the writers that MacSwan sees as 'deconstructivist' uses the term themselves.

Structures and Practices

MacSwan (2020, p.321) is concerned that a translingual perspective is 'at odds with a civil rights orientation, the backbone of language education policy in the United States'. So although both MacSwan (2020) and Otheguy and colleagues (2018) see themselves as engaged in language political struggles in the USA, MacSwan stresses the need to operate with the terms laid down by language policy over the last few decades as part of a civil rights orientation, while Otheguy and colleagues stress the need to question the language ideologies and socially and politically defined entities that may or may not be useful in struggles for equality. To reiterate the arguments in Chapter 2, particularly as explained by Haslanger (2012), just because gender or race or language are very obviously social constructs, and potentially social constructs that need to be resisted, this does not mean they are not real. As Li Wei (2018, p.27) explains, translanguaging 'does not deny the existence of named languages, but stresses that languages are historically, politically, and ideologically defined entities'. The argument is about what it is that exists rather than whether it exists. As Cummins (2021) suggests, neither the social construction of languages nor their reality for students, teachers, politicians and most people is under dispute. Aside from MacSwan's (2022a) assertion that critical constructivists see languages as social fictions rather than social facts, there seems little difference among these positions up to this point: languages are social constructions that are very real. The difference hinges on how that reality is understood, and the assertion that despite these social realities, people have a unitary language system at their disposal (Otheguy et al., 2018). From this perspective, although languages have social reality, we do not need to see them as separate internally: people have a unitary 'linguistic system', a term covering both 'linguistic structure and linguistic competence' (Otheguy et al., 2018, p.629).

This position needs some further probing. The argument that a dual ontology of two separable named languages is based on sociocultural beliefs, while internally people only have a unitary competence, creates a second dual ontology between external practices and internal structures. For Otheguy and colleagues (2018, p.629), 'system, structure, or competence is the assembly of features that, in cooperation with other resources, enables linguistic practices'. As van Leeuwen (2008) points out (discussed further in the next section), linguistics is something of an exception among social sciences in suggesting in this fashion that systems and structures make social practices possible, rather than the other way round. While this is indeed a common linguistic approach – the long history of separation of language from its social and political contexts has made this possible – it sits uncomfortably alongside a focus on language as a social practice. If we take a practice-based position seriously, languages are the products of social activity rather than the projection of internal competence. Indeed, neither system nor competence nor structure sits comfortably with a practice-oriented focus. A practice-based language ontology starts with social practices and then looks at what is produced by such practices as emergent (language, cognition). Linguists working from an *emergent grammar* framework similarly suggest that grammar is a consequence rather than a precondition of communication: grammar is *emergent* since 'structure, or regularity, comes out of discourse and is shaped by discourse in an ongoing process. Grammar is, in this view, simply the name for certain categories of observed repetitions in discourse' (Hopper, 1998, p.156).

If we take language as a social practice as primary – (trans)languaging – then the more obvious argument would be that the cognitive product of social activity is related to the social practice of translanguaging and the social construction of languages. The unitary system argument suggests that because languages are social constructs, they don't really exist in the head, where, by contrast, there are 'psycholinguistic properties of the underlying system' (Otheguy et al., 2018, p.628) or 'the internal categories of lexical and grammatical structure' (Otheguy et al., 2015, p.297). This arguably falls into the trap of suggesting that because languages are social rather than structural facts, an internal unitary competence (an idea that is not comfortably compatible with a view of the primacy of social practice) may underly the social production of languages, unhelpfully separating linguistic/cognitive and social/ideological aspects of language. These problems are evidently a result of trying to address these questions from varied ontological dispositions. Both sides of these debates get caught up in these confusions. Bhatt and Bolonyai (2022) argue that the strict differentiation between internal (one system) and external (socially differentiated languages) suggested by Otheguy and colleagues (2018) is not sustainable, since the dialogue between external languages and the internal construction of languages must reflect different grammatical systems. This is an equally implausible position: on the one hand, a unitary competence that bifurcates into socially constructed languages when used; on the other hand, incommensurable internal and external grammatical systems.

Critics of a strong translanguaging position often ask how it can be possible to question the ontological status of languages while simultaneously using language labels to discuss data. How, one might ask, could Hiratsuka and I (2020) talk about a translingual family repertoire (a repertoire of linguistic items shared across a family) while also using labels such as Japanese, Spanish and English? Bhatt and Bolonyai (2022) insist that Blackledge and Creese's (2010) and García and Li Wei's (2014) discussion of English and Gujarati mixing in terms of translanguaging is contradictory because they name the languages that are being mixed (if there is one underlying system, this could not be the case). To use socially significant language labels is not inconsistent, however, with a view that these are social practices. This common critique of translingual and other approaches that they both reject languages and use language names (Auer, 2022; MacSwan, 2022a) overlooks the point that to suggest languages are socially constructed also suggests the social inevitability of language labels. The difference concerns what is meant by reference to certain named languages: whether one assumes that a linguistic item is part of a pre-existing linguistic entity or whether one sees it as a term whose belonging is socially produced.

Arguments around the status of codeswitching are similarly inconsistent. Some proponents of translanguaging seem quite content to accept codeswitching as a translingual practice (Li Wei, 2018), though others are more sceptical about using the two in conjunction. For some, it has always been important to maintain faith with the tradition going back to Gumperz (1964) that the codes of codeswitching are open-ended semiotic systems (Auer, 1995) rather than languages, and that 'equating of the codes in codeswitching with "named languages" is unwarranted' (Auer, 2022, p.134). Likewise, Blommaert (2013, p.2) insists on the 'perpetual processes of creative coding, of the continuous production of new codes not – at least sociolinguistically – in any salient way tied to "languages" in the classic sense of the term'. Once codes and codeswitching are seen in these terms – as processes distinct from the use of languages as more traditionally understood – codeswitching and translanguaging may not be very far apart. For others, however, codeswitching is understood as 'a speech style in which bilinguals alternate languages between or within sentences' (MacSwan, 2017, p.168, 2022b, p.90). Here we are back to 'bilinguals' (people who speak two languages), the alternation of languages (it is either one language or the other), within or between sentences (the switches occur at clearly identifiable structural junctures).

Such contradictions occur in part because of the ortholinguistic habits of linguistic thought (Pennycook, 2016). An open-ended view of codeswitching or languages with porous boundaries gets pulled back into more orthodox views of language structures. An open-ended view of translanguaging, meanwhile, gets tied to a view of unitary competence. If one views language in ontological terms as a structure, then ideas such as codeswitching will almost inevitably slide back into a vision of two systems rubbing up against each other, of bilinguals alternating between languages within sentences. Most of the translanguaging literature, however, is concerned with language as a social practice, that is to say not whether we have different systems in contact or whether we have one or two language systems in our head depending on how many languages we speak, but what people do with the language options available to them. To explain further what this means, I will discuss in the next section the ontology of language as a practice.

3.7 LANGUAGE AS SOCIAL PRACTICE

I made a case in Section 3.5, following Li Wei (2018), to consider translanguaging as a practical theory of language in that it derives from accounts of practice in educational and other settings. It is also concerned with language as a practice rather than a structure, though as also became clear in the previous section, the distinction is often confused. It is important to distinguish these two positions: a practical theory of language is an epistemological stance that draws on and can be applied to contexts of language use. A practice ontology assumes language to be an activity, something that is done, rather than an entity. The idea of language as a social practice is not equivalent to the sociolinguistic ideas of language use or language in context. Much of the history of sociolinguistics has involved the attempt to map language structures onto social structures. Sociolinguistics is often taken to mean 'language use' – languages being used in the world – but this is not the same as language practice. The idea of 'language use' still operates with a prior concept of language that is then deployed in social environments, whereas the idea of *language practices* takes social activity first and then looks at what role linguistic aspects may play.

While a focus on practice, on 'what people do', has been seen as a foundational category in sociology and anthropology, in linguistics by contrast, 'things have generally been the other way around, with systems (grammars, paradigms) generating processes (syntagms), rather than processes (practices) generating systems (institutions and objectified forms of knowledge)' (Van Leeuwen, 2008, p.5). Ahearn makes a similar distinction between the approach to language of 'most linguists' as a formal system or structure and the view of linguistic anthropologists, which is to view language as 'social action' (2001, p.110). From a standard (socio)linguistic point of view, language as structure and entity pre-exists its use, so it is possible to think about language as a social activity in terms of languages being used by people. This is not at all what van Leeuwen or Ahearn are pointing to. Their point is that while a linguistic point of view starts with a system or structure as given, and then adds issues of usage to the basic picture, from a social or anthropological point of view, the starting point is the social activity, and any structures and regularities that may derive from social practices are secondary. This is also why from an integrational linguistic point of view, 'first-order' activity is seen as communicative practice, while languages as structures are only 'second-order' concepts (Love, 2017; Thibault, 2011).

Sociolinguistics went through a major series of changes, however, shaped by its reconvergence with linguistic anthropology (*sociocultural linguistics* as Bucholtz and Hall, 2008, call this new configuration). The earlier separation, whereby social relations were given a structural emphasis and tied to language through a variationist mapping exercise while questions of culture, politics, ideology and social practices were left to anthropologists, finally started to collapse as the two fields began to talk to each other again.[3] This brought linguistic ethnography – the demand to study language events from an ethnographic perspective – to the field; it gave us language ideologies and an understanding that how people understand their languages might be as important as outsider descriptions; it insisted that we needed to focus not only on language practices, but language as a practice. As Blommaert (2013) – one of the major figures in this shift – made clear, this brought ideas such as *complexity* into play, and necessitated an understanding that a so-called cross-linguistic encounter could not be adequately accounted for from a codeswitching point of view since 'participants walk away from such encounters with fundamentally, ontologically, changed repertoires' (2013, p.1)

It has long been a problem (particularly in English) that the idea of language has no easy way of becoming an activity. One way forward here has been to use terms such as 'languaging'. This need to make language into an activity, as Cowley (2019) notes, has a long history

---

[3] The massive growth of the Sociolinguistics Symposium from the early 2000s was partly a result of this. From a fairly small variationist-oriented meeting of mainly European sociolinguistics, it expanded rapidly into a much bigger and much wider conference looking at politics, ideology, gender, sexuality, race and so forth.

that far predates its recent take-up either on its own or in terms such as *polylanguaging* (Jørgenson, 2008; Jørgenson et al., 2011) or *translanguaging*. The idea of languaging, Cowley (2019, p.2) suggests, 'challenges appeal to language-systems, use, and usage'. Translanguaging has always made this idea of an activity central to its definition. The other option – also found in the phrases *translingual* or *translinguistic practices* (Lee and Dovchin, 2020) – is to add the term *practices* to language (or literacy or other terms). García explains *translanguaging* as 'firmly rooted in the multilingual and multimodal language and literacy practices of children in schools in the 21st century' (García, 2009, p.8). The term *practices*, however, does far more than just turn ideas such as language into an activity: it invokes a much wider realm of practice as a social activity, as a social theory and, ultimately, as an ontology. As Joseph (2006, p.9) puts it, 'a language is not a thing, but a practice always characterized by diversity, into which attempts at imposing unity are introduced'.

According to Schatzki (2001), instead of talking in terms of systems, structures or discourses, social scientists increasingly employ the term practices to describe the ways in which human activity is organized around shared practical understanding. The notion of practices locates human behaviour in terms of activity rather than more abstract concepts of system and discourse, hence the tendency to talk not only of social practices but also of language practices, discursive practices, literacy practices and so on. The idea of practices invokes repeated social and linguistic activities (Pennycook, 2010) as well as the ways in which social activity is organized and embodied (Bourdieu, 1977). As de Certeau (1984) argues in *The practice of everyday life*, 'everyday practices, "ways of operating" or doing things' should no longer 'appear as merely the obscure background of social activity' but rather should be seen as a key to understanding social and cultural relations (p.xi). As some sociological thinkers started to move away from the broad generalizations of social structures (sociology has its own structuralist epistemologies and ontologies), the point was not then to turn to the individual, family or community as a more manageable social entity but to focus instead on how everyday practices such as walking, talking, reading, writing, dwelling or cooking are organized. Schatzki (2002) points to the key understanding that social life is 'plied by a range of such practices as negotiation practices, political practices, cooking practices, banking practices, recreation practices, religious practices, and educational practices' (p.70).

The idea of (social) practices, therefore, is far more than a means of turning a noun into a verb. As Fowler (1996) explains in relation to work in critical language studies, their aim was to theorize language as a social practice in the sense that the term *practice (la pratique)* had acquired in the work of Althusser (1971), derived from Marx's (1972 [1845]) argument that materialist reality needed to be grasped in terms of concrete human action (practice). This was therefore a question of how to bring language, social theory, ideology and politics together. Practices shed light on how social relations are reproduced, how humans do the same things over and over. For Bourdieu, in his *Outline of a theory of practice* (1977), as for others who have engaged with the idea of practice, the question was how to get away from ideas such as 'structure' with its predetermined constituents, but also how to avoid the apparent alternative that placed human activity only at a level of individual action. The idea that mediated between the two for Bourdieu was the *habitus*, an idea that emphasized habitual action influenced by and productive of larger social forces. Practice is not therefore mere behaviour or activity; and neither is it juxtaposed with theory. Rather, this notion of practice attempts to make the observable doings of the everyday central to an understanding of social life, and simultaneously to view such activity in terms of regulated and sedimented social conduct.

Practices are conceived as 'embodied, materially mediated arrays of human activity centrally organized around shared practical understanding' (Schatzki, 2001, p.2). The various approaches to practice have a number of things in common: they make central the world of the everyday, eschewing structural ontologies in favour of an understanding of how people achieve daily life (Schatzki, 2010). They take seriously the ways we walk, eat and talk. As Thrift (2007) describes practices, they can be seen as things we do that have gained stability over time through the establishment of routines. We are schooled in practices and they continue to reproduce themselves if only because the general social default is to continue as before. This is not, however, to argue for an idea of static performance, as if things will always continue because they have done so up to now. Practices are 'continually being rewritten, as unusual circumstances arise' (2007, p.8); they are 'constructed out of all manner of resources' and 'provide the basic intelligibility of the world' (ibid.). Translanguaging, seen from this perspective, takes us 'beyond the linguistics of systems and speakers to a linguistics of participation' (Li Wei, 2018, p.15). As Gurney and Demuro (2019) argue, a shift towards thinking about language in terms of practice is an ontological shift as much as an ideological one, since it presents a very different account of language and languages.

3.8 REPERTOIRES, REGISTERS AND RESOURCES

As has been widely observed, the shift towards practices has brought about a proliferation of new terminology – not only translanguaging, but also *polylanguaging* (Jørgenson, 2008), *metrolingualism* (Pennycook and Otsuji, 2015) and others – much to the detriment of the field for some who would rather maintain the old vocabulary of sociolinguistics rather than these 'uncouth neologisms' (Edwards, 2012, p.37). As can be seen in some of the quotes in the previous section, it led at the same time not only to these neologisms but also to a reinvigoration of terminology such as repertoires, resources and registers. Once the idea of languages, or the equally compromised codes, was questioned, alternatives were needed to account for language practices in terms that didn't predefine languages. While discourse and genre had arguably done some of this work, both were often nevertheless seen as occurring within specified languages and were often pulled back towards structural accounts of their formation rather than practice-based accounts of their social significance: discourses and genres were language-specific textual organizations rather than social practices. The idea that people had repertoires of linguistic resources organized into social registers became a more useful way to conceive of language practices since all three could be used without necessary reference to separate languages (Pennycook, 2018b).

Neither register nor repertoire specifies or implies languages: repertoires are seen as collections of linguistic options, while registers are seen as ways of using language that suggest social commonalities. The notion of repertoire goes back to the work of Gumperz and others in the 1960s, as 'the totality of linguistic forms regularly employed in the course of socially significant interaction' (Gumperz, 1964, p.137). This determination to deal with 'actual speech instead of with *langue*' obliged the researcher 'to recognize the existence of a plurality of codes or code varieties in the same linguistic community' (Giglioli, 1972, p.15). Likewise emerging from work in the 1960s, the idea of register has also seen something of a revival in the new sociolinguistics. Registers could be understood as 'systems of speech style, and to non-linguistic accompaniments (such as dress) that constitute larger semiotic styles' (Agha, 2007a, p.147). While earlier work on registers to refer to ways of using language such as legalese, sport commentary, baby talk, street talk and so on (social rather than regional variation) has rather fallen out of favour in recent sociolinguistics (Coupland, 2007), Agha's idea of *enregisterment* made it possible to see not only how a way of speaking might be identified from its features but also how it was recognized from a wider perspective that might involve dress, bodies, location and much more.

While these terms have enabled sociolinguists to talk about diverse linguistic elements without resort to talking about languages, various tensions remain. On the one hand, while it has been easy to see repertoires as comprising elements drawn from multiple linguistic or semiotic *reservoirs* (to use a distinction from Bernstein, 2000), it has been more common to maintain a view that registers still occur *within* languages. As research on call centres (Hultgren, 2011) or aviation communication (Estival et al., 2016) has suggested, however, it may make more sense to look at such language use in terms of styles or practices rather than as involving particular languages. Registers can therefore be understood as social ways of using linguistic and other elements that are more dependent on social practices that occur across languages. On the other hand, while registers can be understood as social styles, the idea of the repertoire has often been pulled away from community use towards the individual. Wardaugh (1986, p.129) suggests that the concept of repertoire 'may be most useful when applied to individuals rather than to groups. We can use it to describe the communicative competence of individual speakers. Each person will then have a distinctive speech repertoire.' This move towards individual repertoires is also evident in some of the new sociolinguistic approaches that seek to account for history, mobility and complexity yet in doing so return to the individual: 'Repertoires are individual, biographically organized complexes of resources, and they follow the rhythms of actual human lives' (Blommaert and Backus, 2013, p.15). This interest in the individual – an emphasis on individual communicative capacity, whether in the form of individual repertoires or *idiolects* (discussed further in the next chapter) – as a reaction against a focus on language structures undermines the emphasis on concrete social activity. Methodological individualism (Ramberg and Røyneland, in press) may be a misstep almost as serious as methodological nationalism (Schneider, 2018).

The commonly used and seemingly neutral 'resources' meanwhile has come under critical scrutiny as a term that may imply extractivist ideologies (of more interest to bankers and mining companies than language users). [4] Despite these concerns, ideas such as repertoires provide useful tools for looking at an expanded notion of what is at stake when we consider *translingual practices* without recourse to the notions of languages or the reduction of diverse semiotic resources to

---

[4] My thanks to Claire Kramsch and Maggie Bullock Oliveira for drawing this to my attention.

a more limited view of language (Canagarajah, 2013). A *communicative repertoire* can then be understood as the collection of ways people 'use language and other means of communication (gestures, dress, posture, accessories) to function effectively in the multiple communities in which they participate' (Rymes, 2014, pp.9–10). An *embodied repertoire* can refer to the 'meaningful orchestration of multiple semiotic repertoires including body movement, rhythm, gesture, eye contact, head movement, pointing, in addition to linguistic ones' (Zhu Hua et al., 2020, p.77). It was on these grounds that we developed the idea of a *translingual family repertoire* (Hiratsuka and Pennycook, 2020) to describe the ways a family shared linguistic and other semiotic possibilities as an assembled community.

3.9 CONCLUSION

I have contrasted two different ontological starting points in this chapter. This is why the translanguaging debates are generally talking past each other: if you start with structures as pregiven things and then ask how people use them, you will end up with things such as codeswitching, in which bilinguals (people who speak two languages) alternate languages (two different language entities) between or within sentences (across linguistic structures) (MacSwan, 2022b). If you start from the position of language practices, the interest is in what people do with their linguistic options, and you will end up with an idea like translanguaging. The 'translingual turn' is much bigger than debates about unitary competence or codeswitching, bringing instead 'greater attention to the reality that the very notion of "language" inherently limits our understanding of the diverse possibilities for communicative practice across cultural and linguistic difference worldwide' (Lee, 2022, p.6). This broader view of translanguaging takes up questions of space by thinking in terms of *translanguaging space* (Li Wei, 2011) or *spatial repertoires* (Canagarajah, 2018; Pennycook and Otsuji, 2015) that start to incorporate a wider set of semiotic, artefactual and material concerns than other language ontologies. This will be the focus of the next chapter, language as assemblage.

4 Linguistic, Semiotic and Sociomaterial Assemblages

I have been arguing that it is useful to see all languages as assemblages since this allows for a more flexible approach to language than a view that assumes languages to be prefabricated entities that we then use. Thinking of language as an assemblage, Wee (2021, p.16) argues, 'affords significant advantages over the view of language as an autonomous bounded system. It provides a coherent account of regularities and fluidities in language while also being open to the idea of what actually constitutes "the linguistic".' While many linguists might not recognize their view of language in this description of 'an autonomous bounded system' – it is after all common to acknowledge the fuzzy edges and social uses of languages – the commitment to a structural ontology, as I have argued in the previous chapter, implies both autonomy and boundedness in any understanding of what languages are. As Wee also suggests, an assemblage orientation can, without invoking bounded structures, provide a coherent account of the push and pull of fixity and fluidity while raising significant questions about where we draw the lines of what constitutes language. An assemblage approach to language can be seen as a third ontological position (Demuro and Gurney, 2021; Kell and Budach, 2024) that differs from the structural and practice ontologies discussed in Chapter 3.

It shares some of the characteristics of a practice-oriented ontology – not assuming the pre-existence of languages that are then put to use, and looking instead at how people use linguistic elements to get things done – but shifting the focus away from social practices to material events. If the first ontology is structural and the second social, this approach to language may be seen as material. An assemblage approach to language can also be seen, like a practice approach, as a better candidate for a practical theory of language. It derives not from an attempt to describe language structures but from an approach to social happenings that seeks to understand how different elements come together at particular moments, and how language becomes part of the material arrangement of an event. There are three slightly different ways that language and languages can be considered in relation to the idea of assemblage: assemblages as combinations of linguistic items (language assemblages), assemblages as semiotic gatherings (semiotic assemblages) and assemblages as material arrangements that involve language (sociomaterial assemblages). Before discussing these in more depth in Sections 4.3-4.5, I will explore the development of the idea of assemblage in relation to forms of new materialism, as well as ideas such as *entanglements* with which it is closely associated.

4.1 ASSEMBLAGES: FROM AUTONOMY TO ENTANGLEMENTS

The idea of an assemblage is not particularly complex or difficult. Some, perhaps trying to give it an extra exotic feel, pronounce it as if it were a French word (like *dressAGE*, with the emphasis on the final syllable), assuming presumably that it is a 'borrowed' French term *assemblage*. The term *assemblage*, however, is a fairly ordinary term that has been used to translate the French *agencement*, as used by Deleuze and Guattari (1987), who are often taken to be the key source for this way of thinking (though this might arguably be better understood as part of an assemblage of connected orientations; McFarlane, 2011). Like many such translations, it is only partially successful: Canut (2021, p.96) considers the English translation *assemblage* much too neutral ('bien trop neutre'), failing to capture the sense of a reconfiguration of collective positions ('une reconfiguration des positionnements collectifs') related to desire, power, society, politics and economy. While the term assemblage has arguably now taken on many of these dynamics in the work of Tsing (2015) and others, it is true that it works in a different register and does not convey the same sense of action (putting things together) (DeLanda, 2016; Phillips, 2006). It also potentially carries overtones of the idea of assemblage art – to which the French term *assemblage* is more closely connected – with its emphasis on art works consisting of found objects, pre-existing materials brought together to form a new whole.

The term *assemblage* in English (not as a translation of *agencement*) is a term used in evolutionary biology to describe a collection of fossil species that were laid down during the same period (Godfrey-Smith, 2020). In the Ediacaran period we have the Avalon assemblage (from about 575 million years ago, in what is today part of Canada), the White Sea assemblage (560 million years; Russia) and the Nama assemblage (540 million years; Namibia). The term assemblage here is used to describe gatherings of fossils during particular periods which may cover millions of years. The notion of the assemblage allows biologists to hedge on whether very early plants and creatures coexisted and encountered each other or have just ended up as fossils in a similar place over a long period of time. Assemblage has also long been used in archaeology to describe 'artifacts that are found near each other' (Burkette, 2021, p.100). An assemblage is 'a collection of material related through contextual proximity' (Joyce and Pollard, 2012, p.292). Again, the notion of contextual proximity allows archaeologists to hedge on whether certain artefacts were used by the same people or co-occurred over a particular period of time.

The move in various domains of social science towards thinking in terms of assemblages similarly suggests an interest in understanding the interconnections among people, things and the world around them. This is an endeavour to understand the world not so much in terms of its separable parts (humans, languages, animals, objects and so on) but rather in terms of their inseparability: a move from *autonomy* to *entanglements*. In his work on *entangled objects*, for example, Thomas (1991) sought to understand the importance of the objects (material culture) that were traded between Pacific Islanders and Europeans – food, tools, weapons and so on – and their interpretations on both sides of these colonial transactions. Objects and material culture, as Ingold (2012) explains, are *entangled* with humans. Archaeologists likewise started to focus on the entanglements of objects and humans, the relationality and dependence among people and things, and among things themselves (Hodder, 2011, 2012). Meanwhile, philosophers of science such as Bruno Latour (2005) were thinking in terms of networks of things and people (Actor Network Theory), and new materialists were similarly taking an interest in the dynamic role of objects, or 'the curious ability of inanimate things to animate, to act, to produce effects dramatic and subtle' (Bennett, 2010, p.6).

These moves to consider the interrelationships among people and things, humans and the environment can be seen as part of wider *posthumanist* and *new materialist* orientations. Posthumanist thought offers us alternative ways of thinking about what is to be human, presenting new political and intellectual possibilities for considering how we can get beyond the anthropocentric assumptions that so constrain our understanding of ourselves and our place in the world. It is a response both to the failed project of humanism – the projection of a particular vision of the human onto the world – and the challenges posed by human destructiveness, environmental degradation, climate change, population growth, resource scarcity, urbanization, diminishing resources and the treatment of other animals (Pennycook, 2018a). Posthumanism is a broad category that can cover different, though at times overlapping, orientations. One concern is with the tenets of humanist political philosophy (what we might call post-humanism). Braidotti (2013, p.16) takes up a specifically anti-humanist position, asking why, as a woman, she would want to be a member of a category (human) that has been so consistently exclusionary: 'I am none too fond of Humanism or of the idea of the human which it implicitly upholds.'

Humanism generally assumes a stable commonality for all humans and, as many critics of this position have remarked, while masquerading as a universal category, it has been both exclusionary (along lines of gender, race, class, sexual orientation, disability and so on) and culturally particular (promoting a Western vision of individuals within a human collectivity). Given that humanism also carries a sense of caring, of embracing humanity, it has also been criticized as a hypocritical stance within colonial and neocolonial relations. For Frantz Fanon (1952, 1961) the idea of the 'human' promoted by colonial powers was anything but emancipatory: it was a deeply racial concept that only served to alienate the colonized. 'All the western nations are caught in a lie', asserts James Baldwin (1972, p.85), 'the lie of their pretended humanism: this means that their history has no moral justification, and that the West has no moral authority'. Drawing on Fanon, Nascimento (2023, p.46) argues that the Enlightenment, capitalism, liberalism and positivism are all examples of colonial humanism whereby 'the white world is humanized whereas the non-white world is racialized'. While one might argue that humanism is still an ideal worth striving for – it just needs to be more inclusive – others would suggest that from a decolonial perspective, this can only be done once we acknowledge the complicity of humanism with colonialism. There are ways of salvaging forms of critical humanism within a more radical or Southern perspective, but at the very least this needs to be in terms of divergent humanisms (Bessone, 2022; Diagne, 2021; Fanon, 1961).

A different strand of posthumanist work has an interest in transformations to what it means to be human brought about by changing technologies, sometimes called *transhumanism* (we might also see this as posthuman-ism). Transhumanism is 'predicated upon a profound dissatisfaction with the current human condition and "the biological chains" that keep human beings from actualizing their fullest potential' (Huberman, 2021, p.22). Major technological changes that both surround us and become part of us are challenging the very idea of what it means to be human. Instrumentation, the growth of data, and new forms of monitoring and sensing around our bodies (wrist-worn health monitors connected to the cloud, for example) are changing the way we understand and perceive humanity, with an ever-increasing monitoring and surveillance of behaviour (Berson, 2015). *Converging technologies* that transcend, enhance and prolong life through a range of augmentations to mind and body (prosthetic limbs, bionic eyes, brain implants) can be seen as body enhancements rather than just replacements, which raises questions about what it now means to be human: not so much a biological given as an improvable body. Transhumanists are 'committed to using science and technology not just to usher in a new kind of culture and society, but also a new kind of posthuman species' (Huberman, 2021, p.22).

For those of us in language studies there are more pressing concerns than these 'technoutopic visions of the future' (Huberman, 2021, p.217). Recent developments in artificial intelligence (AI) have already posed serious moral and political challenges. The realization that AI-based programs were making racist and sexist assumptions shone a light back on humans and the discriminatory world we have made. Other questions have emerged to do with the legal rights of robots or the responsibilities of self-drive cars or how indeed we can ensure that the monster we have created will continue to be on our side (Walsh, 2022). What is the future for *Humanity 2.0* (Fuller, 2011) or *Life 3.0* (Tegmark, 2018)? Of major significance for applied and sociolinguistic projects, however, are new forms of communication, from our smart phones to the rise of AI-driven language generation. The combination of Large Language Models (LLM) and AI has led to recent developments such as ChatGPT, 'an AI-powered language model developed by OpenAI, capable of generating human-like text based on context and past conversations' (Chat, 2023). It's the 'human-like text' in such descriptions that is causing something of a humanist panic. Indeed, a case might be made that we would be better off worrying about this challenge to the ontology of language than worrying about the extent to which we want to consider languages themselves as inventions.

At one level this concern is quite pragmatic for domains such as education: how do we know that an assessment task is in fact the product of a particular person or is this now an outmoded idea? Will this bring the end of the essay assignment (good riddance, some say)? Of more concern is that it has become much less clear who may be producing text, so that publishers are now compelled to spell out that authorship (accountability for content, consent and contracts concerning integrity of the work) entails 'uniquely human responsibilities that cannot be undertaken by AI tools' (Taylor and Francis, 2023, np). The advice continues that AI tools cannot be listed as co-authors but must be appropriately acknowledged. Similar issues concern online security. As one Australian government site warns: 'You must be a natural person' to have an account. 'This means you are an individual human being. You are not, for example, a corporate entity, robot, or a software program' (MyGov, 2023). This arguably raises much broader concerns since the capacity to produce language has been one of the defining features of what it means to be human (Pennycook, 2018a) so the production of 'human-like' language may be an ontological threat to humanity. It is one thing to augment the physical capacity of the body, but once that supposedly sacrosanct element of humanity that separates us from all the rest – language – can be generated by non-humans, what then defines humanity? 'At the heart of AI's challenge to communication research', Guzman and Lewis (2020, p.73) suggest, 'is a blurring of the ontological divide between human and machine'.

As a result, we are currently at a particular moment of crisis about what constitutes the human. For publishers, educational institutions, major organizations and many others, these changes pose serious threats to integrity and security and unless we push back with a strong sense of what is and is not human, we will be lost in a world of digital flows. From a transhumanist perspective, by contrast, this has been a long time coming and the onus is now on us to accept and work with this new world of unclear boundaries between language, people and machines. The fact that these new technologies pose challenges to what *authorship* means should not in the larger scale of things come as a surprise since the particular conjunction between authorship and authenticity was arguably a passing phase of modernist ideology: premodern and postmodern eras of textual production have not insisted on an author as a guarantor of either provenance or meaning (Kearney, 1988; Pennycook, 1996). How, Wee (2021) asks, do we start to think about communicative practices – even when we start with automated forms of communication on a more mundane level, such as signs in car parks that inform us of the number of available spaces – in relation to prior assumptions about sociolinguistic and pragmatic norms of communication? These new technologies – from AI and speaking robots to brain implants and computer-facilitated telepathy – may fundamentally change not only how we communicate but also what language becomes (Seargeant, 2023).

If the transhumanist interest is in interactions between humans and new technologies, as well as where humans now sit in relation to ever more capable forms of AI, a new materialist orientation recalibrates the relations between humans and the non-human world more generally. This line of thinking questions the boundaries between what is seen as inside and outside, where thought or language occur, and what role a supposedly exterior world may play in thought, action and language. The point is not to discount humans in the search for a more object-oriented ontology but to reconfigure where humans sit, in order to unsettle the position of humans at the ontological apex (the most important forms of being) and to see humans as *entangled* and *implicated* in other things (Bogost, 2012). From this perspective, things, objects, artefacts are not seen as separate from humans or each other but as part of integrated wholes (Barad, 2007). New materialism challenges anthropocentric assumptions that matter is passive, secondary, incapable of action, doesn't matter: 'the only thing that doesn't seem to matter anymore is matter' (Barad, 2007, p.132). New materialism thus 'shifts the focus from questions of correspondence between descriptions and reality ... to matters of practices, doings and actions' (Barad, 2007, p.135). New materialist perspectives allow us to rethink the relative weight we give to different aspects of the material world, how they are related and where humans may (or may not) fit into this picture. This will be discussed further in Section 4.2 in relation to assemblages.

Posthumanism is not giving up on humans, or announcing the end of humanity, but rather calling for a rethinking of the relationship between humans and everything else. Posthumanism asks what our relation is to the planet, to other animals, to the objects around us, and re-evaluates ideas such as human agency, human nature, human language or universalism. In a long line of thinking that has decentred the position of humans as separate from other animals (Darwin, 1872), in control of their history (Marx, 1867), in charge of their own minds (Freud, 1901) or, more recently, distinguishable from the machines they have produced (Turing; see Copeland, 2004), posthumanism continues the work of repositioning humans where they belong, not as monarchs of all they survey but as equal cohabitants of the earth. The challenge is to disidentify from anthropocentric norms and the unearned privileges that have come with humanist assumptions. No longer is the human mind assumed to be the exclusive place of knowledge, or the human psyche to be something under human control, or agency to be distinct, voluntary and solely human, or human life and language to be absolutely different from all other forms of life (Kell and Budach, 2024; Schatzki, 2002). Posthumanist ideas are not therefore so much anti-human as opposed to *human hubris* (Pennycook, 2018a, 2018d).

4.2 ASSEMBLAGES AND DISTRIBUTED LANGUAGE, COGNITION AND AGENCY

Instead of viewing language and thought as internal, this line of thinking suggests that they may be better understood as *distributed* across a wider range of domains which from a humanist point of view had been considered to be exterior, secondary, outside. Distributed cognition operates not only on a spatial scale larger than the individual but expands such insights beyond immediate time and space towards broader cognitive ecosystems. Cognition, Hutchins (1995) argues, involves much more than the brain, including external artefacts, other people and cultural systems for interpreting reality. Cognition is not therefore something to be studied in isolation but rather needs ethnographic understandings of people, place, things and language. Navigation – discussed at greater length in Chapter 5 – is a good example of this, involving far more than a mind-internal capacity to compute direction: navigation involves the senses, the body, the interrelationship with instruments, an ability to read the world around us. Distributed cognition 'begins with the assumption that all instances of cognition can be seen as emerging from distributed processes' (Hutchins, 2014, p.36). Cognition therefore 'draws on brains, bodies and surroundings, including other cognizers, artefacts, social relations and environmental structures' (Steffensen, 2012, p.186).

Agency can also be seen in these terms. This is to view agency not only, as Enfield (2017, p.9) suggests, as 'radically distributed' beyond the individual – agency occurs interactively so that people's goals may be shared or someone can be held accountable for another's action – but also in terms of 'an elemental, material agency distributed across bodies human and nonhuman' (Bennett, 2009, p.2). Such a view suggests that the material world has agentive possibilities, simultaneously rendering agency not just as an ability to act among humans and other animals but also part of a dynamic among people and the world, while also shifting what it means to talk of agency (no longer personal, possessed or volitional). The point is not that objects have agency in the same way that human agency has been understood – as a conscious and deliberate will towards action – but that once we consider agency in relational terms, it becomes evident that many more things may be *actants* in the world than just humans and other animals. Agency is no longer a solely human and conscious will to action but rather a property of an interrelated network. Likewise when we consider cognition, it is not that objects think along human lines but rather that they become material anchors in our distributed processes of cognition. There is therefore a constant dynamic between distribution and assemblage, the one seeking to account for ways in which agency, cognition and identity operate beyond the human, the other drawing attention to the ways in which particular configurations of people, places, things and linguistic resources are drawn together. This is an ontological position where such processes are understood to be part of the material world.

Among other processes that we can consider as distributed, such as identity (Pennycook and Otsuji, 2022), of central importance for the discussion here is language. The idea of *distributed language* challenges a conceptualization of language as structure, internalized system or individual competence. Viewing language – like cognition – as embodied, embedded, enacted and extended (Joseph, 2018), it becomes far more than representational activity in the mind but involves bodies, surrounds and activities (Steffensen, 2012). Human communication, from this perspective, is '*embodied* in a *biological* sense, as well as in a *social* and *cultural* sense' (Ritchie, 2022, p.6; emphasis in original). A distributed language perspective brings together, in Cowley's (2012) account, distributed cognition (Hutchins, 2014) and integrational linguistics (Harris, 1998a). Material surrounds, from this standpoint, are not mere contexts in which we interact but rather part of an interactive whole that includes people, objects and space. This is the idea of language as part of an assemblage, a grouping or temporary arrangement of diverse elements, which will be discussed at greater length in the next section. As part of a more general move towards understanding how supposedly human properties – language, cognition, agency and identity – are part of a wider set of material processes, part of a world of interacting objects and artefacts, these lines of thinking lead to a re-evaluation of the role of objects and space in relation to human thought and action. Identity is concerned with 'our material being in the world' (Block, 2022, p.62).

For Deleuze and Guattari, assemblages are 'concrete collections of heterogeneous materials that display tendencies towards both stability and change' (Adkins, 2015, p.14). They were interested in the dynamics of an 'assemblage of bodies, of actions and passions, an intermingling of bodies reacting to one another' as well as a 'collective assemblage of enunciation, of acts and statements of incorporeal transformations attributed to bodies' (Deleuze and Guattari, 1987, p.88). Their understanding of assemblage refers to entanglements of related entities, implying a relational ontology (see Chapter 2): 'things are as they are (while also constantly changing) because of their interrelations and their entanglements with other things' (Toohey, 2019, p.939). For Deleuze and Guattari (1987), who were particularly sceptical about modern linguistics, language can be seen in terms of relations between semiotic sequences, associations of power and social struggles. The ideas of language and languages can be replaced by an understanding of local and particular uses of slang, registers, patois and so on.

In her study of *matsutake* mushrooms – where they grow (among pine trees in partially cleared forests), how they are gathered (foraging work on often steep slopes), who goes in search of them (peripheral communities of the unemployed, refugees, war veterans and so on) and how global forces affect markets (the Chernobyl nuclear fallout had a big effect on European stocks and Japanese markets) – Tsing (2015, p.23) argues that thinking in terms of assemblages 'urges us to ask: How do gatherings sometimes become "happenings," that is, greater than the sum of their parts?' The idea of the assemblage enables us therefore to see how multiple factors come together at particular moments, producing an event that is more than just a conglomeration of things. There is 'nothing necessarily critical about notions of assemblage' McFarlane (2011, p.205) reminds us, just as there is nothing 'necessarily critical about notions like capital, labour, space or urbanism', but the notion of assemblage makes it possible to see both the complexity and the dynamics of particular combinations of factors. For Tsing (2015, p.24), assemblages 'drag political economy inside them, and not just for humans'; they are 'sites for watching how political economy works', not through a predefined operation of capital but by the juxtaposition of people, things and life trajectories.

Thinking in terms of assemblages therefore has a number of implications. It draws attention to how different things come together in particular ways, and that these may be quite dissimilar kinds of things, not just people and artefacts, but objects, passions, words, policies, economies. It questions the divisions that have been made between humans and things, between nature and culture, or between nature and humans that has so hindered the natural and social sciences throughout the modernist era (Latour, 2015). It questions 'the fallacy of assuming a crisp dividing line between the communication behaviors of humans and those of other organisms' (Ritchie, 2022, p.8). The 'animal turn in linguistics' has started to provide an 'opportunity to develop a theory of a relational framework focusing on language as local meaningmaking distributed among and between species, materiality, place and time' (Cornips, 2022, p.209). Assemblage thinking points to ways that life happens as an unfolding set of uneven practices that are never inevitable. It insists that we look locally, not at broad abstractions about language, society or culture but at local combinations of things that become happenings. This does not mean turning our back on languages or social or political relations but it does mean that these things only make sense when looked at in their local entanglements. Thinking in terms of assemblages means a move from autonomy, structure and bounded systems to entanglements, distribution and relationality.

4.3 LANGUAGE ASSEMBLAGES

There are a number of different ways of thinking specifically about language and assemblage. The first is to look at the ways 'speakers assemble language in ways that reflect their own encounters with and understandings of particular constructions' (Wee, 2021, p.21). That is to say, languages are not pregiven entities that are used but rather sets of communicative possibilities that are assembled by speakers from their own histories of linguistic activity. With a particular transhumanist interest in new technologies, Wee argues that 'what we think of as language is being constantly assembled and reassembled through the joint contributions of humans, technologies and inherited conventions of language use' (2021, p.39). In some ways this is a fairly minimalist account that stresses the ways speakers assemble language according to their own encounters with linguistic elements. Unlike more structuralist accounts, it gives a greater role to the active work of language users, who assemble languages as they go. Language is not therefore an entity that prefigures human engagement, and no one 'can be said to ever encounter a language system or variety in its totality; encounters are only ever with constructions' (Wee, 2021, p.21).

This last point is by no means new: although structural ontologies suggest that languages can be conceived in terms of totalities (at least as far as possible grammatical structures are concerned), it is not clear whether many linguists would go so far as to suggest that, even if a totality exists, anyone actually encounters it. Corder made a similar point in his introduction to applied linguistics fifty years ago: no one 'commands a knowledge of any language "as a whole"' but rather 'possesses a repertoire, or set of overlapping codes' (Corder, 1973, p.66). The point has been reiterated by Blommaert (2010, p.103), more recently, suggesting that no one 'knows *all* of a language ... no one needs all the resources that a language potentially provides' (emphasis in original). In many ways this is an uncontroversial observation: languages are bigger than any one person's knowledge, and encounters with languages can only be partial. In lexical terms this partiality becomes the fodder of quiz and trivia competitions: what do you call a collection of starlings in English? What about a collection of owls? Most people never encounter such things (particularly groups of owls) and certainly don't have a word for them. In what sense are a *murmuration of starlings*[1] or a *parliament of owls* part of the language? This raises various questions about where and what languages are. I suspect that most people who know these terms do so because they come up on quizzes. They are evidently part of very few people's repertoire nor of many speech communities (reservoir, in the terms of Bernstein, 2000). The problem lies with the concept of a language 'in its totality', 'as a whole' or '*all* of a language': it is unclear what this could ever really refer to, and certainly none of us will ever encounter it. It can only ever be an abstraction beyond human experience.

The dilemma that languages are distributed across social environments, and never encounterable as a whole, has been circumvented by focusing on the individual instead. For a number of linguists, indeed, the idiolect (or I-language in Chomskyan terms) is the starting point for linguistic analysis, with external language (E-language) a secondary abstraction. From this perspective, I-language is 'the actual grammar, lexis, phonology etc., that we each carry around in our heads' (Hall, 2020, p.17) and can be understood in ontological terms as part of an internal, cognitive *language capacity* (Hall, 2020). For Otheguy and colleagues (2015, p.288), since linguists '*cannot* legitimately address matters relating to language in the social sense of the term' (emphasis in original), their real focus has to be on idiolects, namely a 'person's own unique, personal language, the person's mental grammar that emerges in interaction with other speakers and enables the person's use of language' (p.289). This is a view of language from an 'internal perspective of the individual' that differs from an

---

[1] As someone who has been lucky enough to witness this remarkable gathering of birds, it was disappointing that no one seemed to have the term to describe it.

'external perspective of the society' and is made up of 'lists of lexical and grammatical features' (p.289), so that the 'only thing anyone actually speaks is his or her own idiolect, something that no one else speaks' (p.294).

This retreat to, and in some cases prioritization of, the individual as the locus of language as something carried around in the head, however, is at odds with a social vision of language: people do not have primary personal language capacities that enable secondary social engagement so much as they engage in language practices as social beings. If, further, we take assemblage-oriented thinking seriously, then these boundaries between inside and outside, social and individual, become difficult to maintain. Once a notion such as agency, for example, is understood beyond the individual not only in terms of 'joint commitment and cooperation toward common goals' (Enfield and Kockelman, 2017, p.xi) but also as 'distributed across an ontologically heterogeneous field, rather than being a capacity localized in a human body or in a collective produced (only) by human efforts' (Bennett, 2010, p.23), then, like similar ideas such as identity, it is hard to see how these can be isolated in some notion of an individual being. Similarly, language may also be seen not only as cooperatively achieved but also more radically distributed. To insist that bilingual idiolects draw on a wider range of lexical or structural elements (Otheguy et al., 2018, p.638) points to internal capacities rather than socially distributed material possibilities. This doesn't mean we don't use language on some personal level or that we all speak in the same way – obviously we don't – but to posit the idea of an idiolect is to submit to a form of *methodological individualism* that gives ontological priority to the individual and which rests on Western liberal assumptions about agency, freedom and society (Ramberg and Røyneland, in press).

From a *languaging* perspective, language is 'a dialogical phenomenon and is not therefore the possessions of individual brains and bodies' (Thibault, 2011, p.214). As Hutchins (2014, p.37) reminds us, while 'language is clearly a cognitive accomplishment', it is 'not one that is accomplished by any individual'. The emergence of a language, he explains, is 'a cognitive process that takes place in an evolving cognitive ecosystem that includes a shared world of objects and events as well as adaptive resources internal to each member of the community'. Thinking in terms of distributed language and assemblages can help us get beyond these awkward divisions that presuppose that languages exist both externally (as either the socially created structures of internal language capacities or as pre-existing structures on which people can draw) or internally (as the underlying structures from which languages are generated or the internal representations of external languages). The notion of distributed cognition and the challenges of new materialism erode this internal/external division, as well as the possibility that the social is outside while some kind of structure is inside. Just as it is useful to get beyond the methodological nationalism (Schneider, 2018) that has so strongly influenced both popular and linguistic thinking about languages, so it is also important to get beyond methodological individualism, which gives to individuals some primordial capacity to contain and use language. The very notion of an idiolect becomes quite implausible from this perspective.

From a language-as-assemblage point of view, there are several important lessons here. A focus on varieties of English from this perspective, for example, can move away from problematic assumptions about the pre-existence of English as a lingua franca (ELF) or Englishes in the outer and expanding circles located in particular geopolitical spaces, and focus instead on 'the incessant assemblings and reassemblings that are part and parcel of language use' (Wee, 2021, pp.41–2). Although ELF proponents have continued to insist that English as a lingua franca avoids the bounded nationalisms of world Englishes and 'is not a variety of English but a variable way of using it' (Seidlhofer, 2011, p.77), more critical evaluations have suggested that the label 'ELF' indicates an ontological assumption about the status of English prior to communication (the 'it' that is being variably used). Terms like 'ELF users' or 'ELF contexts' refer to clearly identifiable people, situations and a pre-utterance entity (O'Regan, 2016). Wee's (2021) contention is that it is more useful to consider these local uses of English in terms of assemblings of features. Rather than viewing language 'as an entity with clear boundaries' or as having 'an autonomous structure', rather than listing varieties of English (Singaporean English, Thai English and so on), it is more useful, Wee (2021, p.42) argues, to think in terms of the 'multiple enactments and assemblages of speakers, language resources and technologies *as well as* a reminder of the complex relationship between these enactments/assemblages and language names' (emphasis in original).

This understanding of language as assemblage, while still arguably maintaining a constricted focus on what constitutes languages, can also include the social and material construction of languages. This is not therefore only a focus on the agentive work of people in making languages out of their encounters with particular linguistic items, since it may also include the wider social making of languages. People's beliefs about language – which, as argued in Chapter 2, are also deeply important and need to be understood as part of *the total linguistic fact* (see the next section) – can from this perspective be seen in terms of *language ideological assemblages*, pointing to the ways in which complexes of beliefs and feelings about a range of factors from a range of sources 'interact with each other to modify language ideologies and linguistic practices' (Kroskrity, 2018, p.134). By avoiding a focus on one particular ideology (such as language purism) or policy (favouring, for example, bilingual schooling) or one particular aspect of political economy (how a community may access certain economic opportunities), and focusing instead on 'the interaction of clusters of ideologies that occur within or across linguistic communities' (p.134), language ideological assemblages point to the ways in which social worlds, political economic disparities, a desire to belong and the remaking of intersectional identities can be intertwined with language and how we think about language.

4.4 SEMIOTIC ASSEMBLAGES

A slightly different perspective to the language-as-assemblage position is offered by an approach that broadens the semiotic domain. Developing the work of Michael Silverstein (1985, p.220), and his insistence on the need to account for the interactions among signs, contexts and language ideologies, Blommaert urges us to consider the 'total linguistic/ semiotic fact' in relation to 'cultural ideology' and 'sociolinguistic stratification' (Blommaert, 2017, p.58). From this perspective, we need to account for the multiplicity of factors that come together around people and place: 'These dense and complex objects are the "stuff" of the study of language in society' (2017, p.59). This move to capture 'adequate contextualization' entails a focus beyond linguistic signs in a narrower sense towards 'semiotic, complex objects', a wider understanding of the *total semiotic fact* (Blommaert, 2017, p.47). Attempts to capture this 'totality' (always impossible) go back at least to Austin's interest in the 'total speech act in the total speech situation' (1962, p.52) as a way to show all that was involved in a speech event. Expanding on Blommaert's interest in *chronotopes* – 'the intrinsic blending of space and time in any event in the real world' (Blommaert, 2017, p.48) – Karimzad (2021, p.26) makes a case for their inclusion in the *total sociolinguistic fact*, so that we can pay more attention to different levels of contexts that are relevant for any interaction and thus provide 'more precise and coherent understandings of experience, memory, imagination, and ideology and their impact on situated practices'.

The trend towards a broader *semiotic landscape* (Eckert, 2018; Jaworski and Thurlow, 2010) can be observed in a number of domains of sociolinguistics. The field of *linguistic landscapes*, for example, has expanded from an earlier focus on languages on signs in the public space – what named languages occur on what public signage? – to a broad understanding of the social semiotics of space. This is a move from signs as signage to signs as semiotics (Pennycook, 2019b), to include 'images, photos, sounds (soundscapes), movements, music, smells (smellscapes), graffiti, clothes, food, buildings, history, as well as people who are immersed and absorbed in spaces' (Shohamy, 2015, pp.153–4). While a lot of the focus around the *translinguistic* turn in sociolinguistics (see Chapter 3) has been on its challenge to linguistic orthodoxies around bilingualism, codeswitching and the ontology of named languages – the idea that 'communication transcends individual languages' – a secondary focus has been on the ways that 'communication transcends words and involves diverse semiotic resources and ecological affordances' (Canagarajah, 2013, p.6). This broad multilingual, multimodal and multisensorial focus (Zhu Hua et al., 2017) has been taken up through an interest *in semiotic assemblages*.

As notions such as linguistic landscapes have expanded to include a wide domain of semiotic possibilities, attention to semiotic assemblages (Pennycook, 2017, 2019a, b) enables an analysis of how language, the street, the sign-makers and the observers are part of a temporary coming-together in a particular place. The concept of semiotic assemblages 'helps us to appreciate a much wider range of linguistic, artefactual, historical, and spatial resources brought together in particular combinations and in particular moments of time and space' (Sharma, 2021, p.68). Sharma's study of the different elements that are assembled in the making of a new Chinatown in Kathmandu – the buildings, workers, artefacts and signs – shows how 'signs and material artifacts operate in a network of relations as assemblages' (p.75), enabling us to see 'how languages are embedded and emergent with other forms of semiosis' (p.79). The invitation to customers to feel the softness of the scarfs on sale suggests the importance of touch. This approach emphasizes the significance not only of the linguistic invitation to feel the scarf, but also of the material feel of the scarf within the bigger context of a new Chinatown. It does not privilege any particular aspect of this – language, artefact, people, space – but rather focuses on the 'network of assemblages' (p.80) at play.

Drawing on the idea of *repertoires*, which, as discussed in Chapter 3, enables an understanding of sets of linguistic elements without defining these in terms of languages or individual capacities, Kusters (2021, p.188) discusses *semiotic repertoires* as neither 'a toolkit of resources' nor 'located in individual people' but rather 'a distributed set of resources that are chained together contingently in activities' (Kusters, 2021, p.188). It has likewise been useful to think in terms of *spatial repertoires* (Canagarajah, 2018; Pennycook and Otsuji, 2014, 2015) to capture the ways that repertoires are not so much a set of individual resources as a set of possibilities assembled in time and space. This focus on semiotic or spatial assemblages has enabled a wide range of studies that aim to grasp as broad a semiotics as possible, to analyse 'the simultaneous co-presence and co-reliance of language and other semiotic resources in meaning-making, affording each equal weight' (Hawkins, 2018, p.64). In our studies of encounters in a corner store in Tokyo, for example, we have shown (Pennycook and Otsuji, 2019) how an understanding of assemblages foregrounds the ways that the fish (various smoked and dried options are offered to the customer), the phones (there are various conversations between the customer and someone advising them on which fish to buy, as well as between the shop workers and others) and the various linguistic resources (French, English, Japanese, Bangla and so on) create a particular spatial and temporal dynamic in these everyday shopping practices.

Looking at street art in these terms takes us not only beyond an analysis of language in the public space, but also beyond an analysis of an artwork itself only in semiotic terms. A focus on the entanglements of street art with a much wider circulation of discourse and material relations, as well as a broader semiotics (including music, for example, or street food), gives us a useful purchase on the ways in which art, the street, the politics and the economy, the artists and the viewers are intertwined (Pennycook, 2022b). This is about how an 'assemblage of architecture, artefacts, and activities' shapes public discourse (Jaworski and Gonçalves, 2021, p.158), allowing us to see how, at any moment, a particular assemblage of people, linguistic resources, products and spatial organization comes together to produce a particular set of interactions (Pennycook, 2017). The Bangladeshi-run shop in Tokyo is interesting not just because of the diversity of languages – Bangla, Hindi, English, Japanese, Nepali, French, and so on – that are part of the spatial repertoire, but also the relations with the products on sale, the spatial arrangement of the counter and till, or the use of mobile phones. These are used to discuss purchases with others elsewhere, to consult shopping lists, to watch sporting events, and may be part of the interactions around the counter. Shopping lists themselves provide rich resources for understanding how cooking and shopping, languages and scripts, products and space interact in constantly shifting assemblages (Pennycook and Otsuji, 2024).

In a comparison of television weather forecasts for hearing and non-hearing viewers, this kind of analysis makes it possible to see the importance of 'sensory ecologies, timing as a semiotic resource, and the construction of semiotic assemblages' (Stone and Köhring, 2021, p.242). While the mainstream hearing audience already get 'a complex interplay of language and gestural resources, indexing, co-occurring with artefacts in the broadcast image' (p.240), for the audience with a deaf sensory ecology, elements such as timing as a semiotic resource become paramount. As will be discussed further in the next section as well as Chapter 6, and as observed by Kusters (2021) and her colleagues, thinking in terms of assemblages in the context of Deaf communities has importance not just for understanding the complexity of communication but also for considering ontologically what language is. The idea of semiotic assemblages broadens the focus from linguistic signs to a wider set of semiotic possibilities, suggesting that it is not only the linguistic form, speakers and setting that matter – as captured in work on the ethnography of speaking (SPEAKING) – but also the social relations, emotional and affective domains, multilingual practices, iterative activity, objects and assemblages, spatial repertoires, interactivity, and sensory relations (SEMIOSIS) (Pennycook, 2023a).

We might still ask, however, whether this focus on meanings – or *semiotic* assemblages – places too much emphasis on human semiosis. Just as Sharma's (2021) interest in the *feel* of the scarf invites us beyond semiotics into the realm of the senses, and a focus on multisensory practices, sensory ecologies or the sociomaterial surrounds when shopping point beyond semiotic domains, so we might ask whether, despite the focus on place, objects, architecture and so on, a semiotic assemblage approach still gives too much prominence to semiotics, suggesting that human meaning-making practices remain central to the process. As far as Pablé (2022) is concerned, to question the centrality of human semiosis – to ask whether objects themselves might play a role – is to undermine the humanist project of linguistics, whether in its segregational or integrational guise. Quoting Harris (2004, p.729) approvingly – 'The black tie I wear at the funeral isn't doing my grieving for me. Nor is it a bit of grief that somehow escaped from inside me and got distributed' – he warns against confusing semiotics and the objects themselves. New materialism, he suggests, with its emphasis on the importance of material objects, 'is diametrically opposed to the integrational semiological approach to signs, which is human- and activity-centred' (Pablé, 2022, p.4).

A black tie at a funeral or rings at a wedding do not do the work of mourning or marrying themselves, Pablé insists. They do not possess either power or meanings themselves but rather only insofar as humans (and only humans) confer meaning on them: no object, he insists, 'can have a semiological function (i.e. that of integrating human activities) by itself, and thus it cannot possess meaning by itself. Only human beings can confer meaning to it' (2022, p.4). From an intercultural perspective, furthermore, when neither ties nor the colour black may be important at funerals, the meaning of a black tie may be very different. Several points are worth further thought here: there are obvious questions to be asked about whether it is indeed the case that only humans give meaning to objects. There is now enough research on non-human animals to suggest that they engage in semiotic practices (Kohn, 2013). In her studies of the meanings of cows' different uses of 'mmmm', Cornips (2022, p.225) makes a case for understanding them in terms of 'local meaning-making which is not human-centred, not language-centred, not praxis-centred' but rather 'distributed among and between species, materiality, place and time'. Integrational linguists can insist that humans and only humans matter semiotically but such a position now needs to justify its focus on humans and humanist assumptions.

These humanist suppositions and insistence that the black tie has only a semiotic rather than a material presence, furthermore, falls into the trap that Barad (2007) warns us about: everything else – language, discourse, semiotics, humans – seems to matter apart from matter itself. From a new materialist perspective, objects do have effects, do participate in the action, and to assume that their only importance is through the semiotic attachments given by humans is to maintain a form of anti-materialism that is being increasingly questioned. This is akin in some ways to the view critiqued by Latour (1999) that the constant catchcry of the National Rifle Association (NRA) in the USA that 'guns don't kill people, people kill people' suggests that guns only have meaning and effect as instruments of human action. Guns do not of course kill people without human intervention, but the point is that guns and people enter into a particular relationship, a network, an assemblage, with particular effects. Likewise, it is not that a black tie sets out to mourn a death of its own volition, but it is the relationship between the tie and the wearer and other people and the event that matters. The black tie is doing some of the mourning and it may be a mistake to assume this depends entirely on human semiosis. In the next section, therefore, I want to move beyond a view that suggests that assemblages are necessarily only *semiotic* and emphasize instead the sociomaterial formations of assemblages.

4.5 SOCIOMATERIAL ASSEMBLAGES

In some ways, a materialist turn in language studies is a reaction against the 'surgical removal of language from context' which produced an 'amputated "language" that was the preferred object of the language sciences for most of the twentieth century' (Kroskrity, 2000, p.5). The division between language as material artefact, process or abstract entity is closely tied to the ontological commitments I have outlined in this book. It is also connected to a longer history of Western (Northern) thought in which distinctions between the material and non-material, the real and the ideal, the concrete and the abstract have long been used to demarcate different approaches to the world (Cavanaugh and Shankar, 2021; Joseph, 2018). As we saw in the previous chapter, in order to construct itself as a respectable discipline within this line of thinking and within the discourses of scientism in the twentieth century, linguistics had to make an extensive series of exclusions, relegating people, history, society, culture and politics to a role external to languages. Through its various satellite domains (sociolinguistics, pragmatics, speech act theory), linguistics has been able to concede that language may have material consequences: language occurs between people in physical contexts, politeness or impoliteness can have social effects, things happen as a result of people using language.

Such moves, however, largely retain a way of looking at language as something that might be combined with material effects – language *and* materiality – but which can also remain separate. For applied linguists, the need to deal with language in its material circumstances and effects compels us to think beyond reassociating a structural language ontology with an external world: language needs to be rethought in more material ways. Alternative approaches deny this separation and insist that language must always be seen in terms of its material instantiation. As Shankar and Cavanaugh (2017) put it, rather than view 'language *and* materiality in tandem by conceptualizing materiality alongside but distinct from language', it is better to focus on 'the material nature of linguistic practice itself – its sounds, shape, and material presences' (Shankar and Cavanaugh, 2017, pp.1-2; emphasis in original). From this point of view, starting with the assumption that language is always in and of the material world, we can start to outline a number of ways of conceiving of language materiality (Cavanaugh and Shankar, 2021; Lamb and Sharma, 2021). One approach looks at language as it is embedded in the material world, pointing not only to the semiotics of the landscape but also the materiality of written signs and the ways they are implanted in physical landscapes. The concern here is with signs as material artefacts (including graffiti, tattoos or sculptures) within physical environments (streets, cities, shops, schools). This is to shift the focus from semiotic landscapes to an appreciation of the *material culture* of 'linguistically defined and linguistically marked objects and events, which are the products of and exist in particular time and space' (Aronin and Ó Laoire, 2013, p.234). The material culture of multilingualism, Aronin and Ó Laoire point out, is made up of materialities relating to multilingual ways of life, from banknotes to billboards, from new technologies to types of food.

Aspects of these approaches were captured by Scollon and Scollon's (2004) notion of *geosemiotics*: discourse in the material world. While they saw their *nexus of practice* as a 'semiotic ecosystem' (Scollon and Scollon, 2004, p.89), it was also a material ecosystem where 'historical trajectories of people, places, discourse, ideas, and objects come together' (p.159). The idea of the nexus of practice, Lamb (2020, p.931) suggests, is 'equivalent to the concept of assemblage' since both 'draw together an array of elements that compose a particular discourse and enable it to spread through the material world'. Pietikäinen (2021, p.237) similarly connects nexus analysis and the idea of assemblage in that both emphasize the ways the 'co-function of different elements – the body, discourses, the interaction order' produce forms of social action. While some ways in which nexus analysis has been taken up stress semiotic elements over others (how discourses are produced, intersect and disperse), Scollon and Scollon (2004) clearly emphasized material, spatial and historical elements in ways that connect to the more recent focus on assemblages and entanglements. From this point, it is also possible to think of all language in material terms and thus to suggest that 'all our experiences with language are only via particular material signs' (Wee, 2021, p.21).

A different element of language materiality is brought by an understanding of the *embodied* nature of language (Bucholtz and Hall, 2016). Rather than being separate from the material world, language is embedded, embodied and emplaced within it. The logocentric tendencies of (socio)linguistic research, drawing on the structural ontology of linguistics, have tended to 'conceptualize the body as secondary to language rather than as the sine qua non of language' (Bucholtz and Hall, 2016, p.174). This perspective opens up a focus on voice as 'the embodied heart of spoken language' that emerges from a body that is located in social space as a particular kind of being (p.178). An embodiment perspective is 'based on the assumptions that mind and communication are functions of the entire physical body' (Ritchie, 2022, p.18). As Kusters and colleagues (2017b, p.9) remind us, 'central in deaf ontologies are corporeality and embodied subjectivity, which means that our bodies influence our experience and thought'. A new materialist viewpoint, Canagarajah (2021, p.207) explains, 'reverses the status of minds, languages, and individuals in communication by materialising them more completely and situating them in social networks and environmental ecologies'. Here too we can see the importance of non-verbal communication and the constant role of facial expression, gesture, interactional synchrony and many aspects of embodied communication (Pennycook, 1985). People 'speak, point, gesture, sign, write, draw, handle objects and move their bodies, in a variety of combinations or aggregates, within diverse social and material contexts' (Kusters et al., 2017a, p.220). Recent studies of sign languages have shown that while the move to see them as equal to spoken languages – all languages are equivalent (see Chapter 3) – was a significant rectification of negative views that sign languages were 'mere gesture', this embrace into the structural fold of linguistics also downplayed the importance of the physical, embodied, spatial aspects of signing that shed light on much that has been missed in the study of spoken languages (Chapter 6).

If we view translingual practices as *multimodal* by attending to the role of 'speech, signs, mouthings, gestures, images, smells, and objects in interactions' (Kusters, 2021, p.184), the point is not just to include gesture within an account of multimodal interaction, but to see these as part of dynamic and interactive assemblages. This opens up a space to appreciate that language materiality needs to be understood both in relation to the body and in relation to 'nonhuman entities, such as animals, other living beings, material objects, and the physical world' (Bucholtz and Hall, 2016, p.184). From Thibault's point of view, languaging 'is not limited to vocalizing but includes a whole range of bodily resources that are assembled and coordinated in languaging events together with external (extrabodily) aspects of situations, environmental affordances, artifacts, technologies, and so on' (2011, p.215). By bringing new materialist perspectives to bear on language, it has been possible to shed light on how Deaf signing is both embodied and located in a material world of places and artefacts (Kusters, 2021). From this perspective, language can be understood as a set of resources that become part of an assemblage involving many other actants, including people, places and objects. The materiality of language is part of the materiality of an assemblage, and 'assemblages of people, human-created objects, and material entities are entangled catalysts for communicative action' (Thorne et al., 2021, p.110).

For Pietikäinen (2021), the advantage of using the idea of assemblages in trying to understand social, economic and linguistic changes in the north of Finland (the 'Cold Rush') is that it makes possible an understanding of how these elements operate in conjunction, as intertwined elements that do not just co-occur but also affect each other. A focus on assemblages, she explains (2021, p.236), 'bypasses old binaries between material/discursive, form/function, and language/society by shifting the focus to relationships and interactions between elements'. In his study of interactions in a metal foundry in the Netherlands, Hovens (2023, p.5) suggests that a 'human–machine assemblage ... can make things happen that neither the human nor the machine can do alone'. This argument is similar to Barad's (2007, p.239) account of factory work in which 'machines and humans differentially emerge and are iteratively reworked through specific entanglements of agencies that trouble the notion that there are determinate distinctions between humans and nonhumans'. From this perspective, workers, machines and managers are 'entangled phenomena, relational beings' and to assume that only humans have agency in such settings is to miss the interconnected role of machines and thereby to overlook 'possibilities for reworking unhealthy and unjust labor conditions'.

For Hovens, thinking in terms of assemblages makes it possible to see the complex arrangements that concern shifting work conditions – the older workers (the 'oude garde' – old guard) are threatened by the influx of casual workers and their languages – and the ways work happens in such an environment – the relations between machines, tools, space, language and people (Hovens, 2020, 2021). This is not therefore by any means to ignore the importance of language and languages in the foundry – there is a shift from the earlier use of related Dutch, Limburgish and German resources (a number of workers crossed the nearby border for work) to languages of wider migration such as Polish, Turkish, Arabic and English – but to see how these are connected to labour policies, machine operation, spatial layouts and so on. Hovens (2023) shows how the linguistic resources, the materiality of work practices, the role of machines, the spatial organization of a workstation, the interactions around a 'cutting table' and so on can be understood in terms of assemblages.

This emphasis on 'the relation between linguistic resources and their entanglement with the tangible world of bodies, material objects, and physical places' (Lamb and Sharma, 2021, p.2) can be understood as a move to see the interdependence between a material world – viewed through a new materialist lens in dynamic terms – and linguistic resources, to show 'how language is not separate from the material world, but irreducibly embedded, embodied and emplaced within it' (Lamb and Sharma, 2021, p.2). The distinctions I have drawn between the material and the semiotic in this section are by no means clear-cut – they are, after all, entangled – and a number of the examples discussed earlier (as semiotic assemblages) can just as easily be included here. It is the emphasis on the semiotic in relation to the material that matters. Thus, Lamb's (2020, 2024) interest in interactions between tourists and turtles on a beach is as much about material as semiotic assemblages, and Sharma's (2021) study of the buildings, buyers, sellers, goods and signs in the new Chinatown in Kathmandu is as much about the materiality of the assemblages – the feel of a scarf, for example, where touching can be interpreted in terms of sensory pleasure – as about the semiotics of garments.

For de Freitas and Curinga (2015, p.254), rather than looking at how language encodes the material world – as in forms of discourse analysis – it is more important to look at *language as material entanglement*, at the ways that 'language is coupled with the material world'. Looking at linguistic assemblages in these terms involves multiple material levels, from speech organs, bodily gestures and words to social effects, surrounds and objects. An analysis of a sign advertising an English school in the back streets of Cebu in the Philippines, for example, can be seen in terms of the *entanglements of English*, drawing attention to the ways the design and physical location of the sign, the contrast with the tangled wires above it or the relation to signs for local Korean-owned businesses connect in multiple ways to power supplies, gendered workforces, migration in and out of the country, local and global inequalities, the political economy of English, and discourses of change, modernization, access and desire (Pennycook, 2020a, 2021b). A sign advertising bitter melons in a Bangladeshi shop in Lakemba, Sydney (Pennycook and Otsuji, 2017; Pennycook, 2019a) is part of a much larger assemblage of market gardens, migration, local economies, religious practices and so on. This approach enables us to focus on the multiplicity of factors – social, semiotic, material, discursive, haptic, architectural – that come to bear on the meanings of things and interactions.

The focus on *sociomaterial assemblages* in language education by Thorne and his colleagues (2021) makes it possible to consider the importance of the materiality of language learning materials and the ways they are entangled with the activities of learners, not just 'what things are, but what they do' (p.111). Sending students out into the world, and using research methods that can capture their interactivity with space and objects around them, they show how various assemblages form – including a water fountain, the size and shape of a metal utility panel embedded in the sidewalk – as the learners talk and move and interact. For Toohey and colleagues (2015, p.466), a similar focus on sociomaterial assemblages in classrooms enables them to see the entanglements among the physical setup of classrooms, furniture, chairs, whiteboards; the bodies of students and teachers; the various materials such as books, paper and computers; the talk and activities in different lessons, as well as the curriculum and what counts as knowledge; pedagogical practices; discourses about teaching and learning; school and district policies, and so on. In each case, it is possible to see the multiplicity of factors involved, as well as their temporality and contingency, the ways they come together at one point and change at different places and times.

4.6 CONCLUSION

An assemblage approach to language suggests an ontological shift from an account of languages as pre-existing structures, or an interest in language as something we do – a social practice – to a view of language as an emergent conjuncture of different components (Demuro and Gurney, 2021). This opens up a space for reconsideration of language and materiality. In structural ontologies, language is an immaterial medium whose relation to the material world is only symbolic or representational. The challenge is not so much to make the case for a materialist approach to language over a non-materialist (structural, cognitive) one – as I have argued, from a relational ontological perspective, the point is to understand different ontologies – but rather to look at different ways of considering language and materiality. To talk of materialism is by no means to subscribe to a doctrine that matter is all there is (everything can be described in physical terms), nor that material relations (particularly in the form of dialectic or historical materialism) define all other concerns. The point, rather, is that *matter matters* (Barad, 2007) and it is incumbent on language studies – and particularly studies from a social or applied perspective – to find ways of connecting language to what Latour (2004) termed *matters of concern*, questions of truth, reality and material relations.

Various approaches to discourse analysis suggest that discourse either reflects the social world (discourses are as they are because of the nature of society) or create the social world (all we can be sure of are discursive constructions of the world) (Sealey, 2014; Teubert, 2013). Both leave us with the problem that we need to reconcile relations of discourse and materiality if critical work is to do more than ideology critique on the one hand and social construction on the other. It is ultimately unproductive to insist on discursive analysis or socioeconomic analysis at the expense of each other, or to insist that one is primary or causative of the other. They are intertwined and complementary, and we would be better served if historical materialist critique of the state and political economy and studies of discursive production worked together. These arguments take us towards a rethinking of the divisions between material and non-material worlds (Barad, 2007; Pietikäinen, 2021), but at the same time urge us to understand the material being and effects of discourse. Rather than working with either an idealist abstraction of discourse (everything is discursively constructed) or a realist reduction of the world (everything is material), we need ways of reconciling and reworking the distinction (Luke, 2013).

New materialist accounts of language view it as embodied, embedded, enacted and extended (Joseph, 2018). An assemblage ontology – whether language is understood as an assemblage of linguistic items, semiotic gatherings or sociomaterial arrangements – is a move towards complexity. To view language as an autonomous system separated from human or other life overlooks the ways linguistic resources participate in certain events. While the idea of repertoire – discussed in the previous chapter as one of the ways of thinking about available linguistic possibilities – may include a wider set of elements than just linguistic, the notion of the assemblage provides a different starting point, decentring the human actor, rendering the idea of idiolects implausible, and emphasizing the dynamic relations among people, things, places and artefacts. The focus on assemblages brings together semiotics, people, objects, things and languages, enables an understanding of the active ways languages may be socially, materially and politically reassembled, and makes possible forms of political analysis based around an ontologically diverse range of actants, 'a style of political analysis wherein the default locus of agency is presumed to be an assemblage of human and nonhuman, of physiological, physical, and technological elements' (Bennett, 2009, p.3). To think differently about how politics may operate, we need to be able to imagine 'new subjectivities that operate increasingly according to a logic of assemblage, defined no longer by their possessions but by their connections' (Hardt and Negri, 2017, p.295).

An assemblage ontology also presents us with various potential difficulties that need to be thought through. Whereas a structural ontology pulls language out of its social and material life and examines it as a bounded, autonomous system, an assemblage ontology attempts to put everything back in. Although the idea of the total linguistic fact never claimed to be able to account for everything, the moves towards the total semiotic fact have sought to provide as wide an account as possible of available resources, leading to a complexity that can be hard to manage. An assemblage focus can also flatten hierarchies: by seeing objects as actants in relational networks, by exploring the entanglements of as much as possible in everyday life, by considering social order and political economy to be part of but not determinant of an assemblage, this approach can make it hard to distinguish between the relative importance of things as they come together. Although as Goico (2021) shows, by connecting assemblages to social practice and showing how 'assemblages that emerge within the routines of everyday life form novel iterations of previous assemblages' (p.270), we can see how assemblages can achieve relative forms of stability, there is nevertheless a concern that the emphasis on the temporary nature of assemblages may lead to an assumption that social forces come and go rather than exist over time.

An assemblage ontology, like a practice ontology, nevertheless presents a much better candidate for a practical theory of language than language as structure. It 'calls on applied linguists to critically examine how the natural world is caught up in our semiotic practices', encouraging the field to 'develop a *green applied linguistics* that investigates the role of language in problematic human–environment relations' (Lamb, 2019, p.2; emphasis in original). It enables studies of language learning, classroom interaction, semiotic landscapes and much more that suggest that language cannot be separated from the material world (Hovens, 2020, 2023; Kusters, 2021; Lamb and Sharma, 2021; Pietikäinen, 2021; Thorne et al., 2021; Toohey, 2019). And finally, though tentatively, I want to draw connections here between assemblage ontologies and the ontological alternatives discussed in the next chapter. While it is important to tread cautiously here – lest this be seen as yet another imposition of Northern thinking onto the Global South (Todd, 2016) – assemblage-oriented thinking, with its focus on material, relational and distributed aspects of language, makes possible a flexibility for thinking about language that may be more compatible with other ontological positions.

5 Other Language Ontologies

It is helpful to look at all languages as assemblages: languages are not so much entities in the world that we use as they are put together through social practices, ideological standpoints, semiotic possibilities and material relations. Both language as a general idea and languages as particular instances may therefore be ontologically plural, different things. As the discussion in Chapter 2 suggested, a major question for language studies is whose knowledge of language counts or, put differently, 'who occupies language?' or what are the lived and embodied experiences of those who occupy a language? (Lee and Makoni, 2022, p.317). While this question has evident importance for understanding generally the kinds of assertions made by linguists, journalists, teachers and a wider public, it has particular significance when we look at this question within a broad global politics of knowledge, asking not just why some versions of knowledge about language are given more credence because of what counts as expertise, academic status or common knowledge, but also how and why some kinds of knowledge have particular status within a global knowledge economy. It also matters because it suggests a relation to language that is about experience, embodiment and place.

What languages are to different communities has considerable practical importance when we turn to questions of language revival or reclamation. If projects to maintain, revive or reclaim languages need practical theories of language to be effective – another key argument of this book – such theories need to be relevant to, and at least in large part to derive from, concerned communities. Indeed, the language endangerment and revival literature has been a major site of critical engagement between different language ontologies: local worldviews have to be made central if the revival of a language is to have real local meaning. When people say their language is sleeping (Leonard, 2017), for example, or that language is deeply connected to the land, there is much more at stake here than possible metaphor: these are statements about language in the world that need to be taken very seriously. This chapter therefore explores the imperative to 'delink from Western notions of "language" as decontextualized and instead think of language as interwoven with bodies and land, and in this sense, alive' (Hermes et al., 2022, p.26). This chapter focuses on alternative, and particularly Indigenous, language ontologies.

While I made a case in the previous chapter that the materiality of assemblage thinking potentially allows for connections with Indigenous and other ways of thinking about language, there are at least two reasons for caution here. First, it is important not to try to explain Indigenous ways of thinking in terms of Western/Northern ontologies or epistemologies or to try to incorporate the former into the latter. Other ways of thinking have to be understood in their own terms, and if connections are to be made this needs to be done on a plane of ontological equality (in the absence of political and epistemological equality) that seeks possible connections. Second, while a material focus can shed light on connections to land, water and surrounds, it runs the danger of overlooking what are often deeply *spiritual* relations. Assemblage-oriented thinking can bridge the gaps between Western rationalist, dualist thought and more grounded views of language, but it is also important to explore ways of thinking that take us beyond forms of materialism. If the language ontologies discussed so far can be seen as structural (system), social (practice) and material (assemblage), this chapter draws connections among social, material and spiritual elements.

5.1 INDIGENOUS THINKING

To take other ontologies seriously is not just to consider different ways of thinking but to accept there may be different ways of being. It is to engage with forms of knowledge and ways of being that have been denigrated, disrupted and disrespected for centuries. It is imperative, as Watts (2013, p.22) makes clear, not to reduce other understandings of the world to 'myths' (and see the discussion in Chapter 2) or to consider stories 'to be an alternative mode of understanding and interpretation rather than "real" events. Colonization is not solely an attack on peoples and lands; rather, this attack is accomplished in part through purposeful and ignorant misrepresentations of Indigenous cosmologies.' On these grounds it is essential to understand colonialism not only in terms of dispossession of lands, livelihoods and ways of being but also in terms of the rejection of forms of knowledge. Any move towards decolonization, in combination with projects to bring languages back to life, has to be open to forms of knowledge and ways of presenting knowledge that have long been disparaged in the institutional ways of knowing that have come to dominate what counts as knowledge.

A starting point is to think outside the boxes of time and space constructed by modernist discourse. This is not about 'traditional' modes of thought: we should not try to compare modernities. Non-Aboriginal Australian temporal ideologies emphasize time in a way that the notion of 'modern' excludes Indigenous people from contemporaneity (Muecke, 2004). Indigenous modernity is not the same as the modernity of the invaders with their political-industrial complex and assumptions about the Enlightenment and science (these co-occurring at the end of the eighteenth century with the invasion of Australia) that already defined these others as non-modern. Indigenous modernity can be understood 'as a predisposition to (both) resistance and adaptation to the rapid changes introduced by invasion and colonialism' (Muecke, 2004, p.5). This is to question what Fabian (1983) called the 'denial of coevalness'[1] – the tendency to see Indigenous ways of being as somehow 'in the past', an unwillingness to accept a contemporary co-presence. Yet 'colonized and peripheral societies produce social thought *about the modern world* which has as much intellectual power as metropolitan social thought, and more political relevance' (Connell, 2007, p.xii; emphasis in original). These are co-existing modes of understanding, since 'so-called indigenous normative systems are, in fact, modern through-and-through', not '*Euro*modern' – that is, adhering to norms of Western modernity – but more generally modern since they are 'aware of the *particularity* of Euromodernity' (Gordon, 2021, p.47; emphasis in original). Perhaps, suggests Muecke (2004, p.6), Indigenous Australians 'were already modern in ways whitefellas still don't have words for'.

The point is not to contrast traditional and modern or cultural and scientific knowledge but to acknowledge on the one hand that Western scientific knowledge has always also been cultural (it is a social practice, as Latour, 1999, and many others have made clear) and that Indigenous knowledge can also be understood as science: 'we are a people of culture. We are also a people of science' (Martin Nakata, cited in Hamacher, 2022, p.13). As the *First Knowledges* books that explore Australian First Nations' knowledge about land, plants

---

[1] Coeval/ness, which he prefers to notions such as simultaneous or contemporary, is a term similar to the more ordinary German term *Gleichzeitig/keit* (happening at the same time) (Fabian, 1983).

and astronomy (Neale & Kelly, 2020; Noon & de Napoli, 2022; Pascoe & Gammage, 2021) make clear, it is time to clear away myths 'that we had no knowledge system or history, only myths and legends; that we had no scientists, doctors or lawyers; that we were incapable of innovation' (Neale, 2021, p.14). It took a long time for astronomers to realize (and only some of them have ever done so) that if people maintain cultural practices stretching back tens of thousands of years, and if they have developed deep understandings of seasons, star configurations and navigation, then, while they may not have the instruments of modern celestial observation, they nevertheless have remarkable knowledge about the night sky and how it changes.

The term 'Indigenous' itself is of course a contested categorization that emerged in the 1970s from struggles for recognition among what are commonly now called First Nations People in North America. The term usefully generalizes a common struggle across the first inhabitants of colonized lands, though may also potentially diminish the differences between radically different people around the world. The identification and classification of people has long been one of the arts of governmentality so that 'the complexity of indigenous identities is invariably reduced to a grossly simplified and legible ontological and cartographical classificatory system that makes governing easier and more effective' (Gomes, 2013, p.10). Definitions of Indigeneity may be either 'criterial' – based on sets of inherent criteria that define the Indigenous, such as evidence of or belief in original inhabitation of a territory – or 'relational' – that is, centred around relations with non-Indigenous others, such as distinguishing themselves from dominant social organizations (Merlan, 2009). Some people are recognized as Indigenous by some authorities and not by others – the Sámi of northern Norway, Sweden, Finland and Russia (the Sápmi region), for example, recognized as the only Indigenous population within the European Union, have different rights in different countries – while others, such as the *Orang Asli* (first people) in Malaysia, are incorporated into the wider concept of *bumiputera* (prince of the land) to ensure that a broad notion of original inhabitants that includes Malays conveys better rights to the land than for later arrivals (particularly Chinese and Indians) (Gomes, 2013).

In part because the term Indigenous is often connected to notions of static or traditional ways of being, and also because of the ways it is used in opposition to colonial modes of thinking – hence Indian or Nigerian sociology, or African philosophy (Patel, 2021), implying an impossible collectivity – some have critiqued such ideas as a form of ethnophilosophy (Hountondji, 1977). As Diagne (2021) explains, the debate in the 1970s about the status of 'African philosophy' centred on a book by the Belgian missionary Placide Tempels, La philosophie bantoue (Bantu philosophy). The two great founders of the négritude movement, Aimé Césaire and Léopold Senghor, had very different reactions, Césaire deriding the work for its political implications (it was, in his view, a rationalization of colonial superiority), Senghor praising it for its insights about African ways of thinking. For Diagne, like Hountondji (1977), this was a confusion between 'real' philosophy and a form of ethnophilosophy that continued, albeit in philosophical language, 'le discours d'une ethnologie coloniale sur la mentalité et la vision du monde des populations "sans ecriture"' (Diagne, 2021, p.91) (the discourse of colonial ethnology on the mentality and worldview of people without written traditions). While Diagne and Hountondji would both later soften their views on this distinction – recognizing their own positionality as African academics educated in the prestigious metropolitan centres of learning in France ('J'étais althussérien, moi aussi' – I too was an Althusserian; Diagne, 2021, p.91) – at stake was an important concern about whether to grant philosophical status to a collective way of thinking and whether, by emphasizing the Indigenous, one was reinforcing a colonial binary.

From Hountondji's perspective it was more important to understand how 'connected knowledge systems immersed in colonial difference have organized exchange and circulation of knowledge across the globe' (Patel, 2021, p.380). Hountondji argues for a more careful critique of knowledge and the building of *endogenous* knowledge. One of the challenges for Indigenous people is to develop an Indigenous position that is not tied to suffocating notions of 'authenticity' or being reduced always to an Indigenous standpoint, and to enable broader participation in discussions of language and knowledge. An Indigenous standpoint, as Nakata (2007) explains, is not just a 'simple reflection of experience' or some sort of 'hidden wisdom that Indigenous people possess' or an assertion of truth 'beyond the scrutiny of others on the basis that, as a member of the Indigenous community, what I say counts' (p.214). Rather, it requires complex analytic skills in order to investigate 'the actualities of the everyday and discover how to express them conceptually from within that experience' instead of using predefined categories (p.215). From this point of view, Nakata goes on to argue, the point is not just to try to 'overturn the so-called dominant position through simplistic arguments of omission, exclusion or misrepresentation' but to develop 'better arguments in relation to my position within knowledge' (p.216).

On one level the Indigenous versus non-Indigenous represents a significant site of social, cultural, economic and political struggle, yet it may also reduce the complexity of this relationship, overlooking ways that 'Indigenous people have more complicated, embodied histories of observing colonial impacts, ignoring or refusing colonial demands, conforming to colonial demands (albeit ambivalently or contradictorily), and appropriating Western understanding for Indigenous purposes and interests' (Nakata et al., 2012, p.125; see also Deloria and Wildcat, 2001). For Nakata and colleagues (2012), an overemphasis on decolonization may present only a cultural agenda of local knowledge without stressing the importance of knowledge of the other: an understanding of how one is positioned in knowledge systems as an Indigenous person. To separate Indigenous and non-Indigenous thought in too extreme a fashion is to overlook the ways that they have influenced each other. One aim of this chapter is to avoid such 'simplistic oppositional analysis between Indigenous and Western knowledge epistemologies as the antithesis of each other' (Nakata et al., 2012, p.127) and to argue instead for relational ontologies and social epistemologies, that is to say to understand the possibility of different kinds of being as well as different ways of knowing without insisting on their absolute difference.

As Northern academics rediscover space, place, things, affect and the significance of embodiment, however, they all too often turn to Northern sources, forgetting that Indigenous people have known all this for a long time. Todd (2016) describes listening to a talk by Bruno Latour, waiting for him to 'credit Indigenous thinkers for their millennia of engagement with sentient environments, with cosmologies that enmesh people into complex relationships between themselves and all relations, and with climates and atmospheres as important points of organization and action' (pp.6–7). And she waited in vain, for while the Northern academy re-engages with the climate, with the earth, with people and places, Indigenous knowledge is almost always still absent. As she goes on to describe this process, as new ways of thinking – particularly the ontological turn and new materialism discussed in the previous chapter – are taken up by Euro-American thinkers, what is actually being rearticulated is 'what many an Indigenous thinker around the world could have told you for millennia: the climate is a common organizing force!' (p.8). On these grounds, Todd challenges the ontological turn as a new form of colonialism. As people draw connections between new materialism, posthumanism and related Indigenous ways of thinking about the more-than-human world (e.g. Hermes et al., 2022), it is crucial that the *first knowledges* that have informed these ways of thinking are given precedence, and that we see these ways of thinking as a convergence, a walking together, an alliance.

The challenge, put another way, is to draw on forms of *Radical Indigenism* which assume that Indigenous 'philosophies of knowledge are rational, articulable, coherent logics for ordering and knowing the world' (Garroutte, 2003, p.113). This Radical Indigenist perspective both challenges Western science and knowledge and calls for Indigenous perspectives to inform language and other projects. An Indigenous standpoint can help 'unravel and untangle ourselves from the conditions that delimit who, what or how we can or can't be, to help see ourselves with some charge of the everyday, and to help understand our varied responses to the colonial world' (Nakata, 2007, p.217). This is about far more than simple charges of omission or misrepresentation (Indigenous languages are not sufficiently discussed or fairly dealt with). It suggests instead the need to think seriously about marginalized knowledge and contemporary theorizing, and to consider that knowledge about Indigenous languages can inform knowledge about language more generally, not as it has often done in the extractivist past in terms of adding to the total archive of linguistic knowledge but rather in terms of unsettling what languages are. Indigenous languages and the lived and embodied experiences of those who occupy them can tell us far more than enhancing colonial knowledge about language (ergativity, recursion, word order, inflection): the ontological implications can change what languages are assumed to be.

5.2 LAND, STARS AND WAVES OF KNOWING

Before turning more specifically to Indigenous language ontologies, it is useful to consider some other kinds of knowledge, particularly astronomy and navigation. These two domains of knowledge can help us see several significant aspects of Indigenous thinking: the length and depth of first knowledges – knowledge of land, sky and plants, for example, dates back tens of thousands of years – and their relational or interconnected aspects – forms of knowledge in one domain are almost always interconnected with other ways of thinking and being; the sky is linked to the land and the land is linked to language. In order to appreciate Indigenous astronomy, you have to understand how the sky relates to the land, or Country (Noon and de Napoli, 2022). First knowledges are typically holistic and relational, viewing the sky, water, land, people and language as integrated and acting on each other (all things have agency and value). Indigenous astronomy has a very long history and is therefore itself subject to change (it is not static): thousands of years of accumulated knowledge also have to embrace change as stars and constellations align differently and at different times. It has therefore also become a very important source for understanding the changing universe. When Western astronomers turned up with their new instruments, they operated with a view of the night sky as largely immobile; it was interaction with Indigenous astronomers, who could draw on traditions over tens of thousands of years, that started to reveal the importance of understanding change (Hamacher, 2022).

Various Aztec ceremonies were linked with the cycle of Venus, and were held every eight years to coincide with the cycles of Venus and the sun (Hamacher, 2022). During the late Southern summer, what is known to Northern astronomers as the Milky Way – a galaxy of stars interspersed by dark areas – becomes prominent. For the Wardaman of the Northern Territory the Milky Way is the Rainbow Serpent, and for the Yolŋu of North-East Arnhem Land a crow, but for many other Aboriginal nations across the vast land mass the space between the stars is the Dark Emu (Gawarrgay in Gamilaraay) (Noon and de Napoli, 2022). For the Gamilaraay, the appearance of the Dark Emu above the horizon is a reminder that this is a time when emus are nesting, a time when some eggs can be gathered. Sky knowledge relates to seasonal and food knowledge. Stories about moon halos (rings around the moon) across the continent (and elsewhere) are connected to rain (halos are a product of ice crystals in the air which result from a warm front meeting cold air, usually leading to rain). Knowledge of the phases of the moon – explained in different parts of the world by a range of different but sometimes quite similar stories – is important for predicting tides, which in turn are important for fishing. Both Lakota in the American Midwest and Torres Strait Islanders (on Mer) explain the orientation of the moon in terms of a dish, sometimes holding water (the dry season), sometimes letting it fall (wet season) (Hamacher, 2022).

Indigenous stories based around stars or land features are often seen by outsiders as 'myths', as little more than fanciful stories, but this is to misunderstand the ways such stories also explain, interpret and retain forms of knowledge, and have enabled both the continuity and changes to long-term astronomical observations. The songs of First Peoples that describe the twinkling of stars (an atmospheric phenomenon) are 'less like nursery rhymes and more like a performative

Other Language Ontologies

scientific text' (Hamacher, 2022, p.98). Knowledge of the stars and their relation to land are also important for navigation. Australian *songlines* are a means of navigation across the land, 'a set of complex arterial connections' that 'comprise an organic network of lines crisscrossing the continent along distributed nodes of concentrated knowledge, often referred to as sites of significance (places) and also known as story places' (Neale and Kelly, 2020, p.35). These sites, like libraries, 'contain stories in which knowledge is embedded', though they are much more than cartographic pathways or written archives. They are route-finding forms of knowledge embedded in stories, songs, dance, art and ceremony that therefore have a deeply different relation to knowledge, community and language than do written texts or drawn maps. Songlines, Noon and de Napoli (2022, p.41) note, are many things, from stories, histories or visas (a means to pass through other people's Country) to navigational tools and archives that document land, sea and sky. They are 'physical stores of memory and knowledge', marked on the ground as well as the sky.

Navigation is a 'holistic process' (Hamacher, 2022, p.194) involving songlines, reading of the land, knowledge of animal behaviour, feeling the wind, ocean currents and wave action, knowing cloud types and movements and much more. Ingersoll's (2016, p.5) *seascape epistemology* suggests an 'approach to knowing presumed on a knowledge of the sea, which tells one how to move through it, how to approach life and knowing through the movements of the world'. This is an 'approach to knowing through a visual, spiritual, intellectual and embodied literacy of the '*āina* ("land") and *kai* ("sea"): birds, the colors of the clouds, the flows of the currents, fish and seaweed, the timing of ocean swells, depths, tides and celestial bodies all circulating and flowing with rhythms and pulsations' (Ingersoll, 2016, p.6). Bringing together Hawaiian practices of *he'e nalu* ('surfing'), *ho'okele* ('way-finding or oceanic literacy') and *lawai'a* ('fishing'), she shows how entering the water is to 'enter an indigenous thought-world stimulated by cultural memory, imagination, perception, and understanding' (Ingersoll, 2016, p.115). Such *waves of knowing* include remarkable navigation skills that enabled Polynesian people to settle and move between the islands of the Pacific (Hutchins, 2005; Thompson, 2019).

Polynesian navigation techniques used a set of common components, including detailed knowledge of stars and star paths, different ways of understanding orientation and various means of finding land (from reading swell and waves to interpreting clouds and knowing feeding habits of seabirds). Some of these can be 'translated into Western conceptual terms', while others 'reflected ways of seeing and thinking with no obvious corollary in the European tradition' (Thompson, 2019, p.265). This is not only a question of knowledge as commonly understood in the Western tradition, but also about how navigation is *experienced* as an embodied practice, a range of learned ways of experiencing the world, coupled to 'the deep, inherited cultural understanding of *island* and *ocean* that was shared by those who for thousands of years lived in and with the sea' (2019, p.272). Such navigational expertise is therefore not just an alternative knowledge but rather '*knowing in a different way*' (2019, p.293; emphasis in original): the models used by Micronesian and Polynesian navigators 'operate in a different frame of reference and on the basis of different fundamental representational assumptions from those that are common in the Western world' (Hutchins, 2005, p.1569). For one Hawaiian navigator, this meant achieving an intuitive sense of sea and sky, of 'thinking not just with his conscious mind but with his body, in some sense *feeling* his way across the ocean' (Thompson, 2019, p.293; emphasis in original).

5.3 LANGUAGE AND COUNTRY

One of the commonalities of Indigenous people (leaving aside the negative commonalities that result from colonial histories of dispossession, such as low life expectancy, poor health outcomes, and high rates of incarceration and suicide; see e.g. Bodkin-Andrews and Carlson, 2016) is a deep connection to the land and water. The struggle over land and sea rights is not only about place but about a much wider cosmology. As Connell (2007, p.198) notes, the 'astonishing tenacity' shown by many Indigenous communities in maintaining their relationship to land in the face of widespread threats from 'pastoralists, missionaries, farmers, miners, the state, the tourist industry' suggests there is far more here than just ownership of territory. It is, rather, a set of deep and spiritual connections. In many 'Indigenous ontologies ... place has agency irrespective of human presence or awareness' (Larsen and Johnson, 2016, p.150). For Watts (2013, p.23), the 'agency that place possesses can be thought of in a similar way that Western thinkers locate agency in human beings' and thus if Indigenous people 'are extensions of the very land we walk upon', there is an obligation to maintain communication with the land. For Topa (Four Arrows) & Narvaez (2022), this can be seen in terms of *kincentrism*, a way of understanding the relations among people, communities and the natural world. This resonates with the discussion in the previous chapter about whether agency is understood only in human terms, shared with animals or a wider property of the material world. In a number of Indigenous ontologies place is active, spiritual and interlinked with language.

Land, from this point of view, is far more than dwelling place, territory or material resource, but rather a living entity that demonstrates living relationships. Land, Styres (2019, p.27) explains, is 'conceptual, experiential, relational, and embodied', both abstract space and concrete place. Land can refer to 'all more than human life forms ... found in the sky, water, and land' (Hermes et al., 2022, p.1 fn 1). From a pedagogical point of view this is not a question of learning *about* the land but learning both '*from* the land and *with* the land' (Simpson, 2014, p.7; emphasis in original), that is to say land is also an active part of the learning; indeed, land is both teacher and pedagogy (Styres, 2011). Indigenous education, Simpson (2014, p.9) insists, is neither Indigenous nor education 'unless it comes through the land'. Humans are late arrivals on the land, where life, relationships and activities were going on long before we entered the world; our role therefore is to listen and learn (Blenkinsop and Fettes, 2020). This implies a shift in the culture of expertise and education: knowledge is in the land rather than certain people (Simpson, 2014).

For Indigenous Australians it is not land, but the Aboriginal English or Kriol term Country that is used: 'Country is a worldview that encompasses our relationship to the physical, ancestral and spiritual dimensions': Country does not belong to people: They belong to Country (Neale, 2021, p.13). For Barbara Napanangka Martin, it is not so much a question of speaking Warlpiri as being Warlpiri, the language being part of the land and of what it means to be Warlpiri (Disbray et al., 2020). *We are our language*, as Meek (2010) similarly puts it in her ethnography of Kaska language revitalization in a Northern Athabaskan community (northern North America). From this point of view, 'what is called "the language" often inheres in what people call themselves, their lands, waters and place' (Nicholas and McCarty, 2022, p.230). Land or Country is not tied only to land. As Hayman and colleagues (2018) suggest, there is a tendency to overlook the importance of people and water. The traditional oral narratives, toponyms and cultural practices of the Tlingit and Tagish (First Nation people of the circumpolar North) suggest an 'alternative ontological water (ice) consciousness' that can 'inform and potentially reimagine contemporary international debates concerning water ethics, water law, water governance, and water management' (p.77). Ingersoll's (2016) *seascape epistemology* likewise illustrates how Indigenous identity emerges and is tied not only to the land but also to the oceans. Indigenous Hawaiian identities, she argues, emerge when they enter the water; 'I become a historical being riding waves, running as a liquid mass, pulled from the deep and thrown forward with a deafening roar. I disappear with fish and strands of seaweed as I course through veins of ocean currents' (2016, p.1). In the ocean, Indigenous Hawaiian communities are able to reconnect with their Kanaka heritage.

For Ingersoll (2016), the goal here is to 'decenter the conversation toward independent and alternative ways of knowing and producing knowledge that allow for empowerment and self-determination within a multisited world' (2016, p.3). Tlingit perspectives on glaciers offer 'an alternative ontological awareness of glaciers as well as a nuanced Indigenous empirical scientific knowledge that moves away from the Eurocentric models of categorizing and understanding the natural world' (Hayman et al., 2018, p.77). The idea of *thinking with glaciers* – akin in some ways to Escobar's (2016) thinking-feeling with the earth – can be understood as 'an effort to re-imagine relationships with water and ice and depart from terracentric histories, and futures' (Hayman et al., 2018, p.87). From this perspective it is also the 'slow activism embedded within Tlingit and Tagish glacial narratives' that can 'disrupt increasingly entrenched notions and narrow definitions of the Anthropocene(s) that reproduce a mono-cultural imaginary' (Hayman et al., 2018, p.87). This sense of the 'slow' is also taken up in Leibowitz and Bozalek's (2018, p.984) notion of 'slow scholarship' – not in a negative sense of going slowly but rather in terms of staying connected and committed to a project – and 'repoliticising and reinvigorating everyday practice in academia'.

Country in Australia encompasses 'the seas, waters, rocks, animals, winds, and all the beings that exist in and make up a place, including people' (Bawaka Country et al., 2022, p.436). Australia was neither terra nullius nor just untended land when the Europeans invaded in 1788: it had already been transformed in many ways by First Nations peoples. 'It was not land, but Country ... Country is physical, communal and spiritual – land, water, sky, habitats, sites, places, totems and relationships, a world of the mind, a way of believing and behaving' (Pascoe and Gammage, 2021, p.53). In northern Australia, as well as many other parts of the continent, two main connections – between land and language on the one hand and between land and people, on the other – are central to how Indigenous people think about themselves and the land. The connection between language and people is 'a secondary product of those two kinds of links' (Rumsey, 2018, p.3).

Other Language Ontologies

People and language are connected only insofar as people and land, and language and land, are connected, and language, having been placed in the land, predates humans. Life and language begin in the land, land that may include the sea, and without land or language there is nothing (Gay'wu Group of Women, 2019).

Summarizing a number of statements about Indigenous languages in North America, Nicholas and McCarty suggest they invoke 'an understanding that the universe is a vibrating energy field in which we are one with the life of the land that includes spiritual ancestors and does not comprehend the notions of a linear history' (Nicholas and McCarty, 2022, p.232). These relations to land (or Country), pedagogy and language suggest that language may be something very different from its status elsewhere as a system amenable to outside analysis. We have to understand 'the role of the land itself in continuing to shape our thoughts and language', a relationship that is 'mostly ignored in revitalization work' (Hermes et al., 2022, p.1). Country includes different forms of water: rivers, creeks, lakes, seas, billabongs and all forms of water that are part of Country. The Aboriginal English term 'saltwater people' refers to many Indigenous groups – from the Gadigal of Warrane (Sydney) and the Bundjalung of Northeast New South Wales to the Gudjuda in Queensland and Larrakia in the Northern Territory – who live in close relationship to the sea. When a speaker of Maringa (Arnhem Land, northern Australia) characterizes the way they speak (and its difference from other ways) as 'saltwater words' (Vaughan, 2018, p.127), this has to be taken seriously in relation to both language and the role of different kinds of water in shaping language. The wuymurri songspiral (a story/song about a whale, but also much more) tells of the saltwater, of being in and with the water and the current (Gay'wu Group of Women, 2019). Songspirals are 'the doing, being, thinking, understanding of Yolŋu life-worlds. They are a generative ontological manifestation of relationality, of the ongoing emergence of everything in relation with everything else, of the co-becoming of time and place' (Bawaka Country et al., 2022, p.437).

This is far more than just a relationship with the land or water, or stories about them. It also points to 'the embodied ways of using language in intergenerational conversation on land while moving' – the importance of talking and walking through land – suggesting a 'compelling alternative to de-contextualized, individualized, linguistic-based, language acquisition methods' (Hermes et al., 2022, p.1). Thus, rather than centring language learning around a teacher-as-expert within a walled classroom, collective ways of learning and 'producing knowledge on and with the land' provide an alternative way of thinking about language, knowledge and learning (and see Topa (Four Arrows) and Narvaez, 2022). As Monaghan (2012, p.53) puts it, language and stories are understood as still being 'in the land, having been placed there by the ancestors' and to reclaim such languages may be as much a spiritual process as one involving documentation. For Yolŋu people from North-East Arnhem Land in northern Australia, songspirals are 'multi-layered articulations passed down through the generations and sung and cried by Aboriginal people to wake Country, to make and remake the life-giving connections between people and place – people and non-human beings emerging together, co-becoming, as Country' (Bawaka Country et al., 2022, p.436).

I have in part embedded discussion of language and pedagogy in this section on Country, land and water precisely because they are, from various Indigenous perspectives, inseparable. To talk of Country in one section and language in another and pedagogical implications in yet another is to draw a distinction that it is hard to maintain. In standard applied linguistic frameworks, it is common to separate language (a system to be acquired) from its surrounds (the context in which language occurs), before moving on to address pedagogical or policy implications (the ways language can be taught or administered, often in other contexts). This kind of conceptual separability may help in focusing on certain aspects of applied questions but may have very little applicability in contexts where language, learning and land are part of a whole. As I have been arguing, furthermore, such insights have implications not just for Indigenous people but for non-Indigenous too. Deep connections to land or water may be hard to achieve for people separated both materially and spiritually from their surrounds, but holistic thinking about how the world fits together can bring renewal to ways of thinking and being in many other contexts.

5.4 LANGUAGE RECLAMATION

It is on the territory of language ontologies that many misunderstandings over language revival have occurred. The disparity is more often framed in different terms – from the more mundane *strategies* to the more comprehensive *ideologies* – but it is centrally a question of alternative ontologies. The problem, as Ennis (2020, p.305) explains, is how 'Euro-derived notions' of language 'interface with Indigenous understandings of the nature of language in revitalization projects'.

This takes us back to one of the questions raised at the beginning of the book: whose version of language counts? In this context it is a question of 'expert knowledge' – based around a particular set of assumptions about what languages are – and very different understandings of language by people with deeply different linguistic, cultural and educational backgrounds (Meek, 2010). Who is listening, asks Hill (2002), and what do they hear? For de Souza (2017, p.206), the problem is still that while some researchers claim a '"pro-indigenous stance" in favour of the preservation of indigenous languages and epistemologies', too much of this thinking remains 'trapped within the bounds of their own Enlightenment epistemologies', or, I would add, ontologies. When these researchers 'claim to listen to the indigenous other, they apparently only hear their own voices and values', unable to escape from the 'bounds of lazy thinking,[2] and thus liable to waste the wealth of experience of the ecology of knowledges that surrounds them but remains invisible to their eyes'.

Recent scholarship and activism around language revival has started to question not only the reliance on language documentation as a central strategy – especially since there is 'scant evidence after 25 years that documentation has played a significant role in saving languages' (Bird, 2020, p.3505) – but also the 'underlying ideologies of how language itself gets defined' (Hermes et al., 2022, p.2). As Henne-Ochoa and colleagues (2020, p.482) make clear, non-Indigenous linguists working with Indigenous communities 'tend to conceive of language as an object', as a 'thing', as a code separable from its context, emphasizing 'structural properties', so that languages can be turned into dictionaries, grammars and texts. As Ndhlovu (2018, p.118) puts it, while 'high-sounding metaphors of human rights, anti-imperialism and biodiversity resonate with contemporary international conversations around social justice and equity issues', such ideas often fail to resonate with local communities' interests because 'standard language ideology remains ensconced as the only valid and legitimate conceptual framework that informs mainstream understandings of what is meant by "language"' Standard language ideology can be understood in two ways, either as processes of linguistic standardization whereby decisions are made between different linguistic options and languages are reduced to forms of literacy, or, as Ndhlovu

---

[2] De Souza (2017) is here taking up Santos' (2012) notion of 'lazy reason' (*razão indolente*) – the critique that dominant modes of thinking cannot understand or engage with alternative modes of thought.

(2018) intends it here, as the process by which languages are viewed through ortholinguistic lenses and reduced to a structural ontology.

On the one hand is the move to standardize languages in revival projects, particularly when connected to literacy and education programmes (Hall, 2019), the 'Faustian bargain' between 'language advocates' and state authorities that create impossible standards and new hierarchies (Costa et al., 2018, p.1). Processes of standardization may seem unavoidable as part of a project to revive a language – if something is to be revived, it needs to be codified, turned into a circumscribed entity – particularly when coupled with what are often taken to be inevitable educational goals. Yet such processes are also connected to practices of silencing, by the state through education policies, by discourses of purism, and from the long-term traumas of discrimination and colonialism (Lane, 2023a). While the potential negative effects of standardization have been noted, this is all too often seen merely as a process of constraint, of making certain structural decisions between language options, without accepting the extent of the ontological challenges it may pose: 'well-intentioned processes of language revitalization place once unstandardized languages into complex ideological assemblages and bring distinct ontologies of language into contact' (Ennis, 2020, p.320). For speakers of types of Ecuadorian Kichwa, for example, such processes of documentation, standardization and education, turning language into a *decontextualized* entity, 'contrasts markedly with their own understanding of language as essentially connected to places and people' (Ennis, 2020, p.320). This is where the two meanings of standard language ideology coalesce when processes of standardization construct a language in ontological terms that is distinct not only in terms of a standard/non-standard division but also in terms of a divide between a decontextualized entity and a set of practices connected to people and place.

In the context of the Northern Kimberley region of Western Australia (and elsewhere), as Rumsey (2018, p.3) explains, one of the main reasons that Northern epistemologies have generally failed to grasp Indigenous relations to land and language is that 'modern European monoglot ethno-nationalist understandings of the relationships among people(s), language and territory' favour people and their relations with territory (nation, homeland) on the one hand and between people and their language on the other (speakers of a particular language). In other contexts, however, the relation may be quite different, favouring land and its relations with people on the one hand and land and its relation to language on the other: the relation between people and language is thereby secondary. Discussing the revival of Wirangu, a South Australian language, Monaghan (2012, p.52) points to the ways the discourse of endangerment 'posits individual languages as denotational codes residing in a bounded ethnic group with a distinctive culture and inhabiting its own ecological niche'. This 'ecologising discourse', he goes on, is underpinned by the myth 'that there are languages, as fixed codes, out there in the world waiting to be discovered, documented, saved, or revived. The language myth is ubiquitous, a foundational myth and ideology in orthodox linguistics' (2012, p.52). This critique takes us back to the language myths discussed in Chapters 2 and 3, longstanding stories told about languages in the Global North that see them as discoverable objects in the world linked to clearly demarcated territories and ethnicities and themselves clearly distinguishable as structural entities.

Hall (2019, p.217) makes a related point with respect to First Nations languages in North America, suggesting that describing 'the syntax of an endangered language using complex concepts may help linguists but it does next to nothing for the reservation community in terms of understanding the language of their heritage'. Wirangu, Monaghan (2012) points out, is a recent construction, an artefact of the colonial encounter. Before the arrival of linguists, whose aim was to fix languages, people's language practices were fluid and the formal concept of a language was quite unnecessary. Language in this sense, he explains, is therefore 'part of an imposed Western analytical framework' with a particular focus on writing over speech (p.52). As Grace (1981, p.263–4) notes, speakers of languages in contexts where processes of standardization have not occurred tend to understand their immediate linguistic reality in terms of 'pools of linguistic resources' rather than as discrete systems. It is quite possible, Bird (2020, p.3509) points out, that 'the parties in a collaboration may view its artefacts differently'. This imposition of Western/Northern linguistic ontologies has been widely critiqued, a 'wicked problem' for linguists in terms of 'what is good for the survival of a particular population in the face of a changing socioeconomic ecology versus what is ideal for the practice of linguistics' (Mufwene, 2016, p.141). The challenge, as Sayers (2023, p.21) puts it, is 'to concern ourselves less with languages in and of themselves, and more with the material well-being of the people who speak them'.

This is not just a question of inappropriate approaches to language but also of the 'extractivist methodologies' (Santos, 2018, p.130) of many social sciences, extracting knowledge like raw material from different parts of the world. The trajectory of linguistics in the future, Agha (2007b) observes, will be shaped by how it formulates its object of study – language – and the breadth or narrowness with which it frames its epistemic project. It can either take a 'largely extractionist-restrictivist-and-exclusionist mode' – narrowing the object of study, extracting it from its surrounds and refusing to engage with other fields of knowledge – or it can take up a more 'integrationist-expansionist-and-collaborative mode' (2007b, p.232) that brings language, space, objects and materiality together. While linguistics 'draws heavily from Native American languages' as part of its interest in adding to the linguistic archive, at the same time it 'normalizes colonial ways of defining, valuing, and analyzing them', overlooking 'Native American communities' ways of defining and engaging with language conceptually' (Leonard, 2021, p.224).

As Albury (2016) remarks in the context of te reo Māori in Aotearoa (New Zealand), if current theories 'continue to define language vitality in western ontological terms, then they will enjoy less applicability in the revitalisation of te reo Māori in Aotearoa' (p.30). Language for Māori, Mika (2016, p.166) argues, is not some 'verbalized outcome of the mind' but rather is 'dense with the full interplay of the world'. One of the greatest deceptions imposed by colonization was to separate language from 'the complete whakapapa (genealogy) of the world'. The challenge, given that there are nonetheless very real reasons why communities want to work on language projects, is how to avoid these 'narrow perspectives on language use and knowledge that are potentially harmful to speech communities' and how to support the 'promotion of minoritised languages by ground-level participants [as] fundamentally a political act through which participants negotiate control over linguistic authority, knowledge production, and self-definition through their linguistic practices' (de Korne and Leonard, 2017, p.7). To operate from this perspective requires an understanding of relational ontologies and a 'much broader view of what is involved in linguistic analysis. It requires a deep listening at discipline level, to hear what other ideologies are important and relevant to our understanding' (Couzens and Eira, 2014, p.332). It is this kind of '*wangan ngootyoong*-informed methodology'[3] – engaging respectfully with diverse ontologies – that makes it possible to work towards a reconciliation of different ways of understanding language.

---

[3] *wangan ngootyoong* is a term meaning 'respect' in the Keerraywoorroong (Victoria, Australia) language.

Ways of categorizing and theorizing 'Indigenous languages using norms for major global languages' or 'Western constructs of what "language" is when engaging in Indigenous language research, teaching, and advocacy' need to be put aside in favour of local control of language reclamation projects (Leonard, 2017, p.15). In short, we have to 'decolonise "language"' (Leonard, 2017, p.32). This also entails, more broadly, decolonizing mainstream understandings of concepts such as multilingualism (Ndhlovu and Makalela, 2021). The aim is not just to expand contexts but to rethink what multilingualism may mean (Makelela, 2018), to understand that the conventional understanding of multilingualism is a colonial construct in need of decolonization, that unlike 'mainstream approaches that proceed through counting putative language-things', an approach to multilingualism that starts with language practices and experiences 'holds the promise for decolonising the field of study' (Ndhlovu and Makalela, 2021, p.173). Once we start to think in terms of relational ontologies, furthermore, it is clear that we are talking here of *multilingualisms* (in the plural) (Kroskrity, 2018; Vaughan and Singer, 2018; Windle et al., 2023), that multilingualisms are different kinds of located practices (Makoni and Pennycook, 2024).

Mufwene (2020, p.290) argues that the idea of *decolonial linguistics* 'entails reducing the Western bias and hegemony in how languages of the global South and the (socio) linguistic behaviours of their speakers and writers are analysed'. Once language revitalization is understood as 'an act of decolonisation' (Stebbins et al., 2018, p.237), the research process can be seen in decolonial terms, involving different language ontologies with respect to relations to community and place, different relations between linguists and community members, different knowledge status between academic and community ways of knowing, different ways of writing and exploring voice, and different ways of approaching ethics (Kwaymullina, 2016). Across the social sciences, it has been acknowledged that research 'needs emancipation from hearing only the voices of western Europe, emancipation from generations of silence, and emancipation from seeing the world in one colour' (Guba and Lincoln, 2005, p.212). As Chilisa (2011, p.1) puts it, 'current academic research traditions are founded on the culture, history, and philosophies of Euro-Western thought' and 'exclude from knowledge production the knowledge systems of formerly colonized, historically marginalized, and oppressed groups'.

This requires the *decolonization* of research methodologies and the development of alternative approaches that include Indigenous ways of doing research, Indigenous ethics, Indigenous control over projects, Indigenous cosmologies and anti-racist education (Armitage, 2022; Bodkin-Andrews and Carlson, 2016; Smith, 2012). It may also be possible, though such propositions remain controversial, for Kaupapa Māori ways of doing research to inform other domains such as Deaf Studies so that research can be far better grounded in the 'ontologies and epistemologies of deaf people and communities' (O'Brien, 2017, p.61). Ndhlovu (2021, p.199) makes a case for *convivial research*, devoted to 'finding connections, points of confluence, and opportunities for transfer of concepts, among members of academic communities, and between them and the nonacademic communities they serve'. For Albury (2017, p.37), one way forward is to take up folk linguistic methodologies (see Chapter 2) that take the voices of Indigenous people seriously: 'folk linguistic research methods can contribute to the decolonisation of sociolinguistic theory and method by understanding, voicing, legitimising, and indeed ultimately applying more ontologies and epistemologies of language' than those that are currently used to frame languages in revitalization projects. This is to take folk linguistics into the domain of decolonization, to take seriously local understandings of language in order to unsettle mainstream ways of thinking about language. Whether citizen linguistics could also be used for the same purposes – particularly given the problematic history of citizenship and Indigeneity (Australian citizenship, granted in 1948 (not 1967 as sometimes claimed), was also constrained) – is an open question, though in its intent – putting research in the hands of the people concerned – it has the potential to become a mode of decolonizing (Svendsen and Goodchild, 2023).

Once different language ontologies are taken seriously, it becomes clear that both language and languages may be very different things. They may include other animals and sounds as well as being understood multimodally. The term *inwewin* in the Ojibwe language, generally translated as meaning 'language', 'does not distinguish human language from the characteristic calls of other creatures' (Hermes et al., 2022, p.4). Heurich's (2020, p.107) study of the Araweté's (Eastern Amazonia in the Brazilian State of Pará) *oporahẽ* songs suggests the need to attend to 'the material wrapping of words – the materiality of sound and voice – in Amazonian ritual singing'. This shifts the focus away from referential and metaphorical meaning common in Northern approaches to language, and foregrounds instead the materiality of sound and voice. This kind of study not only gives us insights into Amazonian language and singing practices but also unsettles Northern modes of thinking about language, asking what it means 'to take seriously the phonetic clothing of a language' (Webster, 2016, p.35).

In Brazil, the Kashinawá, in contrast with modernist traditions of literacy, integrate different symbols in their multimodal literacies, including not only words but also figures, patterns, colours and spatial arrangements (de Souza, 2009). As Dias (2019) explains, to understand local conceptions of language in parts of South America, we need to incorporate multimodality, senses beyond speaking and listening, animal sounds, a capacity to hear the songs of animals and so on. The *sand stories* (*tyepety* in some Arandic languages) told by women in Central Australia include much more than speech: songs, gestures, space and drawings in the sand are all part of a complex multimodal whole (Green, 2014). As First Nations artists have long insisted, dance, song, painting and singing have to be understood together, an assemblage of forms. Just as Fijian Australian hip-hop artist MC Trey connects Fijian practices of dancing, art and storytelling to various modes of hip-hop, so Indigenous Australian (Gumbangirr) Wire MC suggests that the elements of hip-hop – break dancing, deejaying, graffiti and rapping – all connect to multimodal aspects of Indigenous cultures (Pennycook, 2007).

When the common trope is invoked that a language is 'sleeping' rather than 'dead' (Perley, 2012), there is a shift in the understanding both of reawakening the language but also what and where language is. As Leonard (2020b, p.495) explains, members of his community 'contested the colonial logic of "extinction"' and, exercising their 'linguistic sovereignty', instead used 'the term sleeping to describe our language during its dormancy'. Thus, when he suggests that 'my tribal heritage language, *myaamia*, was sleeping for a long time' (Leonard, 2017, p.17), it is important to consider the different ways of thinking that this invokes, the implications for language in relation to landscape and people and use. If, as Monaghan (2012, p.53) suggests, languages have been placed in the land by the ancestors, and if they may predate the arrival of those late arrivals, humans, then processes of reclamation are for more about land, community and spiritual connections than about documentation. This 'broader cultural reclamation story has come to be called *myaamiaki eemamwiciki* "(the) Miamis awaken"' (Leonard, 2020b, p.495; emphasis in original). According to Nunukul and Munaldjali artistic director of the dance group Bangarra, Stephen Page, talking about Yugambeh (a language of what is now Southeast Queensland), previous generations 'were forbidden to speak language but they still had language growing inside them' (Page, 2022, p.26).

For Leonard (2017, 2020a, b), the idea of *reclamation* here is more useful than revitalization since it points to the wider political process of reclaiming the knowledge production around language as well as reawakening a sleeping language. Languages, from these perspectives, are connected to the land, alive, active and not limited to humans. The Navajo phrase *nihizaad hiná*, 'our language is alive' points to this orientation towards languages as living beings rather than communicative tools (McKenzie, 2020, p.506). A central *ontological innovation* in the work of Hermes and colleagues (2022, p.2) was to define 'language as alive – meaning that the relationships of land and language are treated as active agents'. Songspirals in North-East Arnhem Land (Australia) are much more than stories about the land since they 'bring us into being and they link us to the land, to Country. They come from the land and they create it too. It's not just that songspirals created our land a long time ago, but they keep on creating it, and us, and everything in our Country' (Gay'wu Group of Women, 2019, p.xvii).

Engaging with the growing amount of work emerging around Indigenous languages, reclamation and learning, particularly from a new generation of Indigenous scholars, it becomes clear that a central theme is decolonization. This is not in itself surprising since it is largely the colonial enterprise that produced the need for definitions of Indigeneity, and the colonial encounter that devastated such people and their ways of life and forms of knowledge. Processes of decolonization, however, have to go deep. They cannot just be about helping to document a language that is not widely spoken or 'endangered'; nor can they just be critiques of Northern epistemologies. Rather, as Hermes and colleagues (2022), Leonard (2020a, b), Mufwene (2020), Ndhlovu and Makalela (2021) and others make clear, such projects have to both challenge Northern ways of thinking about language and sociolinguistic practices, and to accept the possibilities of different language ontologies, different relations between land and people and language, and different understandings of who and what may be involved in languages.

5.5 CONCLUSION: FROM METAPHOR TO MATERIAL RELATIONALITY

One might argue that 'my language is sleeping' is in fact a metaphor. In common ways of understanding metaphor, this would suggest that 'sleeping' is here standing in for something that it is not (languages cannot sleep). Studies of conceptual metaphor, particularly the work of Lakoff and Johnson (1980), suggest not so much something seen in terms of what it is not, but understanding something in terms of something else, relations of meaning in discourse between an incongruous and a more suitable term: in English, life has its ups and downs, we move forward, we look back, we devour a book, digest ideas and so on. These can then be classified in more general terms to show how we use conceptual metaphors to think: life is a container or a journey, ideas are food, understanding is seeing and so on. 'A large proportion of everyday and scholarly argumentation in a language such as English is dominated by a small number of basic metaphorical concepts (e.g. time is money, languages are systems)' (Mühlhäusler, 1995, p.282). There are obvious difficulties in deciding between what is literal and what is metaphorical, or between what is expected and unexpected, normal or inappropriate, but as Mühlhäusler's second example – languages are systems – shows, just as viewing time as money may be considered metaphorical, so is viewing language as a system or structure.

We can therefore consider that 'all of our concepts of language are in fact metaphorically constructed' (Underhill, 2011, p.15) and that conceptual metaphors play a significant role in the process of 'language making' in both the formation of linguistic theories and common conceptions of language (Jakobs and Hüning, 2022, p.29). When we talk of saving dying languages or looking at language structures, we are talking in metaphors. The idea of 'language use', for example, 'one of the most fundamental conceptual frameworks used to conceive of language as an object of scientific study' (see Chapter 3), presupposes a 'historically situated, mechanistic, utilitarian conception of language' and it is only by reaching beyond such conceptions that we will come to see 'the limits of our metaphor-bound definition which frames our debates on language in contemporary linguistics' (Underhill, 2011, p.175). The metaphor of structure assumes languages can be treated in isolation, as 'complete and closed with determinate boundaries' (Mühlhäusler, 1995, p.285). Underpinning the broad language myths discussed in Chapter 2 are conceptual metaphors that form 'communally shared narratives' as part of an ideological set of beliefs about the 'structure of language and/or the functional uses to which language is put' (Watts, 2011, p.8).

From this point of view, then, as long as we also treat language structure and use as metaphors – that is to say, we also consider central concepts of Northern linguistics as equally metaphorical, as part of a set of conceptual metaphors that view the world in particular ways – we might equally accept that 'my language is sleeping' is metaphorical, and that 'different linguistic communities conceive of "language" differently, and those differences are, of course, metaphorically bound' (Underhill, 2011, p.175). Despite relativizing all language talk as metaphorical, however, this position remains unsatisfactory. As I have argued throughout this book, I want to take ontological claims seriously. Just as Tuck and Yang (2012, p.3) insist that 'decolonization is not a metaphor' – absorbing real processes of decolonization into white settler projects of social justice 'kills the very possibility of decolonization; it recenters whiteness, it resettles theory, it extends innocence to the settler, it entertains a settler future' – so processes of language decolonization cannot be pulled back into projects of language revival that resettle linguistic theory. To talk in terms of conceptual metaphors is to work from a position of epistemological relativism: the world is one but we view it from different cultural perspectives.

Leonard's (2017) view that *myaamia* is sleeping, however, is not, as I understand it, intended metaphorically: languages can sleep. Languages can grow inside you. Languages can be alive. These are different language ontologies rather than different worldviews, metaphors or language ideologies. On political and ontological fronts, therefore, sleeping languages, or languages being in the land or water, are not metaphors: they are realities. A 'relational approach to language rights', suggest Nicholas and McCarty (2022, p.233), does not imply a bounded notion of language as object, but an understanding of language that draws on Indigenous understandings of language and tribal sovereignty while confronting settler colonialism and its history. At stake is a set of deep-seated language ideological assemblages that require 'understanding Indigenous multilingualisms within the complex of language beliefs, feelings, and practices that actually contextualize them' (Kroskrity, 2018, p.134). Or, as I have been arguing in this book, it is not only a question of language ideologies, metaphors or epistemologies, but rather of ontologies. Like Yunkaporta's (2019, p.167) injunction 'to avoid putting all your cognitive eggs in one basket', it is important at the very least to avoid putting all our linguistic eggs in one basket. It is not useful to commit only to one ontological framework.

It is important to contest the colonial logic of extinction (Leonard, 2020b), both for Indigenous languages and for languages such as Kernewek (Cornish), with claims to historical priority, colonial dispossession and minority status, rather than Indigeneity. Cornish is a language claimed to have suffered 'language extinction' (Maher, 2021, p.111), to have 'died in 1777' though to have undergone revival (Jones and Singh, 2005, p.134). It may be true that 'herwydh konygyon yethow' (according to linguists) the most important thing 'rag an termyn a dheu dhe yethow minoryta' (for the future of minority languages) is to 'threusperthi dhe'n henedh nessa heb falladow' (transfer them to the next generation) rather than just 'dyski yethow yn skol' (teach languages in school) or in 'klassow gorthugherweyth rag tevesigyon' (evening classes for adults) (Broadhurst, 2020, p.20). Yet the issue for Cornish is still about creating new speakers and accepting that languages in contexts of revival or reclamation will inevitably be reconstructed, changed or reassembled (Sayers, 2023). It may be that this very use of Cornish itself rather than the advice of linguists or the notion of intergenerational transmission – Fishman's (1991) influential model that rests on a fixity of both language (threatened languages) and process (reversing language shift) – is more important for Cornish, as well as a capacity to ask different questions about its ontological being. 'A eus le rag hwedhlow dyffrans/ A eus le rag hwedhlow koth/ Hwedhel an re na wrug gwaynya/ Agan hwedhel ni oll' (Is there room for different stories/ Is there room for ancient stories/ The story of the ones who didn't win/ The story of us all) asks Gwenno Saunders (2018) in her Cornish language album *Le Kov* (first line cited in Maher, 2021, p.105).

Some of these concerns around Indigenous and other language reclamation can be taken up in practical terms: if we want to do better in language revival projects, we need to have better dialogues between Indigenous and other ontologies. There are also some caveats to consider in any push towards Indigenous or Southern ways of thinking. As suggested at the beginning of this chapter, and discussed in Chapter 2, when we ask whose knowledge of language counts, the goal is to reclaim forms of subjugated knowledge rather than to dismiss all dominant forms: the aim in decolonization is not necessarily to throw out all kinds of colonial knowledge but, rather, as Chakrabarty (2000) argues, to *provincialize* them, to put Northern knowledge where it belongs. There is a danger, furthermore, as we seek alternative ways of thinking from a Southern perspective that in a rush to reject mind–body dualism or forms of rational and scientific thinking, we end up projecting a world of bodies and emotions onto Southern epistemologies, a project that can start to look uncomfortably like a perpetuation of the colonial distinction between the rational European mind and its bodily others (Nandy, 1983). Indigenous standpoints (Nakata et al., 2012) also include Indigenous knowledge of the colonial other and knowledge of where Indigenous people sit within the colonial archive. The entanglements of forms of knowledge cannot always be undone.

This also plays out on more local levels as Indigenous people have to negotiate colonial and Indigenous epistemologies and ontologies in their daily lives, making decisions, for example, about education and language in relation to schooling.

Indigenous ontologies, however, also urge us to reconsider why we think of languages in particular ways. As Blenkinsop and Fettes (2020, p.1037) remark, the alienation from the other-than-human world in the Global North leads to 'anthropocentrism, species elitism, deep nature/culture binaries, romantic concepts of wilderness ... and an underlying utilitarian, imperialistic, colonial orientation'. As López-Gopar and colleagues (2023) suggest with respect to the Ayuk people of Mexico and their capacity to communicate with the mountain, the river, the land and the corn, we need in applied linguistics to be able to grasp what language means within these relations. These ways of thinking about language, 'with their connections to tracts of country, descent-based custodianship and set within social, spiritual, and multilingual practice, are distinct from Western, particularly Anglo, conceptions of "language"' (Disbray et al., 2020, p.520). Meek (2015, p.458) urges us to ask, 'who benefits and who loses from understanding languages the way we do' and what is at stake for whom in these different ways of thinking about language?

If we take Yunkaporta's (2019, p.169) position seriously that 'nothing exists outside of a relationship to something else', it is important to consider the relational ontologies of language (and compare Tynan, 2021), the fact that languages may be different things. Yunkaporta's exposition of different forms of learning from a Wik Mungkan (Cape York Peninsula, Northern Queensland) perspective further suggests the need to engage seriously with other forms of knowledge: these ways of learning are multifaceted social and cognitive processes. Such a perspective takes us away from complex models to represent simple ideas – mainstream models of language and language learning, pushed by academic insistence towards intricacy, take simple ideas and make them diagrammatically complex – when instead we might aim to come to simple representations of complex ideas (Pennycook, 2023b). An Ojibwe language ontology, Hermes and colleagues (2022, p.4) explain, 'is grounded in materiality – a way of thinking in which humans and more-than-humans are connected as relatives in an interlocking web of relationship as one of many, not one apart'. Such engagements with epistemologies of the South and political ontology, Escobar (2016, p.29) explains, are 'efforts at thinking beyond the academy, with the *pueblos-territorio* (peoples-territory) and the intellectual-activists linked to them'. For Escobar (2020), if we are to find ways out of our current crises, we need alternative ways of thinking, alternative possibilities, to do so. And if this is true for political science, the environment and the climate, it is equally so for language.

6 Applied Linguistics as Practical Assemblage

I have been arguing in this book that all languages are assembled, and that as a result they may not be cut from the same cloth. In the previous chapter, I made a case for the importance of understanding, acknowledging and engaging with Indigenous ways of thinking about language. There are several reasons for doing so: as discussed in Chapter 2, an important part of any linguistic enterprise – particularly from anthropological, sociolinguistic and applied perspectives – is to understand how people themselves think about languages. To study language though a scientific lens that distances itself from the communities involved may potentially bring insights for an understanding of some aspects of language, but it equally misses the point that if this is not what language means to those communities, then any such study of a language cannot in any meaningful way be a study of more than a very narrow slice of what language means. This requirement to take on board local meanings of language becomes even more important when we are dealing with languages of the Global South, be these the languages of First Nations in Australia or the northern circumpolar regions (Lane, 2023b). There are moral and political obligations to listen to and understand forms of knowledge that have long been dismissed, disparaged and discarded.

This is about expanding the possibilities of understanding what language and languages are. The relational ontological perspective that I have argued for in this book – *perspectivism* in Viveiros de Castro's (2015) terms – 'works on an ontologically plural level without privileging one ontology. Western science and philosophy have extraordinary merits, but so too do the Tlingit and Tagish cultures. Perspectivism is about acknowledging worlds, and not worldviews' (Hayman et al., 2018, p.83). This ontological pluralism means that it is not necessary to insist on one position over another, or to make a case for a particular epistemological case but to seek to understand different ways of being. Relational ontologies enable us to consider what languages are rather than dwell centrally on epistemologies or ideologies (different ways of thinking about language). It is not therefore a question of deciding what language really *is* (as if this was so easily decided) or *should be* (as if ideology critique could answer our question) but rather of what it *could be* (engaging with possibilities) (Holbraad et al., 2014). The relational focus has made it possible to consider that languages are all of these things. It is not that languages aren't structures or that we don't learn a lot by thinking structurally, but rather that this by no means exhausts the possibilities of what languages are.

This is also important from a practical or applied point of view, since the idea of language reclamation can only really make sense if whatever is being reclaimed is done so in terms that make sense to that community. It is therefore vital for 'critical applied linguists to develop new strategies for attending to the language practices of racialized communities in efforts to surface alternative decolonial genres of the human that have existed and continue to exist in these communities but have often been misrecognized in scholarly efforts to identify competence' (Flores and Rosa, 2022, p.19). This implies a commitment in applied linguistics to 'question colonising ways of conceiving of language' (Dias, 2019, p.100) and to consider with care how other ways of knowing and being matter, how relations to land and water are deeply held spiritual understandings that involve language. 'Reducing language to a communication device, a vehicle for messages expressible in an ideally abstract verbal code, or a system for naming or reflecting a reality which supposedly precedes it, rules out an array of local communicative practices' that resonate with an assemblage approach to language that includes sensorial, kinesic, affective and other aspects of communication (Dias, 2019, p.91).

The connections between First Nation views of language and the idea of assemblages need to be drawn with caution. There are many resonances with a new materialist openness to understand the importance of artefacts, to move away from human-centric visions of the world and in doing so to appreciate a world of things and animals and language that predate human arrival. A more respectful relation to language, land, water, animals and other things that animate the world is surely crucial for all our survival. The danger, however, is that in drawing such connections, the notion of assemblage or of new materialism starts to take precedence, to claim that it can incorporate Indigenous thinking within its framework. This would both overlook the importance of Indigenous thinking in developing forms of new materialism, as well as make yet another colonizing move to reclaim Indigenous knowledge. The relational ontologies that run through this book, by contrast, can point to the similarities here, without seeing them as the same thing: the ontology of language as an assemblage, like the ontology of language practices, is in many ways much closer to these ways of thinking than a structural ontology but it is not the same thing.

Thinking in terms of language assemblages more broadly, however, can provide fruitful ways forward. Any kind of language is assembled though social and ideological practices, a result of ongoing processes of communication, identification, performance and survival. Assemblages describe the way things are brought together and function in new ways, and provide a way of thinking about how agency, cognition, language and identity can all be understood as distributed beyond any supposed human centre. Identities, therefore, are not merely assembled in the way that poststructuralist approaches insist on their discursive production – identities can be seen as temporal and contingent assemblages of discursive elements – but rather as part of sociomaterial assemblages that bring language, people, places and things together. Identities are distributed across people, places and things and then assembled in temporary entanglements of linguistic resources, spatial relations and objects. Identities, from this point of view, are not nameable characterizations – teacher, citizen, mother – but distributed effects of diverse elements. The point is not just that languages are assembled in an active process of human engagement with language elements (Wee, 2021), not just that many different forms of semiosis come together in semiotic assemblages (Pennycook, 2017), but that linguistic resources are but one part of the dynamic processes of assembling. As Toohey (2019, p.953) suggests, ideas born of new forms of materialism, such as *assemblages* or *entanglements*, have major implications for applied linguistic pedagogy and research, encouraging us 'to ask new questions, and be alert to innovate, experiment, and learn new ways of teaching, researching, and being'.

6.1 ONTOLOGICAL CURIOSITY

Wee (2021, p.60) draws a contrast between ontological naivety and curiosity and argues that an ontologically curious position 'takes seriously rather than skirts the question of just how languages, including standard English and its non-standard counterparts, are constituted'. Such a position, he goes on 'avoids taking the name of a variety at face value' and 'refrains from accusing those who wish to inquire into the nature of a variety as "enemies"'. In the same vein, it is important to resist ontological naivety and the ontological panic that has suggested that to question what languages are, to entertain *language suspicion* (Ramberg and Røyneland, in press), is to undermine the hard-fought gains made in bilingual education, language rights, multilingualism and so on. The argument that to challenge languages as commonly defined is 'at odds with a civil rights orientation, the backbone of language education policy in the United States' (MacSwan, 2020, p.321) is akin to suggesting that because affirmative action programmes are based around common understandings of race and gender in the USA, we should not therefore question the ways race and gender are understood. Surely we need to work from both perspectives: political action to rectify contemporary injustices along the lines that have been laid down in the past and at the same time critical inquiry into the ways such differences have been constructed. This by no means suggests that affirmative action should be weakened (alas it is already being eroded) or that bilingual education should be cancelled (it too has been under threat in many contexts) but rather that if we cede the ground to normative definitions of language, race or gender, we are failing in our challenge towards change.

In light of the many questions that have been raised about languages and what they are, we need to have sensible discussions about ontological questions (Ramberg and Røyneland, in press). The problem, as I have suggested, is that an ontological panic has led to a number of unproductive arguments. The position that Makoni and I (Makoni and Pennycook, 2007, p.2) took, for example, that languages are 'the inventions of social, cultural and political movements' with 'very real material effects' has been taken to be 'detrimental to non-dominant-language speakers' opportunities for social equity and language rights since a high level of proficiency in languages of power is usually a necessary condition for social mobility' (Tannenbaum and Shohamy, 2023, p.10). It is not clear, however, why ontologically curious questions about what languages are and what the material effects of such constructions may be can have a detrimental role for language learners. Perhaps the idea of invention is too strong, suggesting too much intentionality in the process of social construction, though the origins of the idea in historical work on the invention of tradition (Hobsbawm and Ranger, 1983) suggest otherwise. Language assemblages offer an alternative way of thinking that maintains the social and political understanding of languages, and sees languages as always being made rather than pre-made. The point remains, however, that if we refuse to ask ontological questions, we also do a disservice to the possibilities of social change.

One implication of taking a relational ontological and social epistemological stance is that it changes the nature of the argument. Rather than claiming that either everyday views or linguistic accounts of language are myths (see Chapter 2), the position I have taken in this book is that we need to account for different ontologies as distinct from epistemological questions about how we understand them. So I do not take the strong position on language myths taken by Harris (1981) or Grace (1987) that both the wider society 'and the science of language in particular ... have a false view of the nature of language' (1987, p.139) or that language as structure is mistaken, but that we have to understand what this means, what work it does and what the implications are for all those language projects for which it does not fit. There are nonetheless various reasons to be cautious about a leap into the ontological turn. Although it arguably presents possibilities for an alternative politics that takes difference seriously rather than dismissing it as just human construction, it also suggests a pluriversal view that is hard to accept for those committed to universality and raises questions of material difference (different worlds) when the focus needs to be on material disparity (differential access to one world).

There are also questions to be asked about the grounds for claiming ontological distinctions. Following Demuro and Gurney (2021), I have made a case here for structural, practice and assemblage ontologies. As we saw in Chapter 2, an increased focus on ontological questions has brought about a range of claims to ontological distinctions, from I-languages and E-languages to fixed versus variable versions of language. Evidently, given that the discussion here is about ontology rather epistemology, we should not start considering all the different ways language is understood in linguistics as having ontological status. Thus, functional versus structural accounts are arguably different ways of approaching the same structural language ontology, but it is worth considering whether, for example, usage-based versions of language – with their focus on how languages are created, sustained and adapted in the interactions among communicative activities and social and cognitive processes (Schmid, 2020) – are just a different way of approaching language structures or a different ontological position on what languages are. We also need to be able to account for the ways ontologies come to be. For Demuro and Gurney (2021, p.5), 'worlds come into existence, ontologically, through practices and enactments. Actions, performances, stories, and so forth, bring particular ontologies into being'. Discussions of the ontological status of the subject 'English' or what constitutes 'good English' in schools make a similar point, suggesting that multiple actors (policy and curriculum documents and their varied enactments, teacher, student and parent interests, as well as the circulation of language ideologies in both local and wider domains) constitute the ontological being of subject English in schools (Cunningham, 2020; Goodwyn, 2020).

Just as it behoves us to be ontologically curious about language, however, we should also be sceptical about the ontological turn itself. It is all too easy to be enveloped by a new turn, either those that emanate more from within the fields of socio- and applied linguistics – such as the multilingual (May, 2014) or translingual (García and Li Wei, 2014) turns – or those that come from elsewhere – such as the spatial, social, somatic, decolonial and other turns. A field such as applied linguistics, arguably defined not so much by its disciplinary solidarity as by its openness to ideas from elsewhere (as an *epistemic assemblage*, see Section 6.3) will always be susceptible to such turns, often with positive effects. This is preferable to being blind to such turns, but they also need to be read critically in terms of what they bring and what they exclude (Pennycook, 2022a). Just as anthropologists have questioned a focus on radical alterity when livelihoods are at stake, and Indigenous scholars have asked whether this is yet another appropriation of Indigenous knowledge, so in language studies we need to be cautious here.

Another concern in thinking in terms of such language ontologies is that while they may challenge and extend the Western tradition of linguistic thought, discussion remains potentially within a single intellectual tradition (the notion of ontology itself needs to be understood in these terms). Contrasting ontologies and epistemologies – the realization, for example, that while linguistics may have moved on from its structuralist epistemological phase, it remains committed to a structural ontology – has been useful but it is a distinction that is often difficult to uphold. As the discussion in Chapter 5 made clear, there are good reasons to challenge such frameworks in more profound ways, a problem that is not overcome by eliding them in terms of onto-epistemologies, as some suggest. The epistemology–ontology divide – knowledge and being – relies on an assumption that humans are 'separate from the world they are in, in order to have a perception of it' (Watts, 2013, p.24). The separation of epistemology and ontology repeats the dualisms of a correspondence theory of truth, with its 'subject-object, culture-nature, word-world dualisms' (Barad, 2007, p.125). Practices of knowing 'cannot fully be claimed as human practices, not simply because we use nonhuman elements in our practices but because knowing is a matter of part of the world making itself intelligible to another part' (Barad, 2007, p.185). Indigenous ontologies may unsettle common linguistic frameworks, but they also unsettle the ontology–epistemology divide itself. This way of thinking 'necessitates a separation of not only human and non-human, but a hierarchy of beings in terms of how beings are able to think as well' (Watts, 2013, p.24). If an ontological focus sits always in relation to an epistemological focus, suggesting that knowing can be separated from being, we may reproduce the conceptual frameworks we aim to supersede.

6.2 THE LIMITATIONS OF THINKING STRUCTURALLY

To be clear, however, the lens of relational ontologies that underpins this book does not mean that such open-ended thinking applies equally to epistemological or political concerns. Unlike the epistemological relativism and judgemental rationalism of Block's (2022) critical realism, my own take on critical social realism evaluates epistemologies in social terms and implications in political terms. As noted in Chapter 1, an applied linguistic scepticism about the reification of languages as separate structures is at least fifty years old (Corder, 1973), yet the implications of structural understandings of language persist: since 'many language educators still hold a structuralist view of language, they are primarily focused on how linguistic signs make conventional meanings, not how speakers and writers get into power struggles over their interpretation' (Kramsch, 2021, p.12). As discussed in Chapter 3, this is the problem of insisting that meaning is guaranteed by a self-governing system rather than part of a social struggle over whose version of the world will hold sway. On one level, then, it is useful to take a relativist stand on ontological questions – languages as structures can coexist with other kinds of language – but on applied, practical, social and political levels, it is equally important to question the implications of thinking structurally.

The liberal egalitarian ideologies of linguistics (see Chapter 3) that have argued forcefully, for example, that all languages are equal have made an important case for the status of languages that were considered inferior, or not even to be languages. This was particularly important for creoles and sign languages in seeking to overcome prejudicial views that decried them as inadequate, deficient, less than real languages: linguists made a compelling case that they were as structurally complex as any others. A similar case has been made that speaking more than one language can lead to a *bilingual advantage*, whereby users of several languages have cognitive advantages over their monolingual counterparts. From a structural and liberal egalitarian point of view, this makes good sense: languages are structural entities and using more than one will exercise the brain more than using one alone. In the social and political domain, this was also part of a significant argument against suggestions that bilingualism or multilingualism might be detrimental to a person since using more than one language could confuse their language, literacy or more general cognitive development. This is all very well but, at the same time, by reducing creoles and sign languages to a notion of structural equality, and by insisting that using two languages must be better than just one, these lines of thinking fail to attend to the situated language practices involved. A shift in how we understand both bilingualism – involving local practices and multiple resources – as well as cognition – in terms of embodied, situated interaction – may still allow us to see the benefits of bilingualism but along the lines of how people are able to interact with the world rather than according to an additive model whereby two must be better than one (Otsuji and Pennycook, 2018; Sanches de Oliveira and Bullock Oliveira, 2022). Bilingual suspicion or ontological curiosity about what it means to speak two languages by no means opposes language learning or the benefits of having available diverse resources, but it questions the grounds on which we assume advantage and the enumerability of advantageous capacities.

While a great deal of work has been done on creole languages, mapping their development or showing how they differ from their lexifier languages, critical questions have emerged concerning the status of this category. Macedo (2019) points to the general process by which the 'standard colonial language' is ideologically distinguished from its varieties which are 'derogatorily labeled as "dialect," "patois," "pidgin," "creole" and "Spanglish," among other labels'. This 'with the mere intent to create an ideological distinction so as to devalue, dismiss, and dehumanize' (2019, p.11). Creole languages are understood 'in opposition to so-called "normal languages" (and especially in opposition to their "lexifiers", which were in many cases the languages of the white colonizers)' (Hollington, 2020, pp.225–6). Such *creole exceptionalism* has been labelled *'linguists' most dangerous myth'* (DeGraff, 2005, p.534; emphasis added). This is the paradoxical process of trying to show that creoles are as structurally complex as other languages while also assuming their distinct status, and the 'exceptional and abnormal characteristics in the diachrony and/or synchrony of Creole languages as a class'. Creole languages, Hollington (2020, p.227) elaborates, are 'an artificially created class of languages'. For Mufwene (2020, p.289), 'creoles are normal language varieties that have speciated in a non-exceptional fashion from their lexifiers'. As Faraclas (2020, pp.79–80) explains, the grounds for the distinction between creole and other languages are tenuous since 'linguists have found no consistent formal criteria which can be used to distinguish Creoles from other languages'.

A similar case can be made for sign languages. The liberal egalitarian ideals that underpin much of linguistic thought aimed to show that such languages are far more than mere gesture, much more than the limited compensatory strategies that had been assumed: sign languages were complex and complete languages like any other. To be literate and deaf was to be bilingual. Once again, the importance of this work should not be underestimated, and yet thinking structurally has meant that all that escapes a structural ontology can be overlooked. Sign languages can help us see how communication operates in spatiotemporal and embodied terms. As Kusters and Sahasrabudhe (2018, p.62) note, academic ideologies about gesture and signing 'have de-localised and de-contextualised fluid language practices; simplified and essentialized their difference; or made distinctions where language users typically do not experience such distinctions'. Looking at 'deaf cosmopolitanism' and particularly the processes by which Deaf people *calibrate* their signs to align with other signers, Moriarty and Kusters (2021, p.287) show how 'calibrating involves the use of diverse semiotic resources that can include International Sign; signing, mouthing, writing and fingerspelling in different languages and scripts; speech; and drawing'.

Such communication is not limited by the notion of fixity implied by bound languages. In contexts of signing, as discussed in Chapter 4, it may be far more useful to think both in terms of a much wider 'semiotic repertoire' of resources that includes a diversity of bodily resources as well as greater flexibility when it comes to using signs in international or cosmopolitan contexts. To argue only that sign languages are as complex as any spoken language is to overlook the ways that such signs can be very different from spoken languages, and more amenable to flexible usage and interpretation. In such contexts people draw on 'an assemblage of shared semiotic resources that they mix and mesh to arrive at shared understanding' (Moriarty and Kusters, 2021, p.290). While a lot of work sought to show that sign languages are more than gesture, at the same time such work downplayed

Applied Linguistics as Practical Assemblage

precisely this importance of embodied signing, overlooking the ways that 'the embodiment of deafness serves to sharply distinguish the reality of sign languages from that of spoken languages' (Kusters and Lucas, 2022, p.90).

Orthodox has sought to do two things: on the one hand define creoles and sign languages in structural terms, showing how they differ from other languages (in both historical and contemporary terms); and, on the other hand, make the case that they are equal structurally to other languages, showing that there is therefore no reason to treat them any differently. It is a worthwhile goal up to a point, but it falls apart on several grounds: it takes as its point of comparison the structural descriptions of languages and aims to demonstrate equal complexity. What this fails to do is acknowledge differences, that creoles or sign languages may entail a range of very different practices or different assemblages of language, people and place. Sign languages, for example, are not just equal to spoken languages but have a range of spatial and gestural implications that could inform linguistic thought in many ways. By understanding how sign languages work, we can rediscover 'the multi-dimensional nature of spoken language – its strategic use of time, of space through gesture and body language, and of tone' (Branson and Miller, 2007, p.119).

All of this is premised on the clear identification of languages along structural rather than on sociocultural or sociopolitical lines. As Hollington (2020, p.225) makes clear, creole linguistics is 'strongly rooted in, and tied to, the colonial discourse, European imperialism, ethnocentric perspectives, and racism'. The term 'Creole', Severo and Makoni (2020, p.63) argue, is a 'racial category that was presented as natural to designate both the people and their language'. It is a word 'saturated with racist and other ethnocentric notions of "contamination" of pure European languages, culture, and bloodlines' leading to 'a growing consensus that it should be discarded as a legacy of colonialism' (Faraclas, 2020, p.80). Given this history and the questionable status of creole languages as a distinct or different class of languages (DeGraff, 2019; Mufwene, 2020), there are challenging questions to be asked of the continued commitment to structural analysis both of the internal workings of these languages and in comparison with others. It is in part the inability to see the construction of creole languages within the broader context of racial classifications and sociopolitical contexts that has enabled this work to carry on regardless. Similarly it is in part the *sensory asymmetries* (Kusters and Lucas, 2022, p.86) between deaf and hearing people that have meant the search to establish equality between sign and other languages has led to an obliviousness to difference. Ultimately, Faraclas (2020, p.80) argues, creole languages should be studied 'as a sociohistorically (rather than structurally) defined set of languages'.

Just as these structural legacies have limited the possibilities for understanding how creole and sign languages have been constructed as distinct yet equal, so applied linguists need to consider very carefully the implications of engaging with structuralist frameworks in applied contexts. For Kramsch (2021) this structural legacy, like Harris' (1981) language myth whereby speakers pass messages back and forth via signs with socially agreed meanings (see Chapter 3), renders language education a process of coding and decoding conventional meanings rather than a struggle over symbolic power, a struggle for language learners and users not just to be understood, but to be valued, taken seriously, treated with respect. Likewise in areas such as language policy and rights, a structural legacy leaves us searching for consensual equality between languages under the label of commonality, rather than a struggle for legitimation of potentially quite different entities amid economic disparities, racial discrimination and a wider struggle for survival. This overlooks the ways in which they might be treated as something different or the wider social and political domains in which these categorizations occur. These attempts to overcome discrimination by appeal to equality fall short in the same way that appeals to humanity or social justice or inclusivity fail to address wider concerns about difference and discrimination (Walcott, 2018).

6.3 REASSEMBLING APPLIED LINGUISTICS

For linguists it has been common to disparage or at least look down on applied linguistics as somehow secondary. Linguists do the theorizing; applied linguists apply the theories. I once worked in a department of Linguistics and Applied Linguistics where the introduction to the department explained things in precisely these terms: linguistics was concerned with the study of language in all its aspects (a rather overstated view of what linguistics actually looks at), while applied linguistics applied such knowledge to real-world contexts. Applied linguists have rather played into this perception, seeing descriptions of language as coming from elsewhere. For some linguists, applied linguistics is just a money-making enterprise connected to (English) language teaching that keeps the linguistic enterprise afloat by conducting 'studies which are claimed to use linguistics in order to help people be better language-teachers' (Sampson, 2017, p.19). Such disdainful formulations are problematic on multiple grounds, reducing applied linguistics to (English) language teaching, suggesting that the only use for such an applied field is its potential commercial benefit, and intimating that applied linguistics may not really be using linguistic knowledge appropriately anyway. Linguists sometimes look down at the popularity of some applied linguistic work: I once inadvisably suggested at a book launch that the several thousand copies sold by the author of her previous work might recommend this new one, only to notice various frowns and shaking heads. High volume book sales, second editions, big h-index numbers, and other markers of both academic and wider popularity can be seen as a sign of recognition which is anathema to the niche interests of dedicated scientists.

One way forward here for applied linguistics has been to emphasize its disciplinary credentials. Indeed, applied linguistics has been subjected to the same kind of disciplinary mechanisms as many other disciplines: handbooks, introductory texts, conferences, symposia and the like, all trying hard to make the case for disciplinary cohesion. It has always been difficult, however, to nail down what applied linguistics really is, and there has never been a really compelling case to consider it a discipline. For some, it is a field of practice informed by real-world language problems, so applied linguists are 'practical people working as a community, and it is their modes of practice and communicating with one another, as much as anything, which define them as a professional group' (McCarthy, 2001, p.118). For others, applied linguistics is better understood as a theory of the practice, suggesting that applied linguistics is 'the practice of language study itself, and the theory that could be drawn from that practice' (Kramsch, 2015, p.455). For others it is an 'interdisciplinary area of inquiry' where research on language-related issues meets wider public concerns (Rampton, 1997, p.11).

A lot of work has nonetheless been done over the years to consolidate applied linguistics as a discipline though, as pointed out in Chapter 1, there were already warnings in introductory texts (Corder, 1973) to be wary of the ways languages were turned into objects that might not suit applied linguistic projects. A revealing part of the process of disciplining applied linguistics has been not only what is placed within the fold – from early concerns with language teaching (and particularly of English) to a broad assortment of interests such as translation, speech pathology, multilingual families, language policies, language revival, language in professional contexts, and more – but also what is kept out. One such exclusion was *critical applied linguistics* (Pennycook, 2001) because of its supposed rejection of theories of language, scepticism towards metanarratives and critique of traditional applied linguistic claims to neutrality (Kaplan, 2002). For Davies (1999), in addition to these concerns, it was the critique of '"normal" applied linguistics' (p.145) as well as 'the attempt since the 1950s to develop a coherent applied linguistics' (Davies, 1999, p.141) that made critical approaches a threat to the disciplinary solidarity of the field. While such handbooks and introductions were clearly unsettled by the overt political orientation taken by critical applied linguists, an equal concern was the challenge to epistemological and ontological assuredness posed by a *transgressive* approach to applied linguistics (Pennycook, 2006).

As another who tried his hand at writing an introduction to the field observed, however, the 'lack of unitary theory and of clear disciplinary boundaries' (McCarthy, 2001, p.21) might be seen as a form of strength, with 'its very openness to outside influences being its strongest and most enduring quality'. The hierarchical organization of knowledge in disciplines through processes of classification and framing plays a significant role in the regulation of access to knowledge (Bernstein, 2000). As May (2014, p.15) suggests, this helps us to see how and why disciplines 'are so often defined (and confined) by a narrowly derived set of research assumptions, approaches, and related models of teaching and learning'. Gordon (2006) critiques *disciplinary decadence* (reductive disciplinary thinking in which practitioners treat their disciplines as either an exclusive standpoint on reality or reality itself) and the ossification of disciplines through *epistemic apartheid* (the segregation of knowledge into intellectual fortresses). It would be better, he suggests, to 'suspend disciplinarity' by halting tendencies towards centrification when confronted by difficult questions (Gordon, 2006, p.34).

Within this broader North/South politics of knowledge (Pennycook and Makoni, 2020), such disciplinary effects can have an even greater negative effect since applied linguistics has been narrowly constructed around particular Western or Northern frames of knowledge and language. Indeed, the attempt to ascertain the origins of applied linguistics as a discipline frequently falls into the Anglocentric trap of assuming its first use must have been in English, and to have emerged somewhere in the USA just after World War II (McCarthy, 2001). As Oda and Takada (2005) make clear, however, the term 応用言語学 ('*Ouyou gengo gaku*': applied linguistics) was in use in the 1930s in Japan, and we could doubtless trace alternative lineages through other languages and traditions. Just as critical work – critical literacy, pedagogy, discourse analysis, applied linguistics – should not be assumed to have emerged only from contexts of enunciation in English in the Global North (Pennycook, 2021a) (the influence of intellectuals and activists from Brazil, the French Caribbean, India and Senegal among many others are equally if not more important), so applied linguistic origins are surely more diverse than Anglocentric histories admit.

Rather than in disciplinary or interdisciplinary or transdisciplinary terms (often proposed as ways out of the disciplinary bind), it may be useful to think of applied linguistics as temporary assemblages of thought and action that come together at particular moments when language-related concerns need to be addressed. This flexible account of applied linguistic practice takes us not only beyond concerns about its disciplinary status but also beyond the idea of an inter/transdisciplinary applied linguistics. It also helps us see how applied linguistic practices, which may appear diverse, confused or undisciplined, are instead the conjoining of language-oriented projects (research where language, broadly understood, is a central concern), epistemes (broad ideas that cut across the humanities and social sciences) and *matters of concern* (Latour, 2004) (things that matter socially and politically). By talking in terms of *epistemes*, I am drawing in part on Foucault's (1966) notion of the *episteme* as a system of thought that provides the conditions of possibility for discourse, thought and action in different epochs (Pennycook, 2018c). Such an understanding makes it possible to see how work that apparently draws on other disciplines is really engaged in emerging epistemes that cut across areas of the social sciences and humanities.

This framing of language-oriented projects, epistemes and matters of concern can be usefully reworked in light of some of the arguments of this book. My earlier interest in epistemes concerned the ways that when we draw on other domains of work (geography, philosophy, sociology, anthropology, gender studies, cultural studies and so on), we generally do so because these fields have been subject to related epistemological shifts, or what we might call social, discursive, somatic, sensorial, spatial, practice and other so-called turns. When we draw on other fields of study, therefore, it is often precisely because those fields are themselves drawing on related schools of thought. Interest in space, practice or ecology is not a result of a new-found concern with geography, sociology or biology but rather with the *epistemic effects* of these areas putting ideas into play across the humanities and social sciences. When geography took a social turn, for example, it made available an account of space as a social category that was taken up in many areas of the social sciences. Aside from more locally derived turns – such as the multilingual and translingual turns (May, 2014, 2022) – increased levels of interest in space, affect, bodies or the senses are not therefore engagements with disciplinary fields as they are an exploration of how emergent ways of thinking may have implications for language-oriented concerns.

I would now prefer to reframe my earlier view of applied linguistics as an epistemic assemblage (language-oriented projects, epistemes and matters of concern; Pennycook, 2018c) in terms of *language matters of concern, practical theories of language*, and *critical and ethical responses*. The first sharpens the old formulation from Brumfit (1995, p.27) that is so often used to define applied linguistics – 'the theoretical and empirical investigation of real-world problems in which language is a central issue' – in relation to Latour's (2004) *matters of concern*. Latour's point, which is similar to the arguments I made particularly in Chapter 2, is that it is important for critical work to move from *matters of fact* – more mundane matters of scientific forms of knowledge – to 'highly complex, historically situated, richly diverse matters of concern' (Latour, 2004, p.237). Such matters of concern are equally real but have more to do with what matters in people's lives, how things and people come together: 'The critic is not the one who debunks, but the one who assembles' (p.246). Just as the framework I have used in this book has taken up a notion of critical social realism, drawing on a mix of thinkers from Haslanger (2012) to Escobar (2018, 2020), so applied linguistics can usefully make claims on reality (beyond the rather naïve 'real-world problems') so as to ensure that these are both things that matter politically and socially, and that they involve language, broadly understood.

Whereas my concern in the earlier formulation of these ideas (Pennycook, 2021c) was particularly with the effects of broad epistemes – or the different 'turns' that affect the humanities and social sciences – this may be better placed in a secondary position alongside the all-important formulation of practical theories of language. As I suggested in Chapter 3, one such theory is translanguaging (Li Wei, 2018) since it emerged from applied linguistic concerns with bilingual education, raciolinguistic discrimination and language use in homes and the streets. It was doubtless partly affected by the 'multilingual turn' – a particular interest in moving from monolingual forms of analysis in the field, flagged by May (2014) and Ortega (2014) – and the social and social justice turns in second language development (Block, 2003; Ortega, 2019), but its origins were in studies of young people in schools (García and Li Wei, 2014). As it addresses matters of concern to do with language, applied linguistics develops theories of language that address these practical concerns. Linguists committed to other ontologies may not like such emergent approaches, and they certainly need to be treated critically themselves, but they are central to applied linguistic endeavours. A case can similarly be made that *raciolinguistics* (Alim, 2016; Rosa and Flores, 2017) is a practical theory of language, emerging from the need to understand how language and race have been entwined. Practical theories of language do not, of course, need to have labels such as these: many practical theories of language remain unnamed in language education, language policy, translation or language in the workplace. The point is that they derive from and turn back towards practice rather than being named in particular ways.

Just as the critical social realist framework insists not only on relational ontologies and social epistemologies but also on critical forms of evaluation, so applied linguistics as a practical assemblage needs a critical and ethical base for considering these applied linguistic projects. This is where the political and ethical concerns that underpin much of critical applied linguistics (Pennycook, 2021a) come in. Part of my argument here is that critical applied linguistics is not a separate activity, a way of doing applied linguistics hoping to have its own handbook, but rather a set of principles that need to undergird all applied linguistic projects. Once we define our work as taking up linguistic matters of concern, and our theories as practical ones that emerge from real-world contexts, then there is no way of avoiding an engagement with politics and ethics and activism. There is no point in working on minority language education, for example, without an element of advocacy (Grenoble, in press; Nicholas and McCarty, 2022). We cannot uncover linguistic inequalities before the law for Indigenous Australians (Eades, 2010) or African Americans (Baugh, 2018) and do nothing about it. Deaf studies cannot ignore the ways communities and educational possibilities or Deaf ways of being are understood, how Deaf refugees cope or how signing rights can be understood (Kusters, et al., 2017b). White normativity is deeply embedded in practices and ideologies of English language teaching (ELT) (Jenks, 2017; Motha, 2014) and we cannot ethically engage with ELT without addressing questions of race and imperialism. When we try to understand language in the context of precarious labour, we have to appreciate the entanglements of class, gender, migration and the global forces that lead women from poorer countries such as the Philippines into domestic work elsewhere (Lorente, 2017).

Putting these two forms of assemblage-related thinking together – languages as assemblages and applied linguistics as assemblage – creates a space for reassembling applied linguistics as a field open to wide-ranging epistemological approaches to a variety of ontological dispositions on language. This critical position is, as Latour (2004) remarks, a question of (re)assembling rather than debunking. This is a point missed by those who reject ontological curiosity or critical endeavours on the grounds that they undermine orthodox approaches, or are not aligned with traditional political approaches, or are only engaged in debunking exercises, when actually at stake are processes of recreation, reconstitution (Makoni and Pennycook, 2007) or reassemblage, ways of thinking about language that engage with the complexity of people, place and politics. This is to see our role, as Williams (2021, p.1135) suggests, as 'public applied linguists' who 'aim to co-cultivate and co-sustain' collaborations in the pursuit of linguistic justice. This opens up applied linguistics to an ethical engagement with alternative ways of thinking about language and context from the Global South, so that renewal of applied linguistics comes not via other disciplines but rather through alternative forms of knowledge.

6.4 CONCLUSION

I have made a case in the previous section for looking at applied linguistics as a practical assemblage. By this I mean it is not best understood in disciplinary terms, as if we had a clear set of methods, forms of analysis, theoretical stances or objects of interest that define our work. Applied linguistics is rather a pulling-together of different possibilities to investigate language-oriented questions. The focus is on language matters of concern, questions of language policy, language and migration, translation, language in the workplace, language and the law, language education, linguistic landscapes and much more. These are not issues best pursued with concepts of languages as bounded structures but rather with language as it operates in the real world. In order to address such questions, we need ways of thinking about language that, as far as possible, derive from those contexts of interest. Rather than linguistic theories developed for other purposes, we need practical theories of language that are intended to shed light precisely on such matters of concern. As applied linguists, we are often involved in suggesting solutions – through research, education or activism – and we need ways of evaluating what it is we are doing, what the effects may be of such proposals.

Applied Linguistics as Practical Assemblage

All of these come together in the process of assembling and reassembling our frameworks for action.

To have workable ways of thinking about language, I have argued in this book for a view of language assemblages. From a broad perspective, all languages are assemblages: they are the products of social and ideological processes, the combinations of varied elements and interests. There are three slightly different ways of thinking about languages as assemblages: a focus on the ways languages are assembled by their users, a focus on a wider set of semiotic elements that combine together, or an understanding of how language fits into a conglomeration of material artefacts. Such an approach to language obviously works well with the idea of applied linguistics as a practical assemblage. It avoids claims to know what languages are prior to working on particular matters of concern and with those who are invested in their own versions of language. This enables us to take up the question of whose version of language matters, not by putting everything in the hands of the users but equally not by assuming we know better. This can be of particular importance when dealing with communities whose understanding of language may appear very different, who see language as deeply connected to land or water, for example. On these grounds we can make a case that these are practical theories of language, theories that derive from practice.

To make such thinking possible, I argued for a focus not only on ontological questions around language – what languages are – but also for a relational approach to ontologies. This is to suggest that we do not live in a uniform world but rather in multiple worlds, or that there is not just one thing called language that is cut up into different languages, but rather different language-things. This shifts the focus away from epistemological relativism – there is one world that we cut up differently according to cultural or ideological patterns – and instead emphasizes ontological plurality. Different approaches to language, therefore, are not just different forms of knowledge about the same thing, but potentially ways of addressing different things. Thus an ontological commitment to language as structure is very different from commitments to language as practice – what people do with linguistic resources – or language assemblages. We can then focus more clearly on the social nature of forms of knowledge – our epistemologies are forged in social relations – as well as the political and ethical implications of our ways of knowing. Framing language and applied linguistics in these terms allows for a flexibility to do what we do but also an accountability to the people we work with.

Suggested readings

CHAPTER 1: WHY LANGUAGE ASSEMBLAGES?

Li Wei (2018). Translanguaging as a practical theory of language. *Applied Linguistics*, 39(1), 9–30.

Wee, L. (2021). *Posthumanist world Englishes*. Cambridge: Cambridge University Press.

CHAPTER 2: LANGUAGE, KNOWLEDGE, MYTHS AND BEING

Harris, R. (1981). *The language myth*. London: Duckworth.

Haslanger, S. (2012). *Resisting reality: Social construction and social critique*. Oxford: Oxford University Press.

Holbraad, M. and Pedersen, M. A. (2017). *The ontological turn: An anthropological exposition*. Cambridge: Cambridge University Press.

Rymes, B. (2020). *How we talk about language: Exploring citizen sociolinguistics*. Cambridge: Cambridge University Press.

CHAPTER 3: STRUCTURES AND PRACTICES

Joseph, J. and Newmeyer, F. (2012). All languages are equally complex: The rise and fall of a consensus. *Historiographia Linguistica*, 39(2/3), 341–68.

Ortega, L. (2018). Ontologies of language, second language acquisition, and world Englishes. *World Englishes*, 37, 64–79.

Otheguy, R., García, O. and Reid, W. (2018). A translanguaging view of the linguistic system of bilinguals. *Applied Linguistics Review*, 10(4), 625–51.

Zhou, F. (2020). *Models of the human in twentieth-century linguistic theories: System, order, creativity*. Cham: Springer.

CHAPTER 4: LINGUISTIC, SEMIOTIC AND SOCIOMATERIAL ASSEMBLAGES

Gurney, L. and Demuro, E. (2019). Tracing new ground, from language to languaging, and from languaging to assemblages: Rethinking languaging through the multilingual and ontological turns. *International Journal of Multilingualism*, 19(3), 305–24. https://doi.org/10.1080/14790718.2019.1689982.

Pennycook, A. (2017). Translanguaging and semiotic assemblages. *International Journal of Multilingualism*, 14(3), 269–82. https://doi.org/10.1080/14790718.2017.1315810.

Toohey, K. (2019). The onto-epistemologies of New Materialism: Implications for applied linguistics pedagogies and research. *Applied Linguistics*, 40, 937–56.

Tsing, A. L. (2015). *The mushroom at the end of the world: On the possibility of life in capitalist ruins*. Princeton, NJ: Princeton University Press.

CHAPTER 5: OTHER LANGUAGE ONTOLOGIES

Henne-Ochoa, R., Elliot-Groves, E., Meek, B. and Rogoff, B. (2020). Pathways forward for indigenous language reclamation: Engaging indigenous epistemology and learning by observing and pitching in to family and community endeavors. *The Modern Language Journal*, 104(2), 481–93.

Leonard, W. (2021). Toward an anti-racist linguistic anthropology: An Indigenous response to white supremacy. *Journal of Linguistic Anthropology*, 31(2), 218–37.

Ndhlovu, F. and Makalela, L. (2021). *Decolonising multilingualism in Africa: Recentering silenced voices from the Global South*. Bristol: Multilingual Matters.

Pennycook, A. and Makoni, S. (2020). *Innovations and challenges in applied linguistics from the Global South*. London: Routledge.

CHAPTER 6: APPLIED LINGUISTICS AS PRACTICAL ASSEMBLAGE

Kramsch, C. (2021). *Language as symbolic power*. Cambridge: Cambridge University Press.

Latour, B. (2004). Why has critique run out of steam? From matters of fact to matters of concern. *Critical Inquiry*, 30(2), 225–48.

Pennycook, A. (2018). Applied linguistics as epistemic assemblage. *AILA Review*, 31, 113–34.

Glossary

Assemblage attempts to understand the world not so much in terms of its separable parts (humans, languages, animals, objects and so on) but rather in terms of their inseparability, a move from autonomy to **entanglements**. It emphasizes the dynamic effects of the conjunctions of different human and non-human elements. See also **language, semiotic and sociomaterial assemblages**. See DeLanda (2016); Tsing (2015).

Bilingual advantage is a term used to suggest that speaking two languages brings certain cognitive advantages. While useful as an argument in favour of bilingualism, the focus on enumerable languages (bilingualism) and cognition overlooks the situated language practices involved. Looking at **distributed cognition** and local language practices, by contrast, makes it possible to see how linguistic resources, cognition and social disparities interact. See Pennycook and Otsuji (2018); Sanches de Oliveira and Bullock Oliveira (2022).

Citizen sociolinguistics focuses on everyday language users and their views on language. Arguing that linguists' views on language should only be one of many voices on language matters, the weak version of citizen sociolinguistics, closer to **folk linguistics**, looks at ordinary people's views on language, while a strong version, following citizen science, puts the analysis in the hands of the people themselves. See Rymes (2020); Svendsen (2018).

Code-switching is the standard linguistic term for mixing two languages. Although the original use of the word *code* was intended to avoid assumptions about languages, the **ortholinguistic** tendencies of linguistics have shifted its meaning from a more open-ended fusion of semiotic codes to a more restricted sense of alternating between languages. Some see it as compatible with **translanguaging**, while others see them as distinct. See Auer (1995); Li Wei (2018).

Creole exceptionalism refers to the assumption that creole languages are an exceptional and abnormal class of languages distinct from all other languages. Critiqued as *one of the most dangerous myths of linguistics*, it has been suggested that creoles are a racial rather than a linguistic category. See DeGraff (2005).

Glossary

Critical constructivism in sociolinguistics, sometimes also called *new sociolinguistics*, describes a shift away from earlier assumptions about whole languages (sometimes called Fishmanian sociolinguistics) in favour of more critical approaches based on language as a social practice, in which speakers draw on a variety of linguistic resources to communicate. See Bell (2014).

Critical realism is a line of thinking often associated with the work of Roy Bhaskar that seeks to combine an account of external reality with an appreciation of the ways reality is understood. Bhaskar's *reclaiming reality* can be contrasted with Haslanger's *resisting reality* in **critical social realism**. See Bhaskar (1989); Block (2022).

Critical social realism, as developed by Haslanger, focuses on the ways that gender, race or language are **social constructions**, that is to say they are produced through social relations. Resisting reality, from this perspective, does not suggest a move against the idea of reality itself so much as a recognition that such socially produced categories can also be opposed and changed. See Haslanger (2012).

Decolonization aims to redress the colonial modes of thought that have outlasted colonialism as a political and economic system. Decolonization projects challenge Western/Northern ways of thinking (about language, for example) and seek alternative forms of knowledge. See Leonard (2017); Mufwene (2020).

Deconstructivism is a term from architecture referring to an orientation away from typical box-shaped buildings towards a more variable set of structures. It has been used in some recent work opposed to aspects of **translanguaging** to refer to **critical constructivism** in sociolinguistics. See MacSwan 2022a.

Disinvention emphasizes that languages do not exist as pre-formed entities in the world, but are rather the inventions of social, cultural and political movements. Such **social constructions** of language are nevertheless real but can be also resisted and ultimately reconstituted as part of a process of **decolonization**. See Makoni and Pennycook (2007).

Distributed cognition, generally associated with the work of Edwin Hutchins, approaches cognition ('in the wild') as involving the world around us, not in representational terms (language and thought reflect reality) but as part of an ecosystem of thinking and action. From this point of view ethnography is the only useful way to study cognition. It has also been developed in relation to **distributed language**. See Hutchins (1995).

Distributed language, in some accounts, combines **distributed cognition** and **integrational linguistics**. More generally, it is an approach to language that focuses on the **entanglements** of language with the world around, suggesting that language is not so much located in human minds as spread across a social and physical environment. See Cowley (2012).

Entanglements is often connected to the idea of **assemblages** and points to the many interconnections between people, language, things and places. While **assemblages** make central the ways things come together in a dynamic configuration, entanglements point to the many connections among different entities. See Pennycook (2020); Toohey (2019).

Episteme is a term in philosophy referring to knowledge or understanding (from which **epistemology** derives). Foucault used the term in a particular way to describe forms of knowledge that in a certain historical era provide the *conditions of possibility* for other ways of thinking. In this book it is used in the term **epistemic assemblage** to describe the ways particular sets of ideas come together in a field such as applied linguistics. See Foucault (1966); Pennycook (2018b).

Epistemology is the study of knowledge and is often contrasted in Western philosophy with **ontology**, the study of being. Some have questioned this distinction between knower and known. This book emphasizes the social nature of epistemology, particularly in relation to **social construction**. See Sveinsdóttir (2015).

Error correction here refers not to correcting language errors but to a position that assumes that providing better information can overcome mistaken **language ideologies**. This fails to engage with social and political contexts and people's beliefs and desires. See Lewis (2018).

Extractivism, in its broadest sense, is a critique of colonial and capitalist modes of production that extracted resources from colonial possessions. Linguistic extractivism refers to ways linguists have plundered languages of the **Global South** in the service of Northern theories of language. See Agha (2007b); Pennycook (2024).

First knowledges refer to *Indigenous cosmologies* or the forms of knowledge of First Nation people in different parts of the world. Such knowledge should not be seen as traditional so much as an evolving set of ideas about the world developed both separate from and in relation to colonial modernity. See Neale (2021).

Folk linguistics is sometimes used negatively to refer to people's inappropriate views about language but is also used in a more positive sense to acknowledge the importance of everyday views about language. It sometimes overlaps with, but can be distinguished from, **citizen sociolinguistics**. By investigating local understandings of language it can also become a tool for **decolonization**. See Albury (2017); Preston (1996).

Glossary

Global North and South are a more recent framing of older concepts such as First, Western or developed (Euro-American) and Third or majority world (the rest). They are geopolitical (to do with global inequalities) rather than geographical terms, and in the form of *Southern theory* are linked to the current emphasis on **decolonization**. See Deumert and Makoni (2023); Pennycook and Makoni (2020).

Idiolect refers to the rather implausible idea of an individual language variety. Linked to ideas such as competence, it is the starting point for some versions of linguistics: everyone has their own internal linguistic system. More social accounts of language reject this kind of *methodological individualism* and suggest that language is a social capacity that people engage with. See Ramberg and Røyneland (2024).

Indigenous multilingualisms are the different kinds of situated language practices found in different Indigenous communities. The phrase points to the plurality of *multilingualism*: it is not so much the use of several different languages but a set of diverse semiotic practices. See Makoni and Pennycook (2024); Vaughan and Singer (2018).

Indigenous standpoint concerns ways of expressing Indigenous concerns from within the lived experience of Indigenous lives. It is neither a mere reflection of experience nor some kind of hidden wisdom based on identity but rather a complex articulation of concepts from **First Knowledge** perspectives in relation to other forms of knowledge. See Nakata (2007).

Integrational linguistics is an approach to language based around the work of Roy Harris, who argued that the idea of languages as fixed and consensual codes though which people communicate was a myth. The segregational account of different linguistic components as well as the idea of languages themselves are all second-order abstractions compared to first-order communicative activity. See Harris (1981, 1998).

Language assemblages, or language as an assemblage, suggest that languages are assembled through varied experiences with language in the world. Languages are not pregiven entities that are used but rather sets of communicative possibilities that are assembled by speakers from their own histories of linguistic activity. See Wee (2021).

Language ideological assemblages point to the ways in which complexes of beliefs about language interact with each other to change **language ideologies** and linguistic practices, suggesting that languages cannot be understood without adequate consideration of the **entanglements** of people, ideology, place and material arrangements. See Kroskrity (2021).

Language ideologies (also linguistic ideology) refer to beliefs about languages and language use held by various people and communities and influenced by cultural and political interests. For some they are an important part of the *total linguistic fact*. See Blommaert (2017).

Language reclamation is a term preferred to some of the older terms such as *language maintenance*, *revival* or *revitalization*, since it suggests a process of reclaiming knowledge about language as well as remaking a language, acknowledging that such projects do not bring language back from the dead so much as produce something new in the process. See Leonard (2017).

Linguistic worldview refers to a common perception that doing things in different languages leads to different ways of thinking and feeling. In its extreme version, it suggests that a whole worldview is tied up in a language, and that languages therefore limit and even determine how we think and act. More sensible approaches ground the effects of language in local social and cultural practices. See Evans (2010).

Materialism, not in the negative sense of consumerism, denotes an interest in how the material world may be related to less obviously material things such as language. Unlike old forms of materialist thinking that emphasized socioeconomic relations, *new materialism* takes the role of objects and artefacts more seriously and asks what roles they play in our lives (or what role we play in theirs). See Barad (2007).

Ontological curiosity, as opposed to ontological naivety, takes the question of how languages are constituted seriously. Such a position does not take the name of a variety at face value and does not see ontological questions as threatening. See Wee (2021).

Ontological turn refers to a move in anthropology to suggest that instead of assuming an external reality that is cut up in different ways culturally or ideologically (a *multiculturalist* perspective), it is more important to engage with the possibility that we may be dealing with different things (a *multinaturalist* perspective). See Holbraad and Pedersen (2017).

Ontology, in philosophy, is the study of being – what it means to exist, what kinds of thing exist and how these things can be related and categorised. It is usually contrasted in Western philosophy with **epistemology**, the study of knowledge. Some have questioned this distinction and its implication that the knower is separable from the known. See Demuro and Gurney (2021); Seargeant (2010).

Ortholinguistic tendencies refer to the propensity in linguistics (as in other fields) to fall back on linguistic orthodoxies, so that concepts with a more open potential, such as *code* or *repertoire*, are considered in terms of languages or competencies as traditionally theorised. See Pennycook (2016).

Glossary

Posthumanism refers to a broad set of ideas that can range from a rejection of humanist ideas (anti- or post-humanism) to an interest in relations among humans and technology (transhumanism) or a concern in understanding the role of humans in relation to the rest of the planet in more equitable terms. See Braidotti (2013); Pennycook (2018a).

Raciolinguistics focuses on race and its relation to language: how language is used to construct race and how ideas of race influence language and language use. Of significant concern are the meanings and implications of speech from a racialized subject. See Alim (2016); Rosa and Flores (2017).

Register has evolved in sociolinguistics from social (as opposed to regional) ways of using language (such as legalese or sport commentary) to broader semiotic styles that may occur across languages. Asif Agha's notion of *enregisterment* – how a register is perceived as such – has reinvigorated the term in recent years. See Agha (2007a); Pennycook (2018c).

Relational ontologies suggest that rather than one, external world, there are multiple forms of existence in relation to each other. Instead of insisting, for example, that there is one thing called language that is subdivided into languages, this position suggests that different languages may not all be the same thing. See Escobar (2018); Hauck and Heurich (2018).

Repertoire shifted from its early use to refer to the totality of linguistic forms available to a community to a narrower sense of an individual's linguistic resources. In the *new sociolinguistics* it has come to include a wider set of communicative and semiotic options and to embrace contexts beyond the individual, as in ideas such as **spatial repertoires**. See Pennycook (2018c); Rymes (2014).

Semiotic assemblages are combinations of different semiotic resources – linguistic, sensory, spatial, artefactual, historical – that come together at particular moments in time and space. This makes it possible to see how linguistic elements can be part of a much wider set of semiotic processes where the whole is greater than the parts. See Pennycook (2017); Sharma (2021).

Social construction is a position that emphasizes the role of sociality in what we take to be real. It is often misunderstood as implying that something is a fiction whereas what it actually suggests is that many realities are social. Gender and race are social constructions, that is to say very real, but only insofar as we take them to be so. It is therefore possible to resist social constructions, such as language, race and gender. See Haslanger (2012).

Sociomaterial assemblages are material arrangements that involve language. Rather than a primary focus on language or semiotics in an

assemblage, the focus here derives from the turn towards **materialism** and the insistence that language elements are both material in themselves and part of wider groupings of material elements. See Hovens (2023); Thorne et al. (2021).

Spatial repertoire captures the ways that **repertoires** are not so much a set of individual or community resources as a set of possibilities assembled in time and space. The idea makes it possible to consider what is linguistically or semiotically available in spatial rather than cognitive terms. See Canagarajah (2018); Pennycook and Otsuji (2014).

Structuralism is a broad epistemological movement that influenced the social sciences in the twentieth century. It focused on structures (of language, culture or society) as internally coherent and autonomous entities that could be separated from the world around them. See Harland (1987); Newmeyer (1986).

Translanguaging focuses on the language practices of plurilingual people and communities and educational approaches that engage with such practices. It describes an ideological position on language, a practical theory of language and a range of pedagogical practices. See García and Li Wei (2014).

References

Adkins, B. (2015). *Deleuze and Guattari's* A Thousand Plateaus: *A critical introduction and guide*. Edinburgh: Edinburgh University Press.

Agha, A. (2007a). *Language and social relations*. Cambridge: Cambridge University Press.

Agha, A. (2007b). The object called 'language' and the subject of linguistics. *Journal of English Linguistics*, 35(3), 217–35.

Ahearn, L. (2001). Language and agency. *Annual Review of Anthropology*, 30, 109–37.

Ahner, H. (1963). *Söhne des Ikarus*. Berlin: Verlag Neues Leben.

Albury, N. J. (2016). Defining Māori language revitalisation: A project in folk linguistics. *Journal of Sociolinguistics*, 20, 287–311. https://doi.org/10.1111/josl.12183.

Albury, N. J. (2017). How folk linguistic methods can support critical sociolinguistics. *Lingua*, 199, 36–49.

Alim, H. S. (2016). Introducing raciolinguistics: Racing language and languaging race in hyperracial times. In H. Samy Alim, J. Rickford and A. Ball (Eds.), *Raciolinguistics: How language shapes our ideas about race* (pp. 1–30). New York: Oxford University Press.

Althusser, L. (1971). *Lenin and philosophy and other essays*. London: New Left Books.

Armitage, J. (2022). Desert participants guide the research in Central Australia. In K. Heugh, C. Stroud, K. Taylor-Leech and P. De Costa (Eds.), *A sociolinguistics of the south* (pp. 215–32). London: Routledge.

Armstrong, N. and Mackenzie, I. E. (2013). *Standardization, ideology and linguistics*. Basingstoke: Palgrave Macmillan.

Aronin, L. and Ó Laoire, M. (2013). The material culture of multilingualism: Moving beyond the linguistic landscape. *International Journal of Multilingualism*, 10(3), 225–35.

Auer, P. (1995). The pragmatics of code-switching: A sequential approach. In L. Milroy and P. Muysken (Eds.), *One speaker, two languages* (pp. 115–35). Cambridge: Cambridge University Press.

Auer, P. (2022). 'Translanguaging' or 'doing languages'? Multilingual practices and the notion of 'codes'. In J. MacSwan (Ed.), *Multilingual perspectives on translanguaging* (pp. 131–59). Bristol: Multilingual Matters.

Austin, J. L. (1962). *How to do things with words: The William James Lectures delivered at Harvard University in 1955*. Oxford: Clarendon Press.

Bade, D. (2021). Edward said, Roy asked, and the peasant responded: Reflections on peasants, popular culture, and intellectuals. In S. Makoni, D. Verity and A. Kaiper-Marquez (Eds.), *Integrational linguistics and philosophy of language in the Global South* (pp. 18–29). New York: Routledge.

Baldwin, J. (1972). *No name on the street*. New York: Dial Press.

Barad, K. (2007). *Meeting the universe halfway: Quantum physics and the entanglement of matter and meaning*. Durham, NC: Duke University Press.

Bauer, L. and Trudgill, P. (1998a). Introduction. In Bauer, L. and Trudgill, P. (Eds.), *Language myths* (pp. xv–xviii). London: Penguin.

Bauer, L. and Trudgill, P. (Eds.) (1998b). *Language myths*. London: Penguin.

Baugh, J. (2018). *Linguistics in pursuit of justice*. Cambridge: Cambridge University Press.

Bawaka Country including Burarrwanga, L., Ganambarr, R., Ganambarr-Stubbs, M., et al. (2022). Songspirals bring country into existence: Singing more-than-human and relational creativity. *Qualitative Inquiry*, 28(5), 435–47.

Bell, A. (2014). *The guidebook to sociolinguistics*. Oxford: Wiley-Blackwell.

Bennett, J. (2010). *Vibrant matter: A political ecology of things*. Durham, NC: Duke University Press.

Bennett, J. and Khan, G. (2009). Agency, nature and emergent properties: An interview with Jane Bennett. *Contemporary Political Theory*, 8, 90–105.

Bernstein, B. (2000). *Pedagogy, symbolic control and identity: Theory, research, critique* (2nd edition). London: Taylor & Francis.

Berson, J. (2015). *Computable bodies: Instrumented life and the human somatic niche*. London: Bloomsbury.

Bessire, L. and Bond, D. (2014). Ontological anthropology and the deferral of critique. *American Ethnologist*, 41, 440–56.

Bessone, M. (2022). Fanon's critical humanism: Understanding humanity through its 'misfires'. *European Journal of Philosophy*, 30(4), 1583–90.

Bhaskar, R. (1989). *Reclaiming reality*. London: Verso.

Bhatt, R. and Bolonyai, A. (2022). Codeswitching and its terminological Other – translanguaging. In J. MacSwan (Ed.), *Multilingual perspectives on translanguaging* (pp. 154–80). Bristol: Multilingual Matters.

Bickerton, D. (1995). *Language and human behaviour*. Seattle, WA: Washington University Press.

Bird, S. (2020). Decolonising speech and language technology. In D. Scott, N. Bel and C. Q. Zong (Eds.), *Proceedings of the 28th International Conference on Computational Linguistics* (pp. 3504–19). Barcelona: International Committee on Computational Linguistics. https://aclanthology.org/2020.coling-main.313/.

Blackledge, A. and Creese, A. (2010). *Multilingualism: A critical perspective*. London: Continuum.

Blackledge, A. and Creese, A. (2014). Heteroglossia as practice and pedagogy. In Blackledge, A. and Creese, A. (Eds.), *Heteroglossia as practice and pedagogy*. (Educational Linguistics series) (pp. 1-20). Dordrecht: Springer.

Blenkinsop, S. and Fettes, M. (2020). Land, language and listening: The transformations that can flow from acknowledging Indigenous Land. *Journal of Philosophy of Education*, 54(4), 1033-46.

Block, D. (2003). *The social turn in second language acquisition*. New York: Routledge.

Block, D. (2022). *Innovations and challenges in identity research*. London: Routledge.

Blommaert, J. (2006). Language ideology. In K. Brown (Ed.), *Encyclopaedia of language and linguistics* (Volume 6, pp. 510-22). Amsterdam: Elsevier.

Blommaert, J. (2010). *The sociolinguistics of globalization*. Cambridge: Cambridge University Press.

Blommaert, J. (2013). *Ethnography, superdiversity and linguistic landscapes: Chronicles of complexity*. Bristol: Multilingual Matters.

Blommaert, J. (2015). Meaning as a nonlinear effect: The birth of cool. *AILA Review*, 28, 7-27.

Blommaert, J. (2017). Chronotopes, scales and complexity in the study of language in society. In K. Arnaut, M. Sif Karrebaek, M. Spotti and J. Blommaert (Eds.), *Engaging superdiversity: Recombining spaces, times and language practices* (pp. 47-62). Bristol: Multilingual Matters.

Blommaert, J. and Backus, A. (2013). Super diverse repertoires and the individual. In I. de Saint-Georges and J.-J. Weber (Eds.), *Multilingualism and multimodality: Current challenges for educational studies* (pp. 11-32). Rotterdam: Sense Publishers.

Bodkin-Andrews, G. and Carlson, B. (2016). The legacy of racism and Indigenous Australian identity within education. *Race Ethnicity and Education*, 19(4), 784-807.

Bogost, I. (2012). *Alien phenomenology, or what it's like to be a thing*. Minneapolis, MN: University of Minnesota Press.

Bourdieu, P. (1977). *Outline of a theory of practice*. Cambridge: Cambridge University Press.

Braidotti, R. (2013). *The posthuman*. Cambridge: Polity.

Branson, J. and Miller, D. (2007). Beyond 'language': Linguistic imperialism, sign languages and linguistic anthropology. In S. Makoni and A. Pennycook (Eds.), *Disinvention and reconstituting languages* (pp. 90-116). Clevedon: Multilingual Matters.

Broadhurst, K. (2020). The death and subsequent revival of the Cornish language. *The Open Review*, 6, 20-7.

Brumfit, C. (1995). Teacher professionalism and research. In: G. Cook and B. Seidlhofer (Eds.), *Principles and practice in applied linguistics*, (pp. 27-42). Oxford: Oxford University Press.

Bucholtz, M. and Hall, K. (2008). All of the above: New coalitions in sociocultural linguistics. *Journal of Sociolinguistics*, 12(4), 401-31.

Bucholtz, M. and Hall, K. (2016). Embodied sociolinguistics. In N. Coupland (Ed), *Sociolinguistics: Theoretical debates* (pp. 173-97). Cambridge: Cambridge University Press.

Burkette, A. (2021). Connections and interdisciplinarity: Linguistic Atlas Project data from an assemblage perspective. In A. Burkette and T. Warhol (Eds.), *Crossing borders, making connections: Interdisciplinarity in linguistics* (pp. 99-110). Berlin: Mouton de Gruyter.

Calvet, L. J. (2006). *Towards an ecology of world languages* (Trans. A. Brown – *Pour une écologie des langues du monde*). Cambridge: Polity.

Cameron, D. (1995). *Verbal hygiene: The politics of language*. London: Routledge.

Canagarajah, S. (2013). *Translingual practice: Global Englishes and cosmopolitan relations*. London: Routledge.

Canagarajah, S. (2018). Translingual practice as spatial repertoires: Expanding the paradigm beyond structuralist orientations. *Applied Linguistics*, 39(1), 31-54.

Canagarajah, S. (2021). Materialising semiotic repertoires: Challenges in the interactional analysis of multilingual communication. *International Journal of Multilingualism*, 18(2), 206-25. https://doi.org/10.1080/14790718.2021.1877293.

Canut, C. (2021). Agencements et indexicalités: Signifier la subjectivation politique. *Langage et société*, 172, 95-123.

Cavanaugh, J. R. and Shankar, S. (2021). Language and materiality in global capitalism. In A. Burkette and T. Warhol (Eds.), *Crossing borders, making connections: Interdisciplinarity in linguistics* (pp. 169-90). Berlin: Mouton de Gruyter.

Chakrabarty, D. (2000). *Provincializing Europe: Postcolonial thought and historical difference*. Princeton, NJ: Princeton University Press.

Chandler, D. and Reid, J. (2020). Becoming Indigenous: The 'speculative turn' in anthropology and the (re)colonisation of indigeneity. *Postcolonial Studies*, 23(4), 485-504.

Chat (2023). https://chat.openai.com/.

Chilisa, B. (2011). *Indigenous research methodologies*. New York: Sage.

Chomsky, N. (1957). *Syntactic structures*. The Hague: Mouton.

Connell, R. (2007). *Southern theory: The global dynamics of knowledge in social science*. Crows Nest, NSW: Allen & Unwin.

Copeland, J. (Ed.) (2004). *The essential Turing: Seminal writings in computing, logic, philosophy, artificial intelligence, and artificial life plus the secrets of enigma*. Oxford: Oxford University Press.

Corder, S. P. (1973). *Introducing applied linguistics*. Harmondsworth: Penguin.

Cornips, L. (2022). The animal turn in postcolonial linguistics: The interspecies greeting of the dairy cow. *Journal of Postcolonial Linguistics*, 6, 209-31.

References

Cornips, L. (In press). Getting to know the dairy cow: An inclusive and self-reflexive sociolinguistics in multispecies emotional encounters. In C. Cutler, U. Røyneland and Z. Vrzić (Eds.), *Language activism: The role of scholars in linguistic reform and social change*. Cambridge: Cambridge University Press.

Costa, J., de Korne, H. and Lane, P. (2018). Standardising minority languages: Reinventing peripheral languages in the 21st century. In P. Lane, J. Costa and H. De Korne (Eds.), *Standardizing minority languages: Competing ideologies of authority and authenticity in the global periphery* (pp. 1–23). New York: Routledge.

Coupland, N. (2007). *Style: Language variation and identity*. Cambridge: Cambridge University Press.

Course, M. (2018). Words beyond meaning in Mapuche language ideology. *Language & Communication*, 63, 9–14.

Couzens, V. and Eira, C. (2014). Meeting point: Parameters for the study of revival languages. In P. Austin and J. Sallabank (Eds.), *Endangered languages: Beliefs and ideologies in language documentation and revitalisation* (pp. 313–33). Oxford: Oxford University Press.

Cowley, S. (2012). Distributed language. In S. Cowley (Ed.), *Distributed language* (pp. 1–14). Amsterdam: John Benjamins.

Cowley, S. (2019). The return of *languaging*: Toward a new ecolinguistics. *Chinese Semiotic Studies*, 15(4), 483–512.

Crowley, T. (1996). *Language in history: Theories and texts*. London: Routledge.

Cummins, J. (2021). Translanguaging – a critical analysis of theoretical claims. In P. Juvonen and M. Källkvist (Eds.), *Pedagogical translanguaging: Theoretical, methodological and empirical perspectives* (pp. 7–36). Bristol: Multilingual Matters.

Cunningham, C. (2020). Beliefs about 'good English' in schools. In C. J. Hall and R. Wicaksono (Eds.), *Ontologies of English. Reconceptualising the language for learning, teaching, and assessment* (pp. 142–61). Cambridge: Cambridge University Press.

Cushing, I. (2022a). *Standards, stigma, surveillance: Raciolinguistic ideologies and England's schools*. London: Palgrave.

Cushing, I. (2022b). Word rich or word poor? Deficit discourses, raciolinguistic ideologies and the resurgence of the 'word gap' in England's education policy. *Critical Inquiry in Language Studies*. https://doi.org/10.1080/15427587.2022.2102014.

Cushing, I. and Snell, J. (2023). The (white) ears of Ofsted: A raciolinguistic perspective on the listening practices of the schools inspectorate. *Language in Society*, 52, 363–86.

Cutler, C. (In press). Labeling ethnolects: Challenges and potentials. In C. Cutler, U. Røyneland and Z. Vrzic (Eds.), *Language activism: The role of scholars in linguistic reform and social change*. Cambridge: Cambridge University Press.

Darwin, C. (1872). *The expression of the emotions in man and animals*. London: John Murray.
Dasgupta, P. (1997). Foreword. In L. Khubchandani, *Revisioning boundaries: A plurilingual ethos* (pp. 11–29). New Delhi: Sage.
Davies, A. (1999). *An introduction to applied linguistics: From theory to practice*. Edinburgh: Edinburgh University Press.
De Certeau, M. (1984). *The practice of everyday life* (S. Rendall, trans.). Berkeley, CA: University of California Press.
De Freitas, E. and Curinga, M. X. (2015). New materialist approaches to the study of language and identity: Assembling the posthuman subject. *Curriculum Inquiry*, 45, 249–65.
de la Cedana, M. and Blaser, M. (2018). Pluriverse: Proposals for a world of many worlds. In M. de la Cedana and M. Blaser (Eds.), *A world of many worlds* (pp. 1–22). Durham, NC: Duke University Press.
de Souza, L. M. (2009). The ecology of writing among the Kashinawá: Indigenous multimodality in Brazil. In A. S. Canagarajah (Ed.), *Reclaiming the local in language policy and practice* (pp. 73–95). Mahwah, NJ: Lawrence Erlbaum.
de Souza, L. M. (2017). Epistemic diversity, lazy reason, and ethical translation in postcolonial contexts. The case of Indigenous educational policy in Brazil. In C. Kerfoot and K. Hyltenstam (Eds.), *Entangled discourses: South–North orders of visibility* (pp. 189–208). New York: Routledge.
DeGraff, M. (2005). Linguists' most dangerous myth: The fallacy of Creole exceptionalism. *Language in Society*, 34(4), 533–91.
DeGraff, M. (2019). Foreword. In D. Macedo (Ed.), *Decolonizing foreign language education: The misteaching of English and other colonial languages* (pp. ix–xxxii). New York: Routledge.
DeLanda, M. (2016). *Assemblage theory*. Edinburgh: Edinburgh University Press.
Deleuze, G. and Guattari, F. (1987). *A thousand plateaus: Capitalism and schizophrenia*. (Trans. B. Massumi). Minneapolis, MN: University of Minnesota Press.
Deloria, V. and Wildcat, D. (2001). *Power and place: Indian education in America*. Golden, CO: Fulcrum Resources.
Demuro, E. and Gurney, L. (2021). Languages/languaging as world-making: The ontological bases of language. *Language Sciences*, 83, 1–13.
Descola, P. (2013). *Beyond nature and culture*. (Trans. J. Lloyd). Chicago, IL: University of Chicago Press.
Deumert, A. and Makoni, S. (Eds.) (2023) *From Southern Theory to decolonizing sociolinguistics: Voices, questions and alternatives*. Bristol: Multilingual Matters.
Deumert, A., Storch, A. and Shepherd, A. (Eds.) (2020). *Colonial and decolonial linguistics: Knowledges and epistemes*. Oxford: Oxford University Press.
Deutscher, G. (2011). *Through the language glass: Why the world looks different in other languages*. London: Arrow Books.

Diagne, S. B. (2021). *Le fagot de ma mémoire*. Paris: Philippe Rey.
Dias, J. (2019). Reshuffling conceptual cards: What counts as language in Lowland Indigenous South America. In M. Guilherme and L. M. Menezes de Souza (Eds.), *Glocal languages and critical language awareness: The South answers back* (pp. 90–103). London: Routledge.
Disbray, S., Plummer, R. and Martin, B. (2020). Languages ideologies and practice from the land and the classroom. *Modern Language Review*, 104, 519–25.
Dixon, R. M. W. (1997). *The rise and fall of languages*. Cambridge: Cambridge University Press.
Dixon, R. M. W. (2016). *Are some languages better than others?* Oxford: Oxford University Press.
Duchêne, A. and Heller, M. (Eds.) (2007). *Discourses of endangerment: Ideology and interest in the defence of languages* (pp. 268–85). London: Continuum.
Eades, D. (2010). *Sociolinguistics and the legal process*. Bristol: Multilingual Matters.
Eckert, P. (2018). *Meaning and linguistic variation: The third wave in sociolinguistics*. Cambridge: Cambridge University Press.
Edwards, J. (2012). *Multilingualism: Understanding linguistic diversity*. London: Continuum.
Ellis, N. (2011). The emergence of language as a complex adaptive system. In J. Simpson (Ed.), *The Routledge handbook of applied linguistics* (pp. 654–67). Abingdon: Routledge.
Enfield, N. (2017). Distribution of agency. In N. Enfield and P. Kockelman (Eds.), *Distributed agency* (pp. 9–14). Oxford: Oxford University Press.
Enfield, N. and Kockelman, P. (2017). Editors' preface. In N. Enfield and P. Kockelman (Eds.), *Distributed agency* (pp. xi–xvi). Oxford: Oxford University Press.
Enfield, N. and Sidnell, J. (2017). *The concept of action*. Cambridge: Cambridge University Press.
Ennis, G. (2020). Linguistic natures: Method, media, and language reclamation in the Ecuadorian Amazon. *Journal of Linguistic Anthropology*, 30(3), 304–25.
Escobar, A. (2016). Thinking-feeling with the Earth: Territorial struggles and the ontological dimension of the epistemologies of the South. *Revista de Antropología Iberoamericana*, 11(1), 11–32.
Escobar, A. (2018). *Designs for the pluriverse: Radical interdependence, autonomy, and the making of worlds*. Durham, NC: Duke University Press.
Escobar, A. (2020). *Pluriversal politics: The real and the possible*. Durham, NC: Duke University Press.
Estival, D., Farris, C. and Molesworth, B. (2016). *Aviation English: A lingua franca for pilots and air traffic controllers*. London: Routledge.
Evans, N. (1998). Aborigines speak a primitive language. In L. Bauer and P. Trudgill (Eds.), *Language myths* (pp. 159–68). London: Penguin.

Evans, N. (2010). *Dying words: Endangered languages and what they have to tell us.* Oxford: Wiley-Blackwell.

Evans, N. and Levinson, S. (2009). The myth of language universals: Language diversity and its importance for cognitive science. *Behavioral and Brain Sciences*, 32, 429–92.

Evans, V. (2014). *The language myth: Why language is not an instinct.* Cambridge: Cambridge University Press.

Fabian, J. (1983). *Time and the Other: How anthropology makes its object.* New York: Columbia University Press.

Fairclough, N. (2003). *Analysing discourse: Textual analysis for social research.* London: Routledge.

Fanon, F. (1952). *Peau noire, masques blancs.* Paris: Éditions du Seuil.

Fanon, F. (1961). *Les damnés de la terre.* Paris: Gallimard.

Faraclas, N. (2020). On colonization and 'awesome materiality': A commentary. In A. Deumert, A. Storch and N. Shepherd (Eds.), *Colonial and decolonial linguistics: Knowledge and epistemes* (pp. 77–83). Oxford: Oxford University Press.

Figueiredo, E. H. D. and Martinez, J. (2019). The locus of enunciation as a way to confront epistemological racism and decolonize scholarly knowledge. *Applied Linguistics*, 42(2), 355–59.

Finkelstein, S. and Netz, H. (2023). Challenging folk-linguistics: Grammatical and spelling variation in students' writing in Hebrew on WhatsApp and in essays. *Applied Linguistics*, 1–22. https://doi.org/10.1093/applin/amac072.

Finnegan, R. (2015). *Where is language? An anthropologist's questions on language, literature and performance.* London: Bloomsbury.

Fishman, J. (1991). *Reversing language shift: Theoretical and empirical foundations of assistance in threatened languages.* Clevedon: Multilingual Matters.

Flores, N. and Rosa, J. (2022). Undoing competence: Coloniality, homogeneity, and the overrepresentation of Whiteness in applied linguistics. *Language Learning*, 1–28.

Foucault, M. (1966). *Les mots et les choses: Une archéologie des sciences humaines.* Paris: Éditions Gallimard.

Foucault, M. (1984). Nietzsche, genealogy, history. In P. Rabinow (Ed.), *The Foucault reader* (pp. 76–100). New York: Pantheon Books.

Fowler, R. (1996). On critical linguistics. In C. Caldas-Coulthard and M. Coulthard (Eds.), *Text and practices: Readings in Critical Discourse Analysis* (pp. 3–14). London: Routledge.

Freud, S. (1901). *Zur Psychopathologie des Alltagslebens.* Berlin: Verlag von S. Karger.

Fuller, S. (2011). *Humanity 2.0: What it means to be human past, present and future.* Houndmills, Basingstoke: Palgrave Macmillan.

Gal, S. (2018). Visions and revisions of minority languages: Standardization and its dilemmas. In P. Lane, J. Costa, and H. De Korne

(Eds.), *Standardizing minority languages: Competing ideologies of authority and authenticity in the global periphery* (pp. 222-42). New York: Routledge.

García, O. (2009). *Bilingual education in the 21st century: A global perspective*. Oxford: Wiley.

García, O. (2011). Educating New York's bilingual children: Constructing a future from the past. *International Journal of Bilingual Education and Bilingualism*, 14, 133-53.

García, O. and Li Wei (2014). *Translanguaging: Language, bilingualism and education*. Houndmills, Basingstoke: Palgrave Macmillan.

García, O., Flores, N., Seltzer, K. et al. (2021). Rejecting abyssal thinking in the language and education of racialized bilinguals: A manifesto. *Critical Inquiry in Language Studies*, 18(3), 203-28. https://doi.org/10.1080/15427587.2021.1935957.

Garroutte, E. M. (2003). *Real Indians: Identity and the survival of Native America*. Berkeley, CA: University of California Press.

Gay'wu Group of Women, Burarrwanga, L., Ganambarr, R. et al. (2019). *Songspirals: Sharing women's wisdom of Country through songlines*. Sydney: Allen & Unwin.

Giglioli, P. P. (1972). Introduction. In P. P. Giglioli (Ed.), *Language and social context* (pp. 7-17). Harmondsworth: Penguin.

Godfrey-Smith, P. (2020). *Metazoa: Animal minds and the birth of consciousness*. London: William Collins.

Goico, S. (2021). Repeated assemblages in the interactions of deaf youth in Peru. *International Journal of Multilingualism*, 18(2), 267-84. https//doi.org/10.1080/14790718.2021.1898617.

Gomes, A. (2013). Anthropology and the politics of Indigeneity. *Anthropological Forum*, 23(1), 5-15.

Goodwyn, A. (2020). The origins and adaptations of English as a school subject. In C. J. Hall and R. Wicaksono (Eds.), *Ontologies of English: Reconceptualising the language for learning, teaching, and assessment* (pp. 101-21). Cambridge: Cambridge University Press.

Gordon, L. (2006). *Disciplinary decadence: Living thought in trying times*. New York: Routledge.

Gordon, L. R. (2021). *Freedom, justice, and decolonization*. New York: Routledge.

Grace, G. W. (1981). Indirect inheritance and the aberrant Melanesian languages. In J. Hollyman and A. Pawley (Eds.), *Studies in Pacific languages and cultures in honour of Bruce Biggs* (pp. 255-68). Auckland: Linguistic Society of New Zealand.

Grace, G. (1987). *The linguistic construction of reality*. Beckenham: Croom Helm.

Graeber, D. (2015). Radical alterity is just another way of saying 'reality'. *HAU: Journal of Ethnographic Theory*, 5, 1-41.

Gramling, D. (2016). *The invention of monolingualism*. London: Bloomsbury.

Gramling, D. (2021). *The invention of multilingualism*. Cambridge: Cambridge University Press.
Green, J. (2014). *Drawn from the ground: Sound, sign and inscription in Central Australian sand stories*. Cambridge: Cambridge University Press.
Greenberg, J. (1963). Some universals of grammar with particular reference to the order of meaningful elements. In J. Greenberg (Ed)., *Universals of language* (pp. 73–113). London: MIT Press.
Grenoble, L. (In press). Activism and endangered language work, with an Arctic focus. In C. Cutler, U. Røyneland and Z. Vrzic (Eds.), *Language activism: The role of scholars in linguistic reform and social change*. Cambridge: Cambridge University Press.
Guba, E. and Lincoln, Y. (2005). Paradigmatic controversies, contradictions, and emerging confluences. In N. K. Denzin and Y. Lincoln (Eds.), *Handbook of qualitative research* (pp. 191–215). Thousand Oaks, CA: Sage.
Gumperz, J. (1964). Linguistic and social interaction in two communities. In J. Gumperz and D. Hymes (Eds.), *The ethnography of communication. American Anthropologist*, 66(2), 137–53.
Gurney, L. and Demuro, E. (2019). Tracing new ground, from language to languaging, and from languaging to assemblages: Rethinking languaging through the multilingual and ontological turns. *International Journal of Multilingualism*, 19(3), 305–24. https://doi.org/10.1080/14790718.2019.1689982.
Guzman, A. and Lewis, S. (2020). Artificial intelligence and communication: A Human–Machine Communication research agenda. *New Media & Society*, 22(1), 70–86.
Hacking, I. (2002). *Historical ontology*. Cambridge, MA: Harvard University Press.
Hall, C. (2020). An ontological framework for English. In C. J. Hall and R. Wicaksono (Eds.), *Ontologies of English: Reconceptualising the language for learning, teaching, and assessment* (pp. 13–36). Cambridge: Cambridge University Press.
Hall, C. and Wicaksono, R. (2020). Approaching ontologies of English. In C. J. Hall and R. Wicaksono (Eds.), *Ontologies of English: Reconceptualising the language for learning, teaching, and assessment* (pp. 3–12). Cambridge: Cambridge University Press.
Hall, R. (2019). Literacy and revitalizing endangered languages. In N. Greymorning (Ed.), *Being Indigenous: Perspectives on activism, culture, language and identity* (pp. 212–27). New York: Routledge.
Hamacher, D. (with Elders and knowledge holders) (2022). *The first astronomers: How Indigenous Elders read the stars*. Sydney: Allen & Unwin.
Hardt, M. and Negri, A. (2017). *Assembly*. Oxford: Oxford University Press.
Harland, R. (1987). *Superstructuralism: The philosophy of structuralism and poststructuralism*. London: Routledge.
Harris, R. (1980). *The language makers*. Ithaca, NY: Cornell University Press.
Harris, R. (1981). *The language myth*. London: Duckworth.

References

Harris, R. (1988). Murray, Moore and the myth. In R. Harris (Ed.), *Linguistic thought in England, 1914-1945* (pp. 1-26). London: Duckworth.

Harris, R. (1990a). On redefining linguistics. In H. Davis and T. Taylor (Eds.), *Redefining linguistics* (pp. 18-52). London: Routledge.

Harris, R. (1990b). The dialect myth. In J. A. Edmondson, C. Feagin and P. Mühlhäusler (Eds.), *Development and diversity: Language variation across time and space.* (pp. 3-10). Dallas, TX: Summer Institute of Linguistics; University of Texas.

Harris, R. (1997). From an integrational point of view. In G. Wolf and N. Love (Eds.), *Linguistics inside out: Roy Harris and his critics* (pp. 229-310). Amsterdam: John Benjamins.

Harris, R. (1998a). *Introduction to integrational linguistics.* Oxford: Pergamon Press.

Harris, R. (1998b). The integrationist critique of orthodox linguistics. In R. Harris and G. Wolf (Eds.), *Integrational linguistics: A first reader* (pp. 15-26). Oxford: Pergamon.

Harris, R. (2002). The role of the language myth in the Western cultural tradition. In R. Harris (Ed.), *The language myth in Western culture* (pp. 1-24). Richmond: Curzon Press.

Harris, R. (2004). Integrationism, language, mind and world. *Language Sciences*, 26, 727-39.

Harris, R. (2009). *After epistemology.* Gamlingay: Brightpen.

Harris, Z. (1951). *Structural linguistics.* Chicago: The University of Chicago Press.

Harris, Z. (1982). *A grammar of English on mathematical principles.* New York: John Wiley and Sons.

Haslanger, S. (1995). Ontology and social construction. *Philosophical Topics*, 23(2), 95-125.

Haslanger, S. (2012). *Resisting reality: Social construction and social critique.* Oxford: Oxford University Press.

Hauck, J. D. and Heurich, G. O. (2018). Language in the Amerindian imagination: An inquiry into linguistic natures. *Language & Communication*, 63, 1-8. https://doi.org/10.1016/j.langcom.2018.03.005.

Hawkins, M. R. (2018). Transmodalities and transnational encounters: Fostering critical cosmopolitan relations. *Applied Linguistics*, 39(1), 55-77.

Hayman, E. with James, C./Gooch Tláa and Wedge, J./Aan Gooshú (2018). Future rivers of the Anthropocene or whose Anthropocene is it? Decolonising the Anthropocene. *Decolonization: Indigeneity, Education & Society*, 6(2), 77-92.

Henne-Ochoa, R., Elliot-Groves, E., Meek, B. and Rogoff, B. (2020). Pathways forward for indigenous language reclamation: Engaging indigenous epistemology and learning by observing and pitching in to family and community endeavors. *The Modern Language Journal*, 104(2), 481-93.

Hermes, M., Engman, M., McKenzie, M. and McKenzie, J. (2022). Relationality and Ojibwemowin in forest walks: Learning from multimodal interaction about land and language. *Cognition and Instruction*. https://doi.org/10.1080/07370008.2022.2059482.

Heurich, G. (2020). Broken words, furious wasps. How should we translate the sonic materiality of Araweté ritual singing. *Journal de la Société des Américanistes*, 106-1, 105–26.

Heywood, P. (2017). Ontological turn, the. In F. Stein, (Ed.), *The open encyclopedia of anthropology*. Facsimile of the first edition in The Cambridge Encyclopedia of Anthropology. http://doi.org/10.29164/17ontology.

Hill, J. (2002). 'Expert rhetorics' in advocacy for endangered languages: Who is listening, and what do they hear? *Journal of Linguistic Anthropology*, 12(2), 119–33.

Hiratsuka, A. and Pennycook, A. (2020). Translingual family repertoires: 'No, Morci is itaiitai panzita, amor'. *Journal of Multilingual and Multicultural Development*, 41(9), 749–63.

Hobsbawm, E. and Ranger, T. (Eds.) (1983). *The invention of tradition*. Cambridge: Cambridge University Press.

Hodder, I. (2011). Human-thing entanglement. Towards an integrated archaeological perspective. *Journal of the Royal Anthropological Institute*, 17(1), 154–77.

Hodder, I. (2012). *Entangled: An archaeology of the relationships between humans and things*. Oxford: Oxford University Press.

Holbraad, M., Pedersen, M. A. and Viveiros de Castro, E. (2014). The politics of ontology: Anthropological positions: Theorizing the contemporary. *Fieldsights*, 13 January. https://culanth.org/fieldsights/the-politics-of-ontology-anthropological-positions.

Holbraad, M. and Pedersen, M. A. (2017). *The ontological turn: An anthropological exposition*. Cambridge: Cambridge University Press.

Hollington, A. (2020). Jamaican postcolonial writing practices and metalinguistic discourses as a challenge to established norms and standards. In A. Deumert, A. Storch and N. Shepherd (Eds.), *Colonial and decolonial linguistics: Knowledges and epistemes* (pp. 225–43). Oxford: Oxford University Press.

Holmes, J. (1998). Women talk too much. In L. Bauer and P. Trudgill (Eds.), *Language myths* (pp. 41–9). London: Penguin.

Home gardeners (2023). Home gardeners become accidental citizen scientists for Wollemi Pine. www.csiro.au/en/news/all/articles/2023/july/wollemi-pine.

Hopper, P. (1998). Emergent grammar. In M. Tomasello (Ed.), *The new psychology of language* (pp. 155–75). Mahwah, NJ: Lawrence Erlbaum.

Hountondji, P. (1977). *Sur la "philosophie africaine"*. Paris: Maspéro (*African philosophy: Myth and reality*. Bloomington: Indiana University Press, 1983).

Hovens, D. (2020). Workplace learning through human-machine interaction in a transient multilingual blue-collar work environment. *Journal of Linguistic Anthropology*, 30(3), 369–88.

Hovens, D. (2021). Language policy and linguistic landscaping in a contemporary blue-collar workplace in the Dutch–German borderland. *Language Policy*, 20, 645–66.

Hovens, D. (2023). Breakdowns and assemblages: Including machine-actants in sociolinguistic ethnographies of blue-collar work environments. *Journal of Sociolinguistics*, 27, 3–23.

Huberman, J. (2021). *Transhumanism: From ancestors to avatars*. Cambridge: Cambridge University Press.

Hultgren, A. K. (2011). 'Building rapport' with customers across the world: The global diffusion of a call centre speech style. *Journal of Sociolinguistics*, 15(1), 36–64.

Hutchins, E. (1995). *Cognition in the wild*. Cambridge, MA: MIT Press.

Hutchins, E. (2005). Material anchors for conceptual blends. *Journal of Pragmatics*, 37, 1555–77.

Hutchins, E. (2014). The cultural ecosystem of human cognition. *Philosophical Psychology*, 27(1), 34–49.

Hutton, C. (1999). *Linguistics and the Third Reich: Mother-tongue fascism, race and the science of language*. London: Routledge.

Hutton, C. (2002). The language myth and the race myth: Evil twins of modern identity politics? In R. Harris (Ed.), *The language myth in Western culture* (pp. 118–38). Richmond: Curzon Press.

Hutton, C. (2022). Can there be a politics of language? Reflections on language and metalanguage. In B. Antia and S. Makoni (Eds.), *Southernizing sociolinguistics: Colonialism, racism, and patriarchy in language in the Global South* (pp. 17–31). New York: Routledge.

Ingersoll, K. A. (2016). *Waves of knowing: A seascape epistemology*. Durham, CT: Duke University Press.

Ingold, T. (2012). Towards an ecology of materials. *Annual Review of Anthropology*, 41, 427–40.

Jakobs, M. and Hüning, M. (2022). Scholars and their metaphors: On language making in linguistics. *International Journal of the Sociology of Language*, 274, 29–50.

Jaspers, J. (2018). The transformative limits of translanguaging. *Language & Communication*, 58, 1–10.

Jaspers, J. and Madsen, L. (2019). Fixity and fluidity in sociolinguistic theory and practice. In J. Jaspers and L. Madsen (Eds.), *Critical perspectives on linguistic fixity and fluidity: Languagised lives* (pp. 1–26). New York: Routledge.

Jaworski, A. and Gonçalves, K. (2021). High culture at street level: Oslo's Ibsen Sitat and the ethos of egalitarian nationalism. In R. Blackwood and U. Røyneland (Eds.), *Spaces of multilingualism* (pp. 135–64). London: Routledge.

Jaworski, A. and Thurlow, C. (Eds.) (2010). *Semiotic landscapes: Language, image, space*. London: Continuum.

Jenks, C. (2017). *Race and ethnicity in English language teaching: Korea in focus*. Bristol: Multilingual Matters.

Johnson, D. C. and Johnson, E. J. (2022). *The language gap: Normalizing deficit ideologies*. New York: Routledge.

Jones, M. and Singh, I. (2005). *Exploring language change*. London: Routledge.

Jørgensen, J. N. (2008). Polylingual languaging around and among children and adolescents. *International Journal of Multilingualism*, 5(3), 161–76.

Jørgensen, J. N., Karrebæk, M. S., Madsen, L. M. and Møller, J. S. (2011). Polylanguaging in superdiversity. *Diversities*, 13(2), 23–37.

Joseph, J. (1997). The 'Language Myth' myth: Or, Roy Harris's red herrings In G. Wolf and N. Love (Eds.), *Linguistics inside out : Roy Harris and his critics* (pp. 9–41). Amsterdam: John Benjamins Publishing Company.

Joseph, J. E. (2006). *Language and politics*. Edinburgh: Edinburgh University Press.

Joseph, J. (2018). *Language, mind and body: A conceptual history*. Cambridge: Cambridge University Press.

Joseph, J. (2022). Afterword: The complementarity of multilingualist and 4T approaches. In W. Ayres-Bennett and L. Fisher (Eds.), *Multilingualism and identity: Interdisciplinary perspectives* (pp. 365–74). Cambridge: Cambridge University Press.

Joseph, J. and Newmeyer, F. (2012). All languages are equally complex: The rise and fall of a consensus. *Historiographia Linguistica*, 39(2/3), 341–68.

Joyce, R. and Pollard, J. (2012). Archaeological assemblages and practices of deposition. In M. Beaudry and D. Hicks (Eds.), *The Oxford handbook of material culture studies* (pp. 291–312). Oxford: Oxford University Press.

Kaplan, R. (2002). Preface. In R. Kaplan (Ed.), *The Oxford handbook of applied linguistics* (pp. v–x). Oxford: Oxford University Press.

Karimzad, F. (2021). Multilingualism, chronotopes, and resolutions: Toward an analysis of the total sociolinguistic fact. *Applied Linguistics*, 42(5), 848–77. https://doi.org/10.1093/applin/amaa053.

Kearney, R. (1988). *The wake of imagination*. Minneapolis. MN: University of Minnesota Press.

Kell, C. and Budach, G. (2024). Materialities and ontologies: Thinking multilingualism through language materiality, post-humanism and new materialism. In P. Makoe, C. McKinney and V. Zavala (Eds.), *The Routledge handbook of multilingualism* (2nd edition, pp. 79–95). London: Routledge.

Kim, Y., Kogan, V. and Zhang, C. (2023). Collecting big data through citizen science: Gamification and game-based approaches to data collection in Applied Linguistics. *Applied Linguistics*. https://doi.org/10.1093/applin/amad039.

Kohn, E. (2013). *How forests think: Toward an anthropology beyond the human*. Berkeley, CA: University of California Press.

Kohn, E. (2015). Anthropology of ontologies. *Annual Review of Anthropology*, 44, 311-27.

Kramsch, C. (2009). *The multilingual subject*. Oxford: Oxford University Press.

Kramsch, C. (2015). Applied linguistics: A theory of the practice, *Applied Linguistics*, 36, 454-65.

Kramsch, C. (2021). *Language as symbolic power*. Cambridge: Cambridge University Press.

Kroskrity, P. V. (2000). Regimenting languages: Language ideological perspectives. In P. V. Kroskrity (Ed.), *Regimes of language: Ideologies, politics and identities* (pp. 1-34). Santa Fe, NM: School of American Research Press.

Kroskrity, P. (2018). On recognizing persistence in the Indigenous language ideologies of multilingualism in two Native American Communities. *Language & Communication*, 62, 133-44.

Kroskrity, P. (2021). Language ideological assemblages within linguistic anthropology. In A. Burkette and T. Warhol (Eds.), *Crossing borders, making connections: Interdisciplinarity in linguistics* (pp. 129-42). Berlin: Mouton de Gruyter.

Kusters, A. (2021). Introduction: The semiotic repertoire: Assemblages and evaluation of resources. *International Journal of Multilingualism*, 18(2), 183-89.

Kusters, A. and Lucas, C. (2022). Emergence and evolutions: Introducing sign language sociolinguistics. *Journal of Sociolinguistics*, 26, 84-98.

Kusters, A. and Sahasrabudhe, S. (2018). Local and academic language ideologies on the difference between gesture and sign. *Language & Communication*, 60, 44-63.

Kusters, A., Spotti, M., Swanwick, R. and Tapio, E. (2017a). Beyond languages, beyond modalities: Transforming the study of semiotic repertoires. *International Journal of Multilingualism*, 14(3), 219-32.

Kusters, A., De Meulder, M. and O'Brien, D. (2017b). Innovations in Deaf Studies: Critically mapping the field. In A. Kusters, M. De Meulder and D. O'Brien (Eds.), *Innovations in Deaf Studies: The role of Deaf scholars* (pp. 1-53). Oxford: Oxford University Press.

Kwaymullina, A. (2016). Research, ethics and Indigenous peoples: An Australian Indigenous perspective on three threshold considerations for respectful engagement. *AlterNative: An International Journal of Indigenous Peoples*, 12(4), 437-49.

Lakoff, G. and Johnson, M. (1980). *Metaphors we live by*. Chicago: University of Chicago Press.

Lamb, G. (2020). Towards a green applied linguistics: Human-sea turtle semiotic assemblages in Hawai'i. *Applied Linguistics*, 41(6), 922-46.

Lamb, G. (2024). *Multispecies discourse analysis*. London: Bloomsbury.

Lamb, G. and Sharma, B. (2021). Introduction: Tourism spaces at the nexus of language and materiality. *Applied Linguistics Review*, 12(1), 1-9.

Lane, P. (2023a). From silence to silencing? Contradictions and tensions in language revitalization. *Applied Linguistics*, 1-20. https://doi.org/10.1093/applin/amac075.

Lane, P. (2023b). The South in the North: Colonization and decolonization of the mind. In A. Deumert and S. Makoni (Eds.), *From Southern Theory to decolonizing sociolinguistics: Voices, questions and alternatives* (pp. 39-55). Bristol: Multilingual Matters.

Larsen, S. and Johnson, J. (2016). The agency of place: Toward a more-than-human geographical self. *GeoHumanities*, 2(1), 149-66. https://doi.org/10.1080/2373566X.2016.1157003.

Latour, B. (1999). *Pandora's hope: Essays on the reality of science studies*. Cambridge, MA: Harvard University Press.

Latour, B. (2004). Why has critique run out of steam? From matters of fact to matters of concern. *Critical Inquiry*, 30(2), 225-48.

Latour, B. (2005). *Reassembling the social: An introduction to actor-network-theory*. Oxford: Oxford University Press.

Latour, B. (2015). Telling friends from foes in the time of the Anthropocene. In C. Hamilton, F. Gemenne and C. Bonneuil (Eds.), *The Anthropocene and the global environmental crisis* (pp. 145-55). New York: Routledge.

Lee, E. and Makoni, S. (2022). Sociolinguistic protests for decolonial future making: Toward centering languaging in the 'streets'. *Bandung: Journal of the Global South*, 9, 300-24.

Lee, J. W. (2022). *Locating translingualism*. Cambridge: Cambridge University Press.

Lee, J. W. and Dovchin, S. (2020). Introduction: Negotiating innovation and ordinariness. In J. W. Lee and S. Dovchin (Eds.), *Translinguistics: Negotiating innovation and ordinariness* (pp. 1-5). New York: Routledge.

Leibowitz, B. and Bozalek, V. (2018). Towards a slow scholarship of teaching and learning in the South. *Teaching in Higher Education*, 23(8), 981-94.

Leonard, W. (2017). Producing language reclamation by decolonising 'language'. In W. Leonard and H. De Korne (Eds.), *Language documentation and description* (Vol. 14, pp. 15-36). London: EL Publishing.

Leonard, W. Y. (2020a). Musings on Native American language reclamation and sociolinguistics. *International Journal of the Sociology of Language*, 2020 (263), 85-90. https://doi.org/10.1515/ijsl-2020-2086.

Leonard, W. (2020b). Learning by observing and pitching in in the context of sleeping language reclamation. *The Modern Language Journal*, 104, 494-7.

Leonard, W. (2021). Toward an anti-racist linguistic anthropology: An Indigenous response to white supremacy. *Journal of Linguistic Anthropology*, 31(2), 218-37.

Levinson, S. (1996). Relativity in spatial conception and description. In J. Gumperz and S. Levinson (Eds.), *Rethinking linguistic relativity* (pp. 177-202). Cambridge: Cambridge University Press.

Lewis, M. (2018). A critique of the principle of error correction as a theory of social change. *Language in Society*, 47(3), 325–46.
Li Wei (2011). Moment Analysis and translanguaging space: Discursive construction of identities by multilingual Chinese youth in Britain. *Journal of Pragmatics*, 43, 1222–35.
Li Wei (2018). Translanguaging as a practical theory of language. *Applied Linguistics*, 39(1), 9–30.
Linguistics Roadshow, The (2023). https://lingroadshow.com/ (last accessed 31 July 2023).
López-Gopar, M., Sughrua, W., Cirilo, C. G. and Hernández, L. C. (2023). 'We tell the river, "Give me back my piece of soul and I give you back your pebble"': The Onto-epistemology and language of the Ayuk Ethnic Group in Oaxaca, Mexico. In S. Makoni, A. Kaiper-Marquez and L. Mokwena (Eds.), *The Routledge handbook of language and the Global South/s* (pp. 110–20). New York: Routledge.
Lorente, B. (2017). *Scripts of servitude: Language, labor migration and transnational domestic work*. Bristol: Multilingual Matters.
Love, N. (1998). The linguistic thought of J R Firth. In R. Harris (Ed.), *Linguistic thought in England, 1914–1945* (pp. 148–64). London: Duckworth.
Love, N. (2017). On languaging and languages. *Language Sciences*, 61, 113–47.
Luke, A. (2013). Regrounding critical literacy: Representation, facts, and reality. In M. Hawkins (Ed.), *Framing languages and literacies: Socially situated views and perspectives* (pp. 136–48). New York: Routledge.
Lyons, J. (1981). *Language and linguistics. An introduction*. Cambridge: Cambridge University Press.
Macedo, D. (2019). Rupturing the yoke of colonialism in foreign language education. In D. Macedo (Ed.), *Decolonizing foreign language education: The misteaching of English and other imperial languages* (pp. 1–49). New York: Routledge.
MacSwan, J. (2017). A multilingual perspective on translanguaging. *American Educational Research Journal*, 54(1), 167–201.
MacSwan, J. (2020). Translanguaging, language ontology, and civil rights. *World Englishes*, 39, 321–33.
MacSwan, J. (2022a). Introduction: Deconstructivism – a reader's guide. In J. MacSwan (Ed.), *Multilingual perspectives on translanguaging*. (pp. 17–55). Bristol: Multilingual Matters.
MacSwan, J. (2022b). Codeswitching, translanguaging and bilingual grammar. In J. MacSwan (Ed.), *Multilingual perspectives on translanguaging* (pp. 90–130). Bristol: Multilingual Matters.
Maher, J. (2021). *Metroethnicity, naming and mocknolect: New horizons in Japanese sociolinguistics*. Amsterdam: John Benjamins.
Makalela, L. (2018). Introduction: Shifting lenses. In L. Makalela (Ed.), *Shifting lenses: Multilanguaging, decolonisation and education in the Global South* (pp. 1–18). Cape Town: CASAS.

Makoni, S. and Pennycook, A. (2007). Disinventing and reconstituting languages. In S. Makoni and A. Pennycook (Eds.), *Disinventing and reconstituting languages* (pp. 1–41). Clevedon: Multilingual Matters.

Makoni, S. and Pennycook, A. (2024). Looking at multilingualisms from the Global South. In P. Makoe, C. McKinney and V. Zavala (Eds.), *The Routledge handbook of multilingualism* (2nd edition, pp. 17–30). London: Routledge.

Martin, L. (1986). 'Eskimo words for snow': A case study in the genesis and decay of an anthropological example. *American Anthropologist*, 88(2), 418–23.

Marx, K. (1867). *Das Kapital: Kritik der politischen Oekonomie*. Hamburg: Verlag von Otto Meisner.

Marx, K. (1972 [1845]). Theses on Feuerbach. In R. C. Tucker (Ed.), *The Marx-Engels reader* (pp. 107–9). New York: W. W. Norton.

May, S. (2014). Disciplinary divides, knowledge construction, and the multilingual turn. In S. May (Ed.), *The multilingual turn: Implications for SLA, TESOL and bilingual education* (pp. 7–31). London: Routledge.

May, S. (2022). Afterword: The multilingual turn, superdiversity and translanguaging – the rush from heterodoxy to orthodoxy. In J. MacSwan (Ed.), *Multilingual perspectives on translanguaging* (pp. 333–44). Bristol: Multilingual Matters.

McCarthy, M. (2001). *Issues in applied linguistics*. Cambridge: Cambridge University Press.

McFarlane, C. (2011). Assemblage and critical urbanism. *City*, 15(2), 204–25.

McKenzie, J. (2020). Approaching from many angles: Seeing the connections for our languages to live. *The Modern Language Journal*, 104, 501–6.

McWhorter, J. (2014). *The language hoax: Why the world looks the same in any language*. Oxford: Oxford University Press.

Meek, B. (2010). *We are our language: An ethnogrpahy of language revitalization in a Northern Athabaskan Community*. Tucson, AZ: University of Arizona Press.

Meek, B. (2015). The politics of language endangerment. In N. Bonvillan (Ed.), *The Routledge handbook of linguistic anthropology* (pp. 447–62). New York: Routledge.

Merlan, F. (2009). Indigeneity: Global and local. *Current Anthropology*, 50(3), 303–33.

Mika, C. (2016). Worlded object and its presentation: A Māori philosophy of language. *AlterNative: An International Journal of Indigenous Peoples*, 12(2), 165–75.

Milroy, J. (2001). Language ideologies and the consequences of standardization. *Journal of Sociolinguistics*, 5(4), 530–55.

Milroy, J. and Milroy, L. (1991). *Authority in language: Investigating language prescription and standardisation* (2nd edition). London: Routledge.

References

Møller, J. S. (2008). Polylingual performance among Turkish-Danes in late modern Copenhagen. *International Journal of Multilingualism*, 5(3), 217-36.

Monaghan, P. (2012). Going for wombat – transformations in Wirangu and the Scotdesco Community on the far west coast of South Australia. *Oceania*, 82(1), 45-61.

Moriarty, E. and Kusters, A. (2021). Deaf cosmopolitanism: Calibrating as a moral process. *International Journal of Multilingualism*, 18(2), 285-302. https://doi.org/10.1080/14790718.2021.1889561.

Motha, S. (2014). *Race and empire in English language teaching*. New York: Teachers College Press, Columbia University.

Muecke, S. (2004). *Ancient and modern: Time, culture and Indigenous philosophy*. Sydney: UNSW Press.

Mufwene, S. (2008). *Language evolution: Contact, competition and change*. London: Continuum.

Mufwene, S. (2016). A cost-and-benefit approach to language loss. In L. Filipović and M. Pütz (Eds.), *Endangered languages and languages in danger: Issues of documentation, policy, and language rights* (pp. 115-43). Amsterdam: John Benjamins.

Mufwene, S. (2017). Language vitality: The weak theoretical underpinnings of what can be an exciting research area. *Language*, 93(4), e202-e223.

Mufwene, S. (2020). Decolonial linguistics as paradigm shift: A commentary. In A. Deumert, A. Storch and N. Shepherd (Eds.), *Colonial and decolonial linguistics: Knowledges and epistemes* (pp. 289-300). Oxford: Oxford University Press.

Mühlhäusler, P. (1995). Metaphors others live by. *Language & Communication*, 15(3), 281-8.

MyGov (2023). https://my.gov.au/ (last accessed 14 December 2023).

Nakata, M. (2007). *Disciplining the savages: Savaging the disciplines*. Canberra: Aboriginal Studies Press.

Nakata, M., Nakata, V., Keech, S. and Bolt, R. (2012). Decolonial goals and pedagogies for Indigenous studies. *Decolonization: Indigeneity, Education & Society*, 1(1), 120-40.

Nandy, A. (1983). *The intimate enemy: Loss and recovery of self under colonialism*. Delhi: Oxford University Press.

Nascimento, G. (2023). On (dis)inventing language as a zone of non-being: Black teachers in ELT and linguistic racism in Brazil. In P. Friedrich (Ed.), *The anti-racism linguist* (pp. 44-63). Bristol: Multilingual Matters.

Ndhlovu, F. (2018). *Language, vernacular discourse and nationalisms: Uncovering the myths of transnational worlds*. Cham: Palgrave Macmillan.

Ndhlovu, F. (2021). Decolonising sociolinguistics research: Methodological turn-around next? *International Journal of the Sociology of Language*, 267-268, 193-201.

Ndhlovu, F. and Makalela, L. (2021). *Decolonising multilingualism in Africa: Recentering silenced voices from the Global South*. Bristol: Multilingual Matters.

Neale, M. (2021). First Knowledges: An introduction. In B. Pascoe and B. Gammage (Eds.), *Country: Future fire, future farming* (First Knowledges Volume 2, pp. 11-14). Melbourne: Thames and Hudson Australia.

Neale, M. and Kelly, L. (2020). *Songlines: The power and the promise* (First Knowledges Volume 1). Melbourne: Thames and Hudson Australia.

Newmeyer, F. J. (1986). *The politics of linguistics*. Chicago: The University of Chicago Press.

Newmeyer, F. J. (1988). *Linguistic theory in America* (2nd edition). New York: Academic Press.

Nicholas, S. and McCarty, T. (2022). To 'think in a different way' - a relational paradigm for Indigenous language rights. In J. MacSwan (Ed.), *Multilingual perspectives on translanguaging* (pp. 229-47). Bristol: Multilingual Matters.

Noon, K. and de Napoli, K. (2022). *Astronomy: Sky country*. (First Knowledges Volume 4). Melbourne: Thames and Hudson Australia.

O'Brien, D. (2017). Deaf-led Deaf Studies: Using kaupapa Māori principles to guide the development of Deaf research practices. In A. Kusters, M. De Meulder and D. O'Brien (Eds.), *Innovations in Deaf Studies: The role of Deaf scholars* (pp. 57-76). Oxford: Oxford University Press.

O'Regan, J. (2016). Intercultural communication and the possibility of English as a lingua franca. In P. Holmes and F. Dervin (Eds.), *The cultural and intercultural dimensions of English as a lingua franca* (pp. 203-17). Bristol: Multilingual Matters.

Oda, M. and Takada, T. (2005). English language teaching in Japan. In G. Braine (Ed.), *Teaching English to the world: History, curriculum and practice* (pp. 93-101). New York: Lawrence Erlbaum Associates.

Oliveira, G. S and Oliveira, M. B. (2022). Bilingualism is always cognitively advantageous, but this doesn't mean what you think it means. *Frontiers in Psychology*, 13. https://doi.org/10.3389/fpsyg.2022.867166.

Ortega, L. (2014). Ways forward for a bi/multilingual turn in SLA. In S. May (Ed.), *The multilingual turn: Implications for SLA, TESOL, and bilingual education* (pp. 32-53). New York: Routledge.

Ortega, L. (2018). Ontologies of language, second language acquisition, and world Englishes. *World Englishes*, 37, 64-79.

Ortega, L. (2019). SLA and the study of equitable multilingualism. *The Modern Language Journal*, 103, 23-35.

Otheguy, R., García, O. and Reid, W. (2015). Clarifying translanguaging and deconstructing named languages: A perspective from linguistics. *Applied Linguistics Review*, 6(3), 281-307.

Otheguy, R., García, O. and Reid, W. (2018). A translanguaging view of the linguistic system of bilinguals. *Applied Linguistics Review*, 10(4), 625-51. https://doi.org/10.1515/applirev-2018-0020.

References

Otsuji, E. and Pennycook, A. (2018). The translingual advantage: Metrolingual student repertoires. In J. Choi and S. Ollerhead (Eds.), *Plurilingualism in teaching and learning: Complexities across contexts* (pp. 71–88). New York: Routledge.

Otsuji, E. and Pennycook, A. (2024). Reassembling meaning while shopping. In G. Rasmussen and T. Van Leeuwen, (Eds.), *Multimodality and social interaction in online and offline shopping* (pp. 85–103). London: Routledge.

Pablé, A. (2019a). Is a general non-ethnocentric theory of human communication possible? An integrationist approach. *Lingua*, 230. https://doi.org/10.1016/j.lingua.2019.102735.

Pablé, A. (2019b). In what sense is integrational theory lay-oriented? Notes on Harrisian core concepts and explanatory terminology. *Language Sciences*, 72, 150–9.

Pablé, A. (2021). Three critical perspectives on the ontology of 'language'. In S. Makoni, D. P. Verity and A. Kaiper-Marquez (Eds.), *Integrational linguistics and philosophy of language in the Global South* (pp. 30–47). New York: Routledge.

Pablé, A. (2022). Linguistics for the apocalypse. *Language & Communication*, 86, 104–110. https://doi.org/10.1016/j.langcom.2022.06.007.

Page, S. (2022). Interview. *The Saturday Paper*, 5–11 February, p. 26.

Pascoe, B. and Gammage, B. (2021). *Country: Future fire, future farming.* (First Knowledges Volume 2). Melbourne: Thames and Hudson Australia.

Patel, S. (2021). Sociology's encounter with the decolonial: The problematique of indigenous vs that of coloniality, extraversion and colonial modernity. *Current Sociology*, 69(3), 372–88.

Pennycook, A. (1985). Actions speak louder than words: Paralanguage, communication and education. *TESOL Quarterly*, 19(2), 259–82.

Pennycook, A. (1996). Borrowing others' words: Text, ownership, memory and plagiarism. *TESOL Quarterly*, 30(2), 201–30.

Pennycook, A. (2001). *Critical applied linguistics: A critical introduction.* Mahwah, NJ: Lawrence Erlbaum.

Pennycook, A. (2006). Uma lingüística aplicada transgressiva. In L. P. Moita Lopes (Ed.), *Por uma lingüística aplicada indisciplinar* (pp. 67–84). Sao Paulo: Parabola.

Pennycook, A. (2007). *Global Englishes and transcultural flows.* London: Routledge.

Pennycook, A. (2010). *Language as a local practice.* London: Routledge.

Pennycook, A. (2016). Mobile times, mobile terms: The trans-super-poly-metro movement. In N. Coupland (Ed.), *Sociolinguistics: Theoretical debates* (pp. 201–16). Cambridge: Cambridge University Press.

Pennycook, A. (2017). Translanguaging and semiotic assemblages. *International Journal of Multilingualism*, 14(3), 269–82. https://doi.org/10.1080/14790718.2017.1315810.

Pennycook, A. (2018a). *Posthumanist applied linguistics.* London: Routledge.

Pennycook, A. (2018b). Repertoires, registers, and linguistic diversity. In A. Creese and A. Blackledge (Eds.), *The Routledge handbook of language and superdiversity* (pp. 3–15). London: Routledge.

Pennycook, A. (2018c). Applied linguistics as epistemic assemblage. *AILA Review*, 31, 113–34.

Pennycook, A. (2018d). Posthumanist applied linguistics. *Applied Linguistics*, 39(4), 445–61. https://doi.org/10.1093/applin/amw016.

Pennycook, A. (2019a). Linguistic landscapes and semiotic assemblages. In M. Pütz and N. Mundt (Eds.), *Expanding the linguistic landscape* (pp. 75–88). Bristol: Multilingual Matters.

Pennycook, A. (2019b). The landscape returns the gaze: Bikescapes and the new economies. *Linguistic Landscape*, 5(3), 217–47.

Pennycook, A. (2020a). Translingual entanglements of English. *World Englishes*, 39(2), 222–35. https://doi.org/10.1111/weng.12456.

Pennycook, A. (2020b). Pushing the ontological boundaries of English. In C. J. Hall and R. Wicaksono (Eds.), *Ontologies of English: Reconceptualising the language for learning, teaching, and assessment* (pp. 355–67). Cambridge: Cambridge University Press.

Pennycook, A. (2021a). *Critical applied linguistics: A critical reintroduction* (2nd edition). New York: Routledge.

Pennycook, A. (2021b). Entanglements of English. In R. Rubdy and R. Tupas (Eds.), *Bloomsbury world Englishes: Volume 2: Ideologies* (pp. 9–26). London: Bloomsbury.

Pennycook, A. (2021c). Reassembling linguistics: Semiotic and epistemic assemblages. In A. Burkette and T. Warhol (Eds.), *Crossing borders, making connections: Interdisciplinarity in linguistics* (pp. 111–28). Berlin: De Gruyter Mouton.

Pennycook, A. (2022a). Critical applied linguistics in the 2020s. *Critical Inquiry in Language Studies*, 19(1), 1–21. https://doi.org/10.1080/15427587.2022.2030232.

Pennycook, A. (2022b). Street art assemblages. *Social Semiotics*, 32(4), 563–76. https://doi.org/10.1080/10350330.2022.2114731.

Pennycook, A. (2023a). Toward the total semiotic fact. *Chinese Semiotic Studies*, 19(4), 595–613.

Pennycook, A. (2023b). From Douglas Firs to giant cuttlefish: Reimagining language learning. In A. Deumert and S. Makoni (Eds.), *From Southern Theory to decolonizing sociolinguistics: Voices, questions and alternatives* (pp. 71–89). Bristol: Multilingual Matters.

Pennycook, A. (In press). Language activism and decolonialism: From extractivist to emergent politics. In C. Cutler, U. Røyneland and Z. Vrzic (Eds.), *Language activism: The role of scholars in linguistic reform and social change*. Cambridge: Cambridge University Press.

Pennycook, A. and Makoni, S. (2020). *Innovations and challenges in applied linguistics from the Global South*. London: Routledge.

Pennycook, A. and Otsuji, E. (2014). Metrolingual multitasking and spatial repertoires: 'Pizza mo two minutes coming'. *Journal of Sociolinguistics*, 18 (2), 161–84.

Pennycook, A. and Otsuji, E. (2015). *Metrolingualism: Language in the city*. London: Routledge.

Pennycook, A. and Otsuji, E. (2016). Lingoing, language labels and metrolingual practices. *Applied Linguistics Review*, 7(3), 259–77.

Pennycook, A. and Otsuji, E. (2017). Fish, phone cards and semiotic assemblages in two Bangladeshi shops in Sydney and Tokyo. *Social Semiotics*, 27 (4), 434–50.

Pennycook, A. and Otsuji, E. (2019). Mundane metrolingualism. *International Journal of Multilingualism*, 16(2), 175–86.

Pennycook, A. and Otsuji, E. (2022). Metrolingual practices and distributed identities: People, places, things and languages. In W. Ayres-Bennett and L. Fisher (Eds.), *Multilingualism and identity: Interdisciplinary perspectives* (pp. 69–90). Cambridge: Cambridge University Press.

Perley, B. (2012). Zombie linguistics: Experts, endangered languages and the curse of undead voices. *Anthropological Forum*, 22(2), 133–49.

Phillips, J. (2006). *Agencement*/assemblage. *Theory, Culture and Society*, 23(2–3), 108–9.

Pickering, A. (2017). The ontological turn: Taking different worlds seriously. *Social Analysis*, 61(2), 134–50.

Pietikäinen, S. (2021). Powered by assemblage: Language for multiplicity. *International Journal of the Sociology of Language*, 267–268, 235–40.

Pinker, S. (1994). *The language instinct*. London: Penguin.

Pinker, S. (2007). *The stuff of thought: Language as a window into human nature*. New York: Viking Press.

Povinelli, E. (2016). *Geontologies: A requiem to late capitalism*. Durham, NC: Duke University Press.

Preston, D. R. (1993). The use of folk linguistics. *International Journal of Applied Linguistics*, 3, 181–259.

Preston, D. (1996). Whaddayaknow? The modes of folk linguistic awareness. *Language Awareness*, 5, 40–74.

Pullum, G. K. (1989). The great Eskimo vocabulary hoax. *Natural Language and Linguistic Theory*, 7, 275–81.

Ramberg, B. and Røyneland, U. (In press). Language activism and social justice – why languages still matter. In C. Cutler, U. Røyneland and Z. Vrzic (Eds.), *Language activism: The role of scholars in linguistic reform and social change*. Cambridge: Cambridge University Press.

Rambukwella, H. (2019). On hybridity, the politics of knowledge production and critical language studies. *Language, Culture and Society*, 1(1), 126–31.

Ramos, A. R. (2012). The politics of perspectivism. *Annual Review of Anthropology*, 41, 481–94.

Rampton, B. (1997). Retuning in applied linguistics. *International Journal of Applied Linguistics*, 7, 3-25.

Ritchie, L. D. (2022). *Feeling, thinking and talking: How the embodied brain shapes everyday communication*. Cambridge: Cambridge University Press.

Rosa, J. and Flores, N. (2017). Unsettling race and language: Toward a raciolinguistic perspective. *Language and Society*, 46(5), 621-47.

Rumsey, A. (2018). The sociocultural dynamics of indigenous multilingualism in northwestern Australia. *Language & Communication*, 62(B), 91-101.

Rymes, B. (2014). *Communicating beyond language: Everyday encounters with diversity*. New York: Routledge.

Rymes, B. (2020). *How we talk about language: Exploring citizen sociolinguistics*. Cambridge: Cambridge University Press.

Sampson, G. (1980). *Schools of linguistics*. London: Hutchison.

Sampson, G. (2017). *The linguistics delusion*. Sheffield: Equinox.

Sanches de Oliveira, G. and Bullock Oliveira, M. (2022). Bilingualism is always cognitively advantageous, but this doesn't mean what you think it means. *Frontiers of Psychology*, 13, 1-23. https://doi.org/10.3389/fpsyg.2022.867166.

Santana, C. (2016). What is language? *Ergo*, 3(19), 501-23.

Santos, B. de S. (2002). *A crítica da razão indolente: contra o desperdício da experiência*. São Paulo: Cortês.

Santos, B. de S. (2004). A critique of lazy reason: Against the waste of experience. In E. Wallerstein (Ed.), *The modern world-system in the long durée* (pp. 157-97). London: Paradigm Publishers.

Santos, B. de S. (2012). Public sphere and epistemologies of the south. *Africa Development*, 37(1), 43-67.

Santos, B. de S. (2018). *The end of the cognitive empire: The coming of age of epistemologies of the South*. Durham, NC: Duke University Press.

Saunders, G. (2018). *Le Kov*. CD. London: Heavenly Recordings.

Savransky, M. (2017). A decolonial imagination: Sociology, anthropology and the politics of reality. *Sociology*, 51(1), 11-26.

Sayers, D. (2023). Using language to help people, or using people to help language? A capabilities framework of language policy. *International Journal of Applied Linguistics*, 1-27. https://doi.org/10.1111/ijal.12463.

Schaller-Schwaner, I. and Kirkpatrick, A. (2020). What is English in the light of lingua franca usage? In C. J. Hall and R. Wicaksono (Eds.), *Ontologies of English. Reconceptualising the language for learning, teaching, and assessment* (pp. 233-52). Cambridge: Cambridge University Press.

Schatzki, T. (2001). Introduction: Practice theory. In T. Schatzki, K. Knorr Cetina and E. von Savigny (Eds.), *The practice turn in contemporary theory* (pp. 1-14). London: Routledge.

Schatzki, T. (2002). *The site of the social: A philosophical account of the constitution of social life and change*. University Park, PA: The Pennsylvania State University Press.

Schatzki, T. (2010). *The timespace of human activity: On performance, society, and history as indeterminate teleological events*. Lanham, MD: Lexington Books.

Schmid, H-J. (2020). *The dynamics of the linguistic system: Usage, conventionalization, and entrenchment*. Oxford: Oxford University Press.

Schneider, B. (2018). Methodological nationalism in Linguistics. *Language Sciences*, 76, 1-13.

Scollon, R. and Scollon, S. W. (2004). *Nexus analysis: Discourse and the emerging internet*. New York: Routledge.

Sealey, A. (2014). Cats and categories – reply to Teubert. *Language and Dialogue*, 4(2), 299-321.

Seargeant, P. (2010). The historical ontology of language. *Language Sciences*, 32, 1-13.

Seargeant, P. (2023). *The future of language: How technology, politics and utopianism are transforming the way we communicate*. London: Bloomsbury.

Seidlhofer, B. (2011). *Understanding English as a lingua franca*. Oxford: Oxford University Press.

Severo, C. and Makoni, S. (2020). Using lusitanization and creolization as frameworks to analyse historical and contemporary Cape Verde language policy and planning. In A. Deumert, A. Storch and N. Shepherd (Eds.), *Colonial and decolonial linguistics: Knowledges and epistemes* (pp. 62-76). Oxford: Oxford University Press.

Shankar, S. and Cavanaugh, J. R. (2017). Toward a theory of language materiality: An introduction. In J. R. Cavanaugh and S. Shankar (Eds.), *Language and materiality: Ethnographic and theoretical explorations* (pp. 1-28). Cambridge: Cambridge University Press.

Sharma, B. K. (2021). The scarf, language, and other semiotic assemblages in the formation of a new Chinatown. *Applied Linguistics Review*, 12(1), 65-91.

Shohamy, E. (2015). LL research as expanding language and language policy. *Linguistic Landscape*, 1(1-2), 152-71.

Silverstein, M. (1985). Language and the culture of gender. In E. Mertz and R. Parmentier (Eds.), *Semiotic mediation*, (pp. 219-59). New York: Academic Press.

Simpson, L. B. (2014). Land as pedagogy: Nishnaabeg intelligence and rebellious transformation. *Decolonization: Indigeneity, Education & Society*, 3(3), 1-25.

Skutnabb-Kangas, T. (2000). *Linguistic genocide in education – or worldwide diversity and human rights?* Mahwah, NJ: Lawrence Erlbaum Associates.

Smith, L. T. (2012). *Decolonizing methodologies: Research and Indigenous peoples* (2nd edition). London: Zed Books.

Smith, N. (1999). *Chomsky: Ideas and ideals*. Cambridge: Cambridge University Press.

Stebbins, T. (2014). Finding the languages we go looking for. In P. Austin and J. Sallabank (Eds.), *Endangered languages: Beliefs and ideologies in language documentation and revitalisation* (pp. 293–312). Oxford: Oxford University Press.

Stebbins, T., Eira, K. and Couzens, V. (2018). *Living languages and new approaches to language revitalisation research*. London: Routledge.

Steffensen, S. V. (2012). Beyond mind: An extended ecology of languaging. In S. Cowley (Ed.), *Distributed language* (pp. 185–210). Amsterdam: John Benjamins.

Stone, C. and Köhring, J. (2021). Sensory ecologies and semiotic assemblages during British Sign Language interpreted weather forecasts. *International Journal of Multilingualism*, 18(2), 226–43. https://doi.org/10.1080/14790718.2020.1867149.

Straaijer, R. (2016). Attitudes to prescriptivism: An introduction. *Journal of Multilingual and Multicultural Development*, 37(3), 233–42.

Styres, S. D. (2011). Land as first teacher: A philosophical journeying. *Reflective Practice*, 12(6), 717–31.

Styres, S. (2019). Literacies of land: Decolonizing narratives, storying, and literature. In L. T. Smith, E. Tuck and W. K. Yang (Eds.), *Indigenous and decolonizing studies in education* (pp. 24–37). New York: Routledge.

Sundberg, J. (2013). Decolonizing posthumanist geographies. *Cultural Geographies*, 21(1), 33–47.

Sveinsdóttir, Á. (2015). Social construction. *Philosophy Compass*, 10(12), 884–92.

Svendsen, B. A. (2018). The dynamics of citizen sociolinguistics. *Journal of Sociolinguistics*, 22, 137–60.

Svendsen, B. and Goodchild, S. (2023). Citizen (socio)linguistics: What we can learn from engaging young people as language researchers. *Working Papers in Urban Language & Literacies*, 314.

Tannenbaum, M. and Shohamy, E. (2023). *Developing multilingual education policies: Theory, research, practice*. London: Routledge.

Taylor & Francis. (2023). https://newsroom.taylorandfrancisgroup.com/taylor-francis-clarifies-the-responsible-use-of-ai-tools-in-academic-content-creation/.

Tegmark, M. (2018). *Life 3.0: Being human in the age of artificial intelligence*. New York: Vintage.

Teubert, W. (2013). Was there a cat in the garden? Knowledge between discourse and the monadic self. *Language and Dialogue*, 3(2), 273–97.

Thibault, P. (2011). First-order languaging dynamics and second-order language: The distributed language view. *Ecological Psychology*, 23(3), 1–36.

Thomas, N. (1991). *Entangled objects: Exchange, material culture, and colonialism in the Pacific*. Cambridge, MA: Harvard University Press.

Thompson, C. (2019). *Sea people: The puzzle of Polynesia*. London: William Collins.

Thorne, S., Hellerman, J. and Jakonen, T. (2021). Rewilding language education: Emergent assemblages and entangled actions. *The Modern Language Journal*, 105, 106-25.

Thrift, N. (2007). *Non-representational theory: Space, politics, affect*. London: Routledge.

Thurlow, C. (2014). Disciplining youth: Language ideologies and new technologies. In A. Jaworski and N. Coupland (Eds.), *The discourse reader* (3rd edition, pp. 481-96). London: Routledge.

Todd, Z. (2016). An Indigenous feminist's take on the ontological turn: 'Ontology' is just another word for colonialism. *Journal of Historical Sociology*, 29(1), 4-22.

Toohey, K. (2019). The onto-epistemologies of New Materialism: Implications for applied linguistics pedagogies and research. *Applied Linguistics*, 40, 937-56.

Toohey, K., Dagenais, D., Fodor, A. et al. (2015). 'That sounds so cooool': Entanglements of children, digital tools, and literacy practices. *TESOL Quarterly*, 49(3), 461-85.

Topa, W. (Four Arrows) and Narvaez, D. (Eds.) (2022). *Restoring the kinship worldview: Indigenous voices introduce 28 precepts for rebalancing life on earth*. Huichin, unceded Ohlone land, aka Berkeley, CA: North Atlantic Books.

Trudgill, P. (1998). The meanings of words should not be allowed to vary or change. In L. Bauer and P. Trudgill (Eds.), *Language myths* (pp. 1-8). London: Penguin.

Tsing, A. L. (2015). *The mushroom at the end of the world: On the possibility of life in capitalist ruins*. Princeton, NJ: Princeton University Press.

Tuck, E. and Yang, K. W. (2012). Decolonization is not a metaphor. *Decolonization: Indigeneity, Education & Society*, 1(1), 1-40.

Tynan, L. (2021). What is relationality? Indigenous knowledges, practices and responsibilities with kin. *Cultural Geographies*, 28(4), 597-610. https://doi.org/10.1177/14744740211029287.

Underhill, J. (2011). *Creating worldviews: Ideology, metaphor & language*. Edinburgh: Edinburgh University Press.

Van Dooren, T. (2019). *The wake of crows: Living and dying in shared worlds*. New York: Columbia University Press.

Van Leeuwen, T. (2008). *Discourse and practice: New tools for critical discourse analysis*. Oxford: Oxford University Press.

Vaughan, J. (2018). 'We talk in saltwater words': Dimensionalisation of dialectal variation in multilingual Arnhem Land. *Language and Communication*, 62, 119-32.

Vaughan, J. and Singer, R. (2018). Indigenous multilingualisms past and present. *Language & Communication*, 62, 83-90.

Viveiros de Castro, E. (2014). *Cannibal metaphysics*. Minneapolis, MN: Univocal.

Vivieros de Castro, E. (2015). *The relative native: Essays on Indigenous conceptual worlds*. Chicago, IL: University of Chicago Press.

Walcott, R. (2018). Against social justice and the limits of diversity: Or Black people and freedom. In E. Tuck and K. W. Yang (Eds.), *Toward what justice? Describing diverse dreams of justice in education* (pp. 85–100). New York: Routledge.

Walsh, T. (2022). *Machines behaving badly: The morality of AI*. Melbourne: La Trobe University Press & Black Inc.

Wardaugh, R. (1986). *An introduction to sociolinguistics*. Oxford: Blackwell.

Watkins, M. (1999). Policing the text: Structuralism's stranglehold on Australian language and literacy pedagogy. *Language and Education*, 13(2), 118–32.

Watts, V. (2013). Indigenous place-thought and agency amongst humans and non-humans (First Woman and Sky Woman go on a European tour!). *DIES: Decolonization, Indigeneity, Education and Society*, 2(1), 20–34.

Watts, R. (2011). *Language myths and the history of English*. Oxford: Oxford University Press.

Webster, A. (2016). The art of failure in translating a Navajo poem. *Journal de la Société des américanistes*, 102(1), 9–41.

Wee, L. (2021). *Posthumanist world Englishes*. Cambridge: Cambridge University Press.

Whorf, B. L. (1956). *Language, thought and reality*. Cambridge, MA: MIT Press.

Wicaksono, R. and Hall, C. (2020). Using ontologies of English. In C. Hall and R. Wicaksono (Eds.), *Ontologies of English: Conceptualising the language for learning, teaching and assessment* (pp. 368–75). Cambridge: Cambridge University Press.

Williams, C. (1996). Secondary education: Teaching in the bilingual situation. In C. Williams, G. Lewis and C. Baker (Eds.), *The language policy: Taking stock* (pp. 39–78). Llangefni: CAI.

Williams, G. (1992). *Sociolinguistics: A sociological critique*. London: Routledge.

Williams, Q. (2021). Into collabs: Public applied linguistics and hip hop language technicians. *Applied Linguistics*, 42(6), 1125–37.

Willinsky, J. (1994). *Empire of words: The reign of the OED*. Princeton, NJ: Princeton University Press.

Winchester, S. (1998). *The surgeon of Crowthorne: A tale of murder, madness and the love of words* (retitled *The professor and the madman: A tale of murder, insanity, and the making of the Oxford English Dictionary* in the United States and Canada). New York: Viking.

Windle, J., Heugh, K., French, M., Armitage, J. and Nascimento dos Santos, G. (2023). Southern multilingual moves in education: Agency, citizenship, and reciprocity. *Critical Inquiry in Language Studies*. https://doi.org/10.1080/15427587.2023.2244099.

Yunkaporta, T. (2019). *Sand talk: How Indigenous thinking can save the world*. Melbourne: Text Publishing.

Zhou, F. (2020). *Models of the human in twentieth-century linguistic theories: System, order, creativity*. Cham: Springer.

Zhu Hua, Li Wei and Jankowicz-Pytel, D. (2020). Translanguaging and embodied teaching and learning: Lessons from a multilingual karate club in London. *International Journal of Bilingual Education and Bilingualism*, 23(1), 65–80. https://doi.org/10.1080/13670050.2019.1599811.

Zhu Hua, Otsuji, E. and Pennycook, A. (2017). Multilingual, multisensory and multimodal repertoires in corner shops, streets and markets: Introduction, *Social Semiotics*, 27(4), 383–93.

Index

actants, 89
action
  communicative, 103
activity
  communication as, 22
Actor Network Theory (ANT), 83
agency
  beyond the individual, 93
  distributed, 88, 93
  entangled, 103
  material, 88
  of place, 118
  posthuman perspectives, 87
  relational, 89
  Western assumptions, 118
  Western individualism, 93
  within assemblages, 107
Agha, 78, 126
Ahearn, 8, 74
Albury, 34, 126, 128
Alim, 10, 151
Althusser, 77
animal
  communication, 2
  semiotic practices, 99
  sounds as part of language, 128
  turn in linguistics, 91
Anthropocene, 120
anthropocentrism, 43, 83, 87, 134
  human hubris, 45
Aotearoa (New Zealand), 34, 69, 126
applied linguistics, 167
  as assemblage, 4, 19, 34, 149-51, 152, 153
  as discipline, 147-9
  critical, 148, 151
  green, 107
  introduction to, 1, 92
  knowledge hierarchies, 3
  language as structure, 7
  language reification, 9
  mainstream, 122
  practical theory of language. *See* language, practical theory of
  reduced to ELT, 146-7
  relation to linguistics, 20
  transgressive, 148
Araweté, 128
Armitage, 128
Armstrong and MacKenzie, 28, 30, 31
Aronin and Ó Laoire, 101
artefacts, 42
  social constructions, 43
artificial intelligence (AI), 85
  ChatGPT, 85
  ontological challenge to language, 85
assemblage vs agencement, 82
assemblages
  and assemblage art, 82
  and distribution, 89
  and entanglements, 14-5, 82-3, 90, 91, 97, 101, 103, 138, 151
  and political economy, 90
  as happenings, 90
  as nexus of practice, 101
  background, 82-3
  human-machine, 103
  in archaeology, 83
  in evolutionary biology, 82
  language ideological. *See* language ideological assemblages
  network of, 96
  semiotic. *See* language assemblages
  sociomaterial. *See* language assemblages
  vs repertoires, 106

Index

astronomy
  Indigenous, 115
Auer, 41, 73
Austin, 95
Australia
  English variation, 21, 25
  first knowledges, 111. *See* knowledge, Indigenous
  hip-hop, 129
  Indigenous citizenship, 128
  Indigenous languages, 27, 60, 64, 136
  Indigenous modernity, 111
  invasion of, 111
  land and language, 120, 124
  land as Country, 18, 119, 120
  law and Indigenous inequality, 151
  saltwater words, 121
  sand stories, 129
  songlines, 117
  songspirals, 122, 130
  Uluru, 42
  Wirangu, 125
authorship
  AI challenges, 86
  and authenticity, 86
Ayuk, 134

Baldwin, 84
Barad, 37, 43, 87, 103, 106, 141
Bauer and Trudgill, 20, 27, 29, 56, 58
Baugh, 151
Bawaka Country et al., 109, 120, 121, 122
Bell, 70
Bennett, 83, 88, 93, 107
Bernstein, 79, 92, 148
Berson, 85
Bessone, 84
Bhaskar, 5, 37, 43, 44
Bhatt and Bolonyai, 72
Bickerton, 64
bilingualism
  bilingual advantage, 143
  bilingual schools, 67
  translingual stance, 68
Bird, 29, 123, 125
black ties
  semiotic or material effects, 99
Blackledge and Creese, 7, 67, 73
Blenkinsop and Fettes, 119, 134
Block, 5, 6, 37, 45, 89, 142, 150

Blommaert, 14, 25, 39, 47, 54, 73, 75, 92, 95
Blommaert and Backus, 79
Bodkin-Andrews and Carlson, 118, 128
body enhancements, 85
Bogost, 43, 87
bounded systems
  languages as, 2, 7, 91
Bourdieu, 62, 76, 77
Braidotti, 84
Branson and Miller, 145
bridge
  as metaphor, 55
Broadhurst, 133
Brumfit, 150
Bucholtz and Hall, 39, 75, 101, 102
Burkette, 83

Calvet, 52
Cameron, 11, 28
Canagarajah, 8, 68, 80, 96, 97, 102
Canut, 82
Cavanaugh and Shankar, 100
Césaire, 113
Chakrabarty, 133
Chandler and Reid, 37
Chilisa, 127
chronotopes, 95
citizen science, 24
citizen sociolinguistics, 23-6
civil rights, 71
codeswitching, 8, 73, 75, 80
coevalness
  denial of, 111
cognition
  distributed, 88, 94
colonial transactions, 83
complexity, 75
Connell, 111, 118
converging technologies, 85
Corder, 1, 3, 9, 92, 142, 147
Cornips, 2, 40, 91, 99
Cornish (Kernewek), 132-3
Costa et al., 124
country, 18. *See* land
  as water, 18
Coupland, 78
Course, 40
Couzens and Eira, 126
Cowley, 8, 75, 89

creole languages, 143-4
creole exceptionalism, 143
critical (social) realism. *See* realism
critical constructivism, 9, 42, 66, 70
critical ethicalities, 45
critical language studies, 77
Crowley, 51, 53
Cummins, 9, 41, 71
Cunningham, 141
Cushing, 33
Cutler, 33
dark emu, 116
Darwin, 87
Davies, 148
de Certeau, 76
de Freitas and Curinga, 104
de Korne and Leonard, 126
de Souza, 34, 123, 129
Deaf communities, 98
deaf cosmopolitanism, 144
deaf ontologies, 38, 102
decolonizing
  decolonial perspective, 84
  indent imperative, 39
  delinking, 110
  knowledge, 110
  language, 14, 18, 127
  language reclamation, 130
  language revival, 132
  linguistics, 127
  multilingualism, 127
  not a metaphor, 132
  overemphasis, 114
  research, 127
  sociolinguistics, 34
deconstructivism, 9, 42, 70
DeGraff, 143
DeLanda, 82
Deleuze and Guattari, 82, 89
Demuro and Gurney, 5, 7, 39, 40, 49, 51, 81, 105, 140
Deutscher, 60
Diagne, 84, 112
Dias, 17, 129, 137
Disbray et al., 119, 134
discourses of endangerment, 125
discrete language communities, 70

disinventing language, 2-3, 9, 41, 127, 139, 152
Dixon, 54, 59, 64, 65
Duchêne and Heller, 62

Eades, 151
Eckert, 60, 96
ecosystem
  cognitive, 88, 93
  material, 101
  semiotic, 101
education
  and standardization, 124
  anti-racist, 128
  bilingual, 55, 139, 150
  classroom entanglements, 105
  Indigenous, 119
  language, 105, 146
  minority language classrooms, 69
  policy, 139
  shifting expertise, 119
Edwards, 78
egalitarianism, 3, 50, 55, 66
  liberal, 13, 17, 32, 50, 64, 66, 142-4
Ellis, 53
embodiment, 101, 145
Enfield, 88
Enfield and Kockelman, 93
Enfield and Sidnell, 22
English
  as a lingua franca (ELF), 47, 94
  as ontological entity, 59
  entanglements, 104
  in Philadelphia, 24
  metaphors in, 131
  ontologies, 48
  school subject, 141
  structural ontology, 48
  varieties, 94
  world Englishes, 47-8
English language teaching (ELT)
  complicity, 69
  White normativity, 151
English-only ideologies, 69
Ennis, 122, 124
enregisterment, 78
entangled objects, 83
epistemes, 149
epistemologies
  Enlightenment, 123

Index

epistemological relativism, 6, 45, 132, 142, 153
   seascape, 117, 119
   social, 6, 10, 45, 114
   structural, 7
epistemology vs ontology. *See* ontology vs epistemology
equality
   as similarity, 66
   ontological, 110
   struggles for, 71
error correction, 12, 23, 28, 32-3
Escobar, 5, 9, 36, 45, 120, 134, 150
Estival et al., 79
ethnophilosophy, 113
Evans and Levinson, 63
Evans, N., 27, 60-2
Evans, V., 56, 61
everyday views on language
   citizen linguistics, 13, 20
   folk linguistics, 20, 24, 25, 34, 128
   lay-oriented, 13, 20, 22, 31
extractivism, 79, 125

Fabian, 111
fact
   total linguistic. *See* totality
Fairclough, 44
Fanon, 84,
Faraclas, 144, 145
Finkelstein and Netz, 23, 27
Finland, 103
Finnegan, 40
First Nations
   knowledges, 115
   worldviews, 45. *See* Indigenous perspectives
Fishman, 133
Flores and Rosa, 137
folk linguistics, 23-6
   as decolonization, 128
   methodologies, 128
Foucault, 48, 149
Four T (4 T) approach, 67
Fowler, 76
Freud, 87
Fuller, 85

García, 2, 67, 68, 76
García and Li Wei, 8, 47, 67, 73, 141, 151

García et al., 68
Garroutte, 115
Gay'wu Group of Women, 121, 130
gender
   as social construct, 9, 10, 41, 43-4, 71
   grammatical, 59
geosemiotics, 101
Giglioli, 78
Global South, 14, 108, 136, 152
   language ontologies, 14
   Southern perspectives, 26
   southern theory, 47
Godfrey-Smith, 82
Goico, 107
Gomes, 112
Gordon, 111, 148
Grace, 18, 51, 55, 57, 58, 63, 125, 140
Graeber, 37
Gramling, 9, 53
grammar
   emergent, 72
   grammatical systems, 72
   grammaticality, 28, 31, 57
   ill-formed, 30
   universal, 63
Green, 129
Greenberg, 63
Grenoble, 151
Guba and Lincoln, 127
Gumperz, 73, 78
Gurney and Demuro, 77
Guugu Yimithirr, 60
Guzman and Lewis, 86

habitus, 77
Hacking, 48
Hall, 46, 92, 125
Hall and Wicaksono, 5, 46, 48
Hamacher, 111, 116-7
Hardt and Negri, 107
Harland, 55
Harris, R., 2, 13, 20-2, 29, 53, 56-8, 63, 89, 98, 140, 146
Harris, Z., 52
Haslanger, 5, 9, 10, 41, 43-5, 71, 150
Hauck and Heurich, 40
Hawai'i
   Hawaiian practices, 117
   Kanaka heritage, 120

Hawkins, 97
Hayman et al., 119, 120, 136
Henne-Ochoa et al., 123
Hermes et al., 110, 114, 121, 123, 128, 130, 134
Heurich, 128
Heywood, 38
Hill, 123
Hiratsuka and Pennycook, 69, 72, 80
Hobsbawm and Ranger, 139
Hodder, 83
Holbraad and Pedersen, 35, 38
Holbraad et al., 36, 137
Hollington, 143, 145
Holmes, 27
Hopper, 72
Hountondji, 112
Hovens, 103, 104
Huberman, 85
Hultgren, 79
humanism. *See* posthumanism
  and colonialism, 84
  divergent humanisms, 84
Hutchins, 88-9, 93, 117
Hutton, 10, 28, 29, 63-4

idealism
  transcendental, 43
identity
  distributed, 89
ideology critique, 106
idiolects, 79, 92
  bilingual, 93
I-language, 92. *See* idiolects
indigeneity
  definitions of, 112
Indigenous
  knowledge. *See* knowledge, Indigenous
Indigenous cosmologies
  misrepresentation of, 110
Indigenous languages, 14, 18, 33, 40, 60, 65, 69, 115, 127, 130, 132
Indigenous modernity, 111
Indigenous multilingualisms, 132
Indigenous perspectives, 17, 115, 122
Indigenous standpoints, 18, 113, 133
individualism, 16, 79
  individual action, 77
  methodological, 79, 94. *See* idiolect

Ingersoll, 117, 119
Ingold, 83
integrational linguistics, 2, 8, 13, 22, 47, 57, 89, 98, 99
  as alternative ontology, 57
  first and second-order activities, 75
  vs segregational, 58
  intercultural perspectives, 99
  invention of tradition, 139

Jakobs and Hüning, 3, 19, 131
Japanese, 69
Jaspers, 67
Jaspers and Madsen, 23
Jaworski and Gonçalves, 97
Jaworski and Thurlow, 96
Jenks, 151
Jones and Singh, 132
Jørgenson, 76, 78
Joseph, 23, 55, 58, 63, 67, 76, 89, 100, 106
Joseph and Newmeyer, 64, 65

Kaplan, 148
Karimzad, 95
Kashinawá, 129
Kathmandu, 96
Kearney, 86
Kell and Budach, 2, 5, 81, 88
Kernewek (Cornish), 132-3
Kichwa, 124
kincentrism, 118
knowledge
  democratization, 32
  disciplinary, 148
  disciplinary decadence, 148
  epistemic apartheid, 148
  global economy, 109
  Global North, 37, 114
  global politics of, 50
  Global South, 67
  hierarchies, 4, 34
  Indigenous, 111-15
  language as storehouse, 60
  marginalized, 18, 115
  North/South politics, 50, 58, 148
  of the sea, 117
  route-finding, 117
  sky, 116
Kohn, 36, 41, 99
Kramsch, 4, 62, 142, 146-7

Index

Kroskrity, 14, 25, 58, 95, 100, 132
Kusters, 38, 97-8, 102-3
Kusters and Lucas, 145
Kusters and Sahasrabudhe, 144
Kusters et al., 102, 151
Kwaymullina, 127

Lakoff and Johnson, 130
Lamb, 101, 104, 107
Lamb and Sharma, 101, 104
land
   as living entity, 119
   as teacher and pedagogy, 119
   more-than-human life, 119
Lane, 124, 136
language
   amputated, 100
   and worldview, 59-62
   as autonomous system, 51, 54, 55, 81
   as bounded object, 54, 81
   as human capacity, 40
   as material entanglement, 104
   as metaphysically invariant, 49
   complexity, 64
   decontextualization, 124, 144
   distributed, 89-91
   embodied, 89
   Euro-derived notions, 122
   everyday knowledge about, 3
   ontological status of, 2, 46
   Platonic abstraction, 46
   practical theory of, 4, 5, 10, 14, 16-7, 19, 31, 34, 50, 67, 69, 74, 81, 107, 109, 150-3
   reification, 2, 48, 142
   standardization, 124
language and thought
   as intertwined, 61
   worldview, 59-62
language as practice, 7, 41, 50, 67, 69, 72, 74-7, 153
language as structure, 7, 18, 41, 50, 51-6, 75, 89, 140, 153
language assemblages
   difficulties, 107
   general, 91-2
   language as assemblage, 41, 91-2, 138, 153
   languages as assemblages, 14, 15, 17, 62, 82, 153
   semiotic assemblages, 15, 82, 95-100, 104, 138
   sociomaterial assemblages, 15, 82, 100-5, 138
language capacity
   cognitive, 92
language change
   internal factors, 54
language gap, 33
language ideological assemblages, 14, 19, 25, 58, 95, 124, 132
language ideologies, 11-3, 21, 23-4, 26, 32, 39, 50, 62, 70-1, 75, 95, 141
   standard, 123
language labels
   as lay category, 23
language learning. *See* also *second language acquisition*
   decontextualized, 121
   materiality, 105
language myths, 11, 12, 23, 27, 56, 140
   archemyth, 58
   as conceptual metaphors, 131
   creole exceptionalism, 143
   dialect, 21
   Eskimo snow, 60
   Global North, 125
   language as fixed code, 125
   linguistic homogeneity, 59
   Western cultural tradition, 57
language ontologies, 38, 39.
   See language assemblages
   approaches to, 46-9
   dual, 70, 71
   ELF, 47
   essentialist vs non-essentialist, 54
   I-language and E-language, 46
language reclamation, 122-30
language revival, 17-8, 61, 69, 109, 122-3, 133
   as decolonization, 127
language universals, 63
   as norms, 63
   refuted, 63
language vs dialect, 54
languages
   as abstract entities, 52
   as artefacts, 43
   as autonomous systems, 53

languages (cont.)
  as colonial constructs, 125
  as containers, 61
  as equally complex, 63–6
  as inventions, 2, 41, 139
  as self-contained entities, 52
  as self-regulating systems, 28, 54
  as social constructs, 2, 41, 42, 43
  as unitary wholes, 61
  fuzzy boundaries, 1, 53, 56, 81
  inclusion and exclusion, 41
  Indigenous. *See* Indigenous languages; Australia
  languagized world, 23
  Native American, 33. *See* myaamia, Navajo, Ojibwe, Tlingit
  ontological status of, 2, 46, 70, 72
  partial encounters with, 92
  primitive, 64
  sleeping, 109, 129
languaging, 8, 72, 75, 93, 102
langue, 78
  vs parole, 51
Larsen and Johnson, 118
Latour, 5, 43, 83, 90, 99, 106, 111, 114, 149, 150, 152
Lee, 8, 25, 80
Lee and Dovchin, 68, 76
Lee and Makoni, 109
Leonard, 14, 18, 33, 109, 126, 127, 129, 130, 132
Levinson, 60
Lewis, 13, 33
Li Wei, 4, 20, 42, 67, 68, 71, 73, 74, 77, 80, 150
Leibowitz and Bozalek, 120
Limburgish, 103
linguistic anthropology, 13, 32, 39, 75
linguistic autonomy, 69. *See* language as autonomous system
linguistic complexity, 65
linguistic ethnography, 39, 75
linguistic knowledge, 3
linguistic landscapes, 96
linguistic natures, 40
linguistic reality, 9, 42
linguistics, 2
  and Native American languages, 126
  animal turn in, 91
  as engineering, 55
  as prisoner of its own invention, 52
  Chomskyan, 22, 46, 52, 92
  descriptive vs prescriptive, 3, 10, 26, 31
  generativist, 22, 46, 52, 56, 65
  integrational. *See* integrational linguistics
  knowledge hierarchies, 20
  mainstream, 7, 13
  normative, 29
  ontological map, 47
  orthodox, 22, 29, 50, 51, 56, 57, 125, 145
  ortholinguistic tendencies, 73, 124
  Saussurean, 46, 51
  structuralist, 51, 65
Linguistics Roadshow, 21, 28, 64
locus of enunciation, 33
López-Gohar et al., 134
Lorente, 151
Love, 52, 75
Luke, 106
Lyons, 28, 51, 54

Macedo, 143
MacSwan, 2, 9, 14, 42, 64, 70–1, 73, 80, 139
  normativity, 29–30
Maher, 132
Makalela, 127
Maki, 126
Makoni and Pennycook, 2, 9, 41, 127, 139, 152
Malaysia, 112
Mapudungun, 40
marginalized knowledge, 18, 115
Maringa, 121
Marx, vi, 77, 87
materialism
  flattened hierarchies, 107
  new, 87–8, 98–9, 102, 104, 106
materiality, 16, 49, 99
  and language, 100
  assemblage as material event, 81
  material anchors, 89
  material arrangements, 14, 15, 82
  material culture, 83
  of language, 101–3, 128
  of signs, 101
  sociomaterial arrangements, 106

Index

matsutake mushrooms, 90
matters of concern, 106, 149
May, 141, 148, 150
McCarthy, 147, 148
McFarlane, 82, 90
McKenzie, 130
McWhorter, 57, 61
Meek, 119, 123, 134
Merlan, 112
metaphors
  and language, 130–4
  conceptual, 130
methodological individualism.
  See individualism
metrolinguism, 78
Milroy and Milroy, 28
modernism
  Euromodernity, 111
Møller, 26
Monaghan, 122, 125, 129
Moriarty and Kusters, 144
Motha, 151
Muecke, 111
Mufwene, 61, 125, 127, 144
Mühlhäusler, 131
multilingual turn, 141
multilingualism
  as invention, 9
  material culture, 101
  multilingualisms, 127
multimodality, 102, 128–9
multinaturalism, 35
multisensory practices, 96, 98
myaamia, 33, 129, 132

Nakata, 18, 111, 113, 115
Nakata et al., 114, 133
Nandy, 133
Nascimento, 84
nationalism
  methodological, 9, 29, 44, 48, 56, 63, 79, 94
nature vs culture, 42
Navajo, 130
navigation
  as distributed cognition, 88
  as embodied practice, 118
  Polynesian, 117
  songlines, 117
Ndhlovu, 123, 128
Ndhlovu and Makalela, 14, 127, 130

Neale, 112, 119
Neale and Kelly, 117
négritude, 113
Netherlands, 103
Newmeyer, 51, 55, 64
nexus of practice, 101
Nicholas and McCarty, 119, 121, 132, 151
non-representational perspectives, 37
Noon and de Napoli, 115
normativity
  linguistic, 12, 28, 57
  ontological, 45

O Brien, 128
O'Regan, 47, 94
Oda and Takada, 148
Ojibwe, 128, 134
ontological curiosity, 2, 35, 138–41
ontological innovation, 130
ontological panic, 1, 3, 5, 66, 139
ontological turn, 5, 6, 35–8, 46, 49, 62, 114, 140–1
  perspectivism, 37, 136
ontologies
  relational, 5, 6, 10, 17, 34, 44–5, 66, 90, 114, 126–7, 134, 136–7, 142, 153
ontologies of language
  essentialist vs non-essentialist, 47
ontology
  historical, 48
  structural, 7, 16, 29, 56, 59, 66, 77, 141
  traditional vs anthropological, 36
  vs epistemology, 8, 35, 37, 47, 51, 55, 141
Orang Asli, 112
Ortega, 46, 47, 48, 54, 150
Otheguy et al., 30, 42, 68, 70–2, 92
Otsuji and Pennycook, 104
owls
  parliament of, 92
Oxford English Dictionary, 21

Pablé, 2, 13, 22, 31, 47, 57, 98–9
Page, 129
Pascoe and Gammage, 120
Patel, 112–3
Pennycook
  applied linguistics as assemblage, 4, 34, 149, 150
  authorship, 86

Pennycook (cont.)
  critical applied linguistics, 5, 19, 141, 148–9, 151
  decolonizing sociolinguistics, 134
  entanglements of English, 104
  hip-hop, 129
  language activism, 39
  language as practice, 22, 76
  non-verbal communication, 102
  posthumanism, 35, 84, 86, 88
  registers, 78
  semiosis, 98
  semiotic assemblages, 96–7, 138
  social semiotics, 96
  translingual practices, 26, 66, 73
Pennycook and Makoni, 26, 58, 148
Pennycook and Otsuji, 23, 78, 80, 89, 97, 98, 143
Perley, 129
Philippines, 104
Phillips, 82
Pickering, 49
Pietikäinen, 101, 103, 106
Pinker, 10, 26, 56, 60–1
pluriverse, 9, 36, 140
politeness
  grammatical, 65
polylanguaging, 8, 76, 78
posthumanism, 83–8
  and human hubris, 88
  as anti-humanism, 84
  transhumanism, 84
Povinelli, 35
practical theory (of language), 4–5, 10, 14–9, 31, 34, 50, 67–9, 74, 81, 107–9, 150–3
praxis, 4
Preston, 24
Pullum, 60

race
  and artificial intelligence, 85
  and creole linguistics, 145
  and humanism, 84
  as social construct, 9, 10, 41, 43–4, 71, 166
  in ELT, 151
  racialized communities, 137
  White normativity, 151
raciolinguistics, 10, 13, 33, 150

racism
  language evaluations, 64–5
radical Indigenism, 18, 115
Ramberg and Røyneland, 47, 79, 93, 139
Rambukwella, 41
Ramos, 37–8
Rampton, 147
rationalism, 6
  judgemental, 45, 142
  razão indolente, 34, 123
realism
  critical, 5, 37, 45, 142
  critical social, 5, 6, 10, 44–5, 142, 150
  ontological, 6, 37, 45
  transcendental, 43, 63
reality
  as plural, 44
  construction of, 5, 37
  discursive production of, 43
register, 78–9
relational ontologies. *See* ontologies, relational
repertoires, 78–80
  communicative, 80
  embodied, 80
  semiotic, 97, 144
  spatial, 68, 80, 97–8
  translingual family, 69, 73, 80
  vs reservoirs, 79, 92
research
  convivial, 128
  decolonizing. *See* decolonizing research
Ritchie, 89, 91, 102
Rosa and Flores, 10, 151
Rumsey, 120, 124
Rymes, 13, 20, 24–6, 80

Sámi, 112
Sampson, 46, 51, 53, 57, 64, 65, 147
Sanches de Oliveira and Bullock Oliveira, 143
Santana, 2, 46, 49, 52
Santos, 34, 125
Saunders, 133
Savransky, 37
Sayers, 125, 133
Schaller-Schwaner and Kirkpatrick, 47
Schatzki, 76–7, 88
Schmidt, 140

Index

Schneider, 9, 29, 48, 56, 79, 94
Scollon and Scollon, 101
Seargeant, 46, 48, 57-8, 86
seascape epistemology, 117, 119
　waves of knowing, 117
second language acquisition (SLA), 46-7
Seidlhofer, 94
semiotic assemblages. *See* language assemblages
semiotic landscape, 96
Senghor, 113
sensory ecologies, 98
　deaf, 98
Severo and Makoni, 145
Shankar and Cavanaugh, 101
Sharma, 96, 98, 104
Shohamy, 96
shopping
　lists, 98
　practices, 97
sign languages, 102, 144-5
　calibration, 144
　sensory asymmetries, 145
silencing, 124
Silverstein, 25, 95
Simpson, 119
Skutnabb-Kangas, 61
Smith, 22, 64
social construction, 6, 9, 44, 45, 71, 72, 106, 139
social practices, 76-7
social semiotics, 96
sociolinguistics, 8, 39, 66
　as language use, 74
　new, 78
　of globalization, 47
　sociocultural linguistics, 39, 75
　traditional, 48
　variationist, 60
sociology, 76
sociomaterial assemblages. *See* language assemblages
songspirals, 121
Spanish, 40
　Colombian, 69
　Spanish-English bilingualism, 30
spiritual relations, 17, 110
standard language ideology. *See* language ideology

starlings
　murmuration of, 92
Stebbins, 21
Stebbins et al., 127
Steffensen, 88, 89
Straaijer, 28
street art, 97
structural ontology. *See* ontology
structuralism, 7, 51-2, 54-5
　in social sciences, 54
Styres, 119
Sveinsdóttir, 6, 44
Svendsen, 13, 25
Svendsen and Goodchild, 128
Sydney
　corner shop, 104
　Harbour Bridge, 55
　Opera House, 42
symbolic power, 146
systemic functional linguistics, 53

Tannenbaum and Shohamy, 3, 139
te reo Māori, 34, 69, 126
Tegmark, 85
Teubert, 43, 106
The language hoax, 60
The language myth, 56
Thibault, 8, 75, 93, 102
thinking with glaciers, 120
Thomas, 83
Thompson, 117
Thorne et al., 103, 105
Thrift, 77
Thurlow, 23
Tlingit and Tagish, 119, 136
Todd, 37, 108, 114
Tokyo
　corner shop, 97
Toohey, 90, 138
Toohey et al., 105
Topa (Four Arrows) and Narvaez, 118
Torres Strait Islanders, 116
totality
　of a language, 91, 92
　of linguistic forms, 78
　total linguistic fact, 25
　total semiotic fact, 25, 95, 107
　total sociolinguistic fact, 95
　total speech situation, 95

translanguaging, 3, 7–9, 30–1, 44, 50, 76, 150
  as practical theory, 20, 66–70
  battles, 70–4
  first language use, 69
  space, 80
  translingual practices, 68, 70, 76, 102
  translingual semiotics, 68
  translingual turn, 80, 96
  translinguistic practices, 68
Trudgill, 28, 54
Tsing, 82, 90
Tuck and Yang, 132
Turing, 87
turns, 149
  animal, 91
  multilingual, 141, 150
  ontological, 114, 136, 140–1
  social, 150
  translingual, 141

Underhill, 131
UNESCO
  World Heritage, 42
unitary views
  competence, 71, 72
  languages as wholes, 61
  linguistic system, 68, 71
United States of America, 71
  National Rifle Association, 99
universality
  and difference, 64
  as cultural norm, 58
  disengagement from, 36
  ontological, 63
  Universal Grammar, 63

Van Dooren, 8
van Leeuwen, 8, 71, 74
Viveiros de Castro, 35, 136
voice, 37, 102

Walcott, 146
Walsh, 85
Wardaugh, 79
Warlpiri, 119
water
  as Country, 121
  consciousness and ethics, 119
  importance of, 119
  saltwater people, 121
Watkins, 53
Watts, R., 13, 57, 58, 131
Watts, V., 38, 110, 118, 141, 142
waves of knowing, 117
Wee, 1, 2, 15, 35, 43, 49, 54, 81, 86, 91, 94, 101, 138
Western ideological frameworks, 17, 100, 124, 125, 127. *See* language myths
Whorf, 62
Wicaksono and Hall, 48
Williams, C., 67
Williams, G., 60, 66
Williams, Q., 152
Windle et al., 67, 127
Wirangu, 125

Yolŋu, 116, 121, 122
Yugambeh, 129
Yunkaporta, 132, 134

Zhou, 52, 56
Zhu Hua et al., 80, 96

Printed in the United States
by Baker & Taylor Publisher Services